CROSSING CULTURAL
FRONTIERS

CROSSING CULTURAL FRONTIERS

Studies in the History of World Christianity

Andrew F. Walls

Edited by Mark R. Gornik

ORBIS BOOKS

Maryknoll, New York 10545

ORBIS BOOKS
Maryknoll, New York 10545

Fathers and Brothers
MARYKNOLL™

Founded in 1970, Orbis Books endeavors to publish works that enlighten the mind, nourish the spirit, and challenge the conscience. The publishing arm of the Maryknoll Fathers and Brothers, Orbis seeks to explore the global dimensions of the Christian faith and mission, to invite dialogue with diverse cultures and religious traditions, and to serve the cause of reconciliation and peace. The books published reflect the views of their authors and do not represent the official position of the Maryknoll Society. To learn more about Maryknoll and Orbis Books, please visit our website at www.maryknollsociety.org.

Grateful acknowledgment is made to the publications in which these essays originally appeared. A list of these credits is included in the sources.

Library of Congress Cataloging-in-Publication Data

Names: Walls, Andrew F. (Andrew Finlay), author. | Gornik, Mark R., editor.
Title: Crossing cultural frontiers : studies in the history of world Christianity / Andrew F. Walls ; edited by Mark R. Gornik.
Description: Maryknoll : Orbis Books, 2017. | Includes bibliographical references and index.
Identifiers: LCCN 2017014252 (print) | LCCN 2017027739 (ebook) | ISBN 9781608337231 | ISBN 9781626982581 (pbk.)
Subjects: LCSH: Christianity. | Church history. | Missions--History.
Classification: LCC BR121.3 (ebook) | LCC BR121.3 .W353 2017 (print) | DDC 270—dc23
LC record available at https://lccn.loc.gov/2017014252

In grateful remembrance of
Harold and Maude Turner

Contents

Contents

Introduction

This book, like its predecessors, *The Missionary Movement in Christian History* and *The Cross-Cultural Process in Christian History*, is a ragbag, reminiscent of those bags of my grandmother's day that held strips of cloth from miscellaneous sources to be used for making clootie mats (rugs, warm if dust retaining). The strips in this case are of writings composed over a long period; the earliest was first published in 1970. All have been revised, in most cases conservatively; one or two have never appeared in print before. All can claim to be in some way studies in the history of World Christianity, a concept that is increasingly being recognized as an essential dimension of the Christian faith, necessary to any satisfactory comprehension of it.

I confess myself to be a late convert to the use of the term "World Christianity" itself, for it is not without dangers. The most obvious of these is that it can too readily be assumed to mean "Christianity somewhere else," rather as "world music" means "music from somewhere else," and supermarkets have aisles dedicated to "world food," meaning "not what your mother used to give you." But no other term readily reflects the fact that Christianity is a significant presence in all six continents and, in principle, has always been addressed to the *oikumene,* the whole inhabited world. This is the more important since the way Christian theology and history have traditionally been studied in the West (and these models have been too readily adopted in other parts of the world) is geographically skewed, obscuring vital aspects of the Christian faith.

Many of the writings that follow take their origin from the transformative development in Christian history, which took place in the twentieth century, when the demographic and cultural composition of Christianity fundamentally changed. Whereas for several centuries previously, Christianity had been characteristic of the peoples of Europe, and their descendants beyond Europe, with a relatively modest Christian presence elsewhere, it became evident by the end of the twentieth century that Africans, Asians, and Latin Americans now formed the majority of the world's Christians, and that Christianity was becoming a principally non-Western religion. Some of the essays examine the processes by which this change took place—usually by developments, microscopic in themselves, in widely separated areas of the world. These developments occurred against the background of geopolitical events, one of the most crucial being what I have called the Great European Migration (a concept too easily subsumed under contingent aspects of it such as colonialism and imperialism). This movement of peoples over a period of some four and a half centuries brought many millions of Europeans from their homelands to other parts of the world and created a world order. This migration has generated another, which I designate the Great Reverse Migration, whereby many millions of people from beyond the West have moved, are moving, and will continue to move to Europe and the lands in which Europeans settled during their own great migration, lands that we group collectively with Europe and call "the West." These developments make migration an essential theme of world Christian history, and the Great Reverse Migration is clearly a vital factor for the future of World Christianity.

Another set of essays discusses the implications of this fundamental change in the demographic composition of the Christian church for theology, theological study, and theological education, and the processes of rethinking, reconceiving, and re-presenting that will be involved. The implications arise from the incarnational nature of Christian faith; when the Word took flesh and dwelt with humanity, he took humanity in a particular time and place, becoming a Jew in first-century Palestine. Even so, as the Word is received by faith in other times and places, he becomes embodied in "the flesh" of those times and places, the language, thought patterns, specificities. From this fact stems another component of the book's title, *Crossing Cultural Frontiers*. Christian history has seen a series of such frontier crossings, the first—and paradigmatic—one taking place in the New Testament period, as demonstrated in the Acts of the Apostles, when the Messiah of Israel was received by Gentiles in the world of the eastern Mediterranean. We can trace some of the new issues this raised: questions about how to act in a Christian way (like the complicated matter in 1 Corinthians about accepting dinner invitations from pagan friends) and then questions about how to think in Greek in a Christian way. These latter questions were to lead to the searches and controversies that produced the great creeds and our formulated doctrines of the Trinity and Incarnation. All these were the intellectual and social products of the crossing of Christianity's first cultural frontier into the Hellenistic world: from the processes of conversion (that is, the turning toward Christ), first of Hellenistic social and family life, and then of Greek intellectual life.

One or two essays consider this process in the Greek world and how far it may offer parallels with our own age, as Christians now wrestle with the what-to-do and how-to-think questions posed by the cultures, traditions, and categories of thought belonging to Africa and Asia. Nor are these theological activities purely of local interest; as the engagement with Greek thought expanded the Christian understanding of Christ without rendering the Jewish conceptions redundant, so the frontier crossings of our own time bring hope of expanded understanding without fear of loss.

So World Christianity is normative Christianity. The first essay seeks to show the remarkable extent (often obscured by traditional Western ways of viewing church history) that this was realized in the multicultural church of the early Christian centuries. Later contributions consider developments in those transitional centuries when Europeans had the central place (later shared with Christians of European descent elsewhere) as the representatives of Christianity. The development of the missionary movement from the West is naturally a recurrent theme here. I believe that the missionary movement from the West is a single story with Catholic, Protestant, and shared phases; and, so far as my knowledge goes, the different phases reflect remarkable degrees of commonalty. I acknowledge that the studies selected very much reflect Protestant developments. Missions have commonly been the sphere of radical Christians, and a recurrent theme is the relation of the missionary movement to radicalizing movements of renewal and revival within the wider church; and particular attention is given to the importance for missionary activity of the interrelated movements of Pietism in continental Europe and Evangelical revival in the Anglo-Saxon world.

Africa plays a larger part in the stories treated than do other parts of the world. Some essays reflect on the fact that Africa has almost two millennia of continuous Christian history; others highlight the significance within that history of one small and often neglected country, Sierra Leone. Some attention is also given to quite recent theological developments relating to Africa, in the conviction that the continent may yet be a theological laboratory of major ecumenical significance.

As Christian faith and experience reflect the Ephesian vision of the new temple of the Spirit that is in the process of construction from geographically, ethnically, and linguistically diverse bits of converted social reality, it becomes increasingly clear that those bits of converted social reality belong to each other, for they all belong to Christ and become complete only in him. Hence the repeated theme of the bicultural—and in principle multicultural—nature of the church, and on the opportunities for giving substance to this aspect of the church that are now opened (not least by the Great Reverse Migration) for returning to the norm of the church of the

New Testament. The very name "Christian" was invented, the Book of Acts informs us, to express a bicultural entity.

The book owes more than I can say to the editor, Mark R. Gornik, Director of the City Seminary of New York. To a very large extent the choice of articles and the general architecture of the book are his; and his quiet and friendly stimulus and his generous opening of the facilities of City Seminary have been crucial to its completion. I am grateful also to William R. Burrows and Robert Ellsberg, successive editors at Orbis Books for their encouragement and patience. My wife, Ingrid, has been essential to the completion of the project.

Thanks are owed to the publishers and editors who have given permission to reprint many of the essays that appear here. To list the friends and colleagues, past and present, all over the world, who have provided inspiration for them, or given substance or improvement to them, would be impossible. The dedication of the book gives me opportunity to attest my particular indebtedness to the late Harold and Maude Turner, who shared collegial years in Sierra Leone, Nigeria, and Scotland.

In a work that reflects studies and developments over more than sixty years, some autobiographical references are perhaps inevitable. I trust these are neither too numerous, sententious, or obtrusive. My deepest gratitude must be for the privilege of being allowed for so long to move around the amazing workshop in which the renewal and construction of World Christianity has been taking place. *Gratias Domino refero.*

Editor's note: Thank you Carrie Myers, Maria Liu Wong, and Sachiko Clayton for your efforts in helping to complete this book.

Part One

THE TRANSMISSION OF CHRISTIAN FAITH

1

World Christianity and the Early Church

An Autobiographical Note

I took my first faltering steps toward the life of learning in the early 1950s. As a new postgraduate student I was urged by my mentor (a great scholar whose memory I revere and whose commitment I desire to emulate) toward an issue which at that time seemed to be at the cutting edge of scholarly debate. It was, what happened to Christianity in the century or so following the apostolic age? Was there really an apostolic deposit, a paradigm handed down from the apostles? One of the keys to this question of apostolic tradition appeared to be a work apparently bearing the title "Apostolic Tradition" written early in the third century by the contentious Rome-based writer Hippolytus. How good was the implicit claim in the title? The trouble was that, while the work had undoubtedly been written in Greek, and in Rome, the Greek text had not survived. There were only versions—or were they rather adaptations?—fragmentary in Latin, fuller in two dialects of Coptic, Arabic, and Ethiopic—and the text had clearly been quarried for their own purposes by Syriac and Greek writers.

Innocently, I set out to separate the wheat from the chaff. The important question, surely, was to get back to the original by restoring the Greek text; and for this purpose, the fragmentary Latin version seemed the most suitable. How readily one turned to a Western language, and one already known. It was axiomatic that a student of the early church must know Greek and Latin. And so, following conventional wisdom, I missed an important point about the early church that the history of this text illustrated: its vast geographical spread and linguistic diversity.

My labors were only modestly prosperous. I did not solve the problem of apostolic tradition. My work on the Latin text suggested only that it too was a version, an adaptation like the others, and that its origin was probably Gothic. Gothic! Here was another sign of the ethnic diversity and geographical range of the early church, but again I missed the point. Coptic, Syriac, Arabic, Ethiopic, Gothic were only distractions, barriers to understanding a problem centered on Rome; they were only serviceable for what they proved or suggested about texts written in Greek or Latin. I had fallen into the trap in which much patristic scholarship has been long enmeshed. I had identified the early church with the Church of the Roman Empire, and identified the determinative, formative processes of the early church as those taking place in the Greco-Roman world.

The texts at the center of my work as an apprentice scholar were pointing to an aspect of the early church that did not penetrate my mind until long afterward; its geographical range, its linguistic profusion, its cultural diversity; and yet its cohesiveness, its sense of mutual belonging. This document had begun its life in Rome, it belonged to the Greek-speaking strongholds of Hellenistic culture; yet it had been appropriated in the vernacular worlds of Upper and Lower Egypt. It had been used in the Syriac-speaking world, and traveled into the Persian Empire; it had been translated into the language of Arabia, it had been taken up in the heart of East Africa. And if I was right about the Latin version, tribespeople from the east, whose language had only recently reached written form, and who still handled Latin with the stiffness of a language recently acquired, were reading it too, as they settled in new homelands.

The New Testament and the Bicultural Model of the Church

What was being revealed was that World Christianity is not a development of the last century; it is the natural Christian condition. Christianity has always been global in principle, and for much of its history, global in practice too. And global inevitably means multicultural. Cultural diversity was built into the church within the New Testament period. This was an inevitable result of the early decision not to require circumcision and obedience to the Torah for Gentiles who came to faith in Jesus. In taking this decision, the early church abandoned the long-standing proselyte model by which Gentiles were incorporated into Israel by assuming Jewish religious culture. The earliest church, the church we meet in the opening chapters of Acts, was Jewish to the backbone. These people had not changed their religion on coming to faith in Jesus; rather, Jesus had renewed, revitalized and given insight and understanding into the religion they had always had. This earliest church therefore delighted in Torah and temple and everything that makes for Jewish identity. This was not a new Israel. They *were* Israel, the morally renewed Israel with the New Covenant written on their hearts that the prophets had declared would arise in the Messianic Age.[1]

The events reflected in Acts 15 and the Epistle to the Galatians meant that Gentile believers in Jesus could be received as fellow Israelites without becoming Jews. This created an entirely new situation: a bicultural religious community. Though the decision was reached in Jerusalem, the principal effects were not felt there, where Gentile believers were so few, but in Antioch, where there were two Jesus lifestyles, one Judaic, one Hellenistic, operating side by side. It was in Antioch that the name Christian was first used[2]; no one had needed such a term in earlier days. But the Antiochene Christians were a single community that was bicultural, with two distinct lifestyles. There were old believers who were circumcised, kept the food laws and the Sabbath, washed before prayer, observed Passover and Pentecost and Hanukkah, and attended the temple for such events whenever they could do so; and there were new believers who did not circumcise their children, ate pork, lived under conditions where Sabbath observance was impossible, and were debarred from joining the community of Israel at worship in the temple.

These two groups together constituted the *christianoi*. They were not two communities, but one; the symbol of their togetherness was the common table at which traditionally Jews and Gentiles did not meet. This was a step too far for some old believers; and even Peter, who was convinced theologically that God had accepted Gentiles as his people, found it difficult to sit at the same table if he thought report of it might get back home.[3] Yet a great deal of the New Testament is, directly or indirectly, concerned with maintaining the bicultural nature of the church. The Epistle to the Ephesians is devoted to the coinherence, the mutual belongingness of Jewish and Gentile believers. Their respective lifestyles, the one converted Judaic culture, the other converted hybrid Hellenistic culture, were equally necessary in the building of a new temple more durable than the one in Jerusalem from which Gentile

---

[1] Cf. Jeremiah 31:31–34. The point is explored in Andrew F. Walls, "Converts or Proselytes? The Crisis over Conversion in the Early Church," *International Bulletin of Missionary Research* 28, no. 1 (2004): 2–6.

[2] Acts 11:26.

[3] Galatians 2:11–14.

believers were excluded. Both were necessary as organs in a functioning body of which Christ himself was the head and brain. Only together, the epistle declares, do we come to the full stature of Christ.[4]

The original bicultural model of the church was a casualty of Christian success, perhaps also of Christian failure. The success lay in the rapid increase in the numbers of Gentile Christians; the failure in the drying up— in the Hellenistic world, at least—of the numbers of Jews turning to Jesus, with increasing hostility between church and synagogue.[5] It was the end of the Jewish way of being Christian. It is clear that influential Greek Christian writers[6] viewed the remnants of Judaic Christianity in Palestine, not as the spiritual descendants of James the brother of the Lord, but as heretics defective in Christology and sunk in legalistic bondage. The future of Jewish Christianity was to be still bleaker; the time came in Europe when Jewish converts would be watched for such telltale signs of the sincerity of their Christian profession as avoiding pork or secret Sabbath keeping. Too often in Europe, the only way a Jew could become a Christian was by becoming a Gentile Christian, a sad reversal of the New Testament pattern.

The Early Church and Multicultural Christianity

But the end of the New Testament bicultural model did not mean the end of multicultural Christianity. As we have already seen, Christians of Hellenistic culture did not constitute the whole church, nor were Greek and Latin the only languages of Christians.

Among the areas early showing rapid Christian growth was the Nile Valley, where the dominant language was Coptic, not originally a literary

---

[4] Ephesians 4:13. The passage, and its place in the argument of Ephesians, is explored in Andrew F. Walls, "The Ephesian Moment," in *The Cross-Cultural Process in Christian History* (Maryknoll, NY: Orbis Books, 2002), 72–81.

[5] That hostility is reflected throughout the Epistle of Barnabas, which cannot be later than c. 140 AD. It is the more striking in view of the latter's probable origin in Alexandria, and the fair assumption that Alexandria's first missionaries were Jews addressing the city's huge Jewish community. In the *Martyrdom of Polycarp*, datable to 156, the author, who writes on behalf of the Church of Smyrna, speaks of the zealous involvement of Jews ("as is their wont") in bringing about the death of the much respected bishop (ed. Lightfoot, section 13). Justin, who knew the Palestine scene, speaks of the savagery of attacks on (presumably Jewish) Christians by the insurgent Bar Cochba (*Apology* 1.31). The vigor with which Ignatius repudiates Sabbath keeping as belonging to another realm than the Christian (*Magnesians* 9.1, ed. Lightfoot) is also eloquent.

[6] See, e.g., Irenaeus, *Against Heresies* 1.26.2 (ed. Harvey); Eusebius, *Ecclesiastical History* 3.27 (a passage apparently dependent on Origen).

language at all. Coptic achieved a new dignity as a language by being used for Christian purposes, the Sahidic translation of the Scriptures providing its first major literature. The Nile Valley produced one of the earliest Christian revival movements, and the life of its archetypal figure, Antony, illustrates some aspects of cultural diversity in the early church.[7]

Antony's "conversion" is not from paganism, but from ordinary Christianity. His story shows charismatic Christianity making a recovery in Africa at a time when the charismatic features seen in the New Testament appeared to have faded as the church disciplined itself with a strengthened episcopate to cope with intellectual anarchy ("heresies") and with state persecution.

We fail to understand Antony if we forget that he was an African peasant, with an African peasant's view of the universe and of the powers behind it. We have noted that Coptic was not a literary language. The bulk of Coptic writing of the period before the Sahidic New Testament consists of magical formulae,[8] spiritual technology to cope with the powers at work behind the universe. Antony, a village Christian, has a way to categorize those powers: they are the devil and his demons, the enemies of Christ. His quest for perfection as a disciple inevitably leads to conflict with those powers. It is only after he is battle-hardened by such conflicts and has experienced Christ's victory in them that he moves out to the desert.

The understanding of Antony has suffered by placing him in a spiritual tradition that seeks disengagement from the world, and thus interprets his move to the desert as escape. Antony is an African peasant, with a worldview in which the pre-Christian Coptic magical material makes perfect sense— that recognizes hostile forces at work in the world and associates them with opposition to Christ. And where are those powers more manifest than in the heartless desert? When Antony goes to the desert in his quest for total discipleship, he is not escaping from the world; he is challenging the devil on his own territory. Antony's story is about spiritual warfare, which is why his desert adventure does not begin until he has experienced total victory over satanic power in the more conventional Christian theater of proximity to village life.[9] When he reaches the desert, the immediate effect is not peace,

---

[7] The main authority for Antony's life remains the *Life of Antony* ascribed to Athanasius. See also *The Coptic Life of Antony*, trans. Tim Vivian (San Francisco: International Scholars Publications, 1995). Antony's extant letters are available in a translation by Samuel Rubenson, *The Letters of St. Antony* (Minneapolis: Fortress Press, 1996).

[8] S. Kent Brown, "Coptic-Greek inscriptions from Christian Egypt," in *The Roots of Egyptian Christianity*, ed. Birger A. Pearson and James E. Goehring, 26–41 (Minneapolis: Fortress Press, 1986).

[9] Antony seems to have begun by visiting holy men who lived outside their villages— detached, but not out of contact.

but such conflict as leaves him bruised, bleeding, lacerated by demonic attack. When, at his own insistence, he is carried from the church to which his shattered body has been conveyed, to the graveyard of a deserted village (where would one expect a more potent concentration of the powers of evil?), it is to claim Christ's victory over the one who rules the wilderness, and the result brings blessing to the area—sick healed, bereaved comforted, old feuds settled.[10] Antony would have no difficulty in understanding the language of spiritual warfare used by modern charismatics. The Christianity he represents is radical, vernacular-speaking, spiritually confrontational, popular in the sense of addressing widely recognized needs. It is literate, but hardly literary; it applies a conviction of Christ's cosmic victory to the worldview of Nile Valley peasants, with their anxieties and terrors, while embodying the simplicity of the Lord's Word to the disciples, "Be perfect, as your Father in heaven is perfect."[11]

Antony was venerated, but the type of Christianity he represented was difficult to control. Pachomius, the next major Christian figure in the Coptic world, was directed by visions, was possessed of second sight, and was even accused of witchcraft. When Shenoute, abbot of the White Monastery, another major figure in the tradition, calls on young and old to "cry Jesus" in joy or sorrow, when they suffer the injustice of a corrupt trial or see horrible sights, the modern reader can hear echoes of many a modern African Pentecostal sermon. And when we read the *Apothegmata Patrum*, which collects sayings of the Desert Fathers, we are visiting the first written corpus of African proverb literature. In this literature, as Peter Brown truly says, the Egyptian peasant finds a voice for the first time.[12] It is a voice readily recognizable in modern African Christianity.

The ancient church of Egypt was bicultural. Alexandria and the urban centers, which bore the brunt of state persecution, were part of the globalizing culture of the Mediterranean: cosmopolitan and Greek-speaking. In the Nile Valley lay a rural, vernacular-speaking population. There was traffic between the worlds: Athanasius, the archetypal Greek theologian, seems to have spoken Coptic; Antony had rejected the chance of a Greek education, and never used the language; Pachomius, an ex-soldier, knew Greek but used Coptic. If the arm of the state was less busy in the rural area, its Christianity knew spiritual warfare of a different, but not necessarily less bruising, kind.

---

[10] *Coptic Life* 14 (Vivian, 47).

[11] Matthew 5:48.

[12] Peter Brown, *Authority and the Sacred: Aspects of the Christianisation of the Roman World* (Cambridge: Cambridge University Press, 1995).

The years of state persecution brought the two cultures of the church together, as church leaders from Alexandria fled persecution in the city and found shelter in desert oases, shared village hospitality, and preached to rural pagans.[13] The end of persecution in 313 removed this engine of fellowship and thereafter signs of cultural strain appear in the Egyptian Church. The Christological controversies of the fifth century exacerbated the divide: Nile Valley Christians, monks (often of peasant background), the Coptic areas generally, identified with the Monophysite cause, the supporters of Chalcedon were most noticeable in the metropolitan area of Alexandria. When the Arabs invaded, many Coptic Christians saw the Muslims as their liberators from the oppression of their Christian neighbors.[14]

Syria also had a bicultural church, metropolitan, cosmopolitan, Greek speaking, on the one hand, vernacular Syriac, on the other. But in much of the western side of the area bilingualism was common, and the Christian cultural picture was more complex than in Egypt. In Syria, the Greek world jostled with other, older influences: with the astral lore of Assyria and Babylon; with Jewish life, ancient and modern, traditional and sectarian, ethnic and proselyte; and with the ancient Iranian religion of the imperial superpower. In all these different cultures, Christian preaching found a response, and Syriac-speaking Christianity produced perhaps the most remarkable missionary movement that Christianity has ever known. It sent the faith to India, across the heart of Central Asia, penetrated the peoples bordering the Chinese Empire, and in 635, reached the capital of that empire and gained the ear of the emperor. In estimating the global reach of Christianity in the early centuries, it is worth remembering that the favorable response of the Chinese emperor to the missionaries of 635 is almost exactly contemporary with the council in Northumbria described by Bede, which resulted in the conversion of King Edwin and the decision makers of that northern English kingdom.[15] At this period, Christianity is a global faith, present, active, and growing from the Atlantic almost to the Pacific and with outposts from Siberia to Sri Lanka.[16]

---

[13] The experiences of Bishop Dionysius of Alexandria under the persecutions of Decius and Valerian are recorded by Eusebius, *Ecclesiastical History* 6.40–6.41, 7.11.

[14] See W. H. C. Frend, *The Rise of the Monophysite Movement: Chapters in the History of the Church in the Fifth and Sixth Centuries* (Cambridge: Cambridge University Press, 1972).

[15] Bede, *Ecclesiastical History* 2.13.

[16] Cosmas Indicopleustes, the sixth century traveler turned monk, refers to a "Church of the Christians" "even in Taprobane, an island in Further India where the Indian Sea is" (*Christian Topography*, ed. McCrindle, 118ff.). Cosmas indicates that the church is of "Persian" immigrants. A sixth-century stone cross has been discovered at Anuradhapura, the old capital of Sri Lanka. See Ian Gillman and Hans-Joachim

The African and Asian Dimensions
of Early Christianity

Early Christianity has important African and Asian dimensions that invite the attention of Western Christians. Asia had almost a millennium and a half of Christian history before the arrival in Asia of Western missionaries, and that history is neither insubstantial nor insignificant. There are good reasons for Western Christians to deepen acquaintance with the earlier Asian Christianity. For one thing, it is the principal example—Africa, especially Ethiopia, produces others—of an expression of Christianity that does not owe its shape and expression to the Greco-Roman inheritance. It is certainly influenced, sometimes strongly influenced, by that inheritance, for it arose in the context of what was already a global Christianity that included the Hellenistic world. But it is not dominated by it. In early Asian Christianity, we see the biblical material and the Christian tradition in inter-action with other cultures: Semitic, Iranian, Indian, Chinese. And if it is good for Western Christians to explore this, how much more significant is it for Asian Christians to encounter a Christianity that has centuries of experi-ence of the life of Asia and that cannot be dismissed as part of the detritus of Western colonialism?

The old Asian Christianity also introduces us to different ways of doing theology, introducing us to theology as poetry and to theology as drama. Take this verse from a second century Syriac hymnbook:

A cup of milk was offered to me
And I drank it in the sweetness of the Lord's kindness.
The Son is the cup; And the Father is he who was milked;
And the Holy Spirit is she who milked him.[17]

Here, in the second century, is an indubitably Trinitarian statement of faith; but it is set out, not in metaphysical, but in poetic terms. The images are bold: the believer takes a cup and his lips make contact with the Son, God Incarnate, but within the cup is the sustaining milk of the life of the Father. Then comes the still bolder image of the Father as milk cow, the ultimate source of the milk on which believers depend. And the milk reaches the cup

---

Klimkeit, *Christians in Asia before 1500* (Ann Arbor: University of Michigan Press, 1999), 33.

[17] *Odes of Solomon*, Ode 19. The translation is from J. H. Charlesworth, *The Odes of Solomon* (Missoula, MT: Scholars Press, 1977). The Odes are extant in a Syriac version, but one ode exists in a Greek version. They may well originate from the bilingual area of Syria.

from which the believer drinks by means of the Divine Milkmaid, the Holy Spirit, who makes the Father's riches available through the Son. (The word for Spirit, *ruch*, being feminine, the Holy Spirit has the pronoun "she.") It is a powerful relational model of Trinitarian belief; but the context is one of worship, of devotion, of adoration.

Some of the greatest figures in early Syriac Christianity are great poets. In Ephrem, hymn merges with sermon and sermon with hymn and both with the drama of the dialogues he sometimes introduces. More than once he describes an argument, rising in stridency all the time, between death and Satan as to which of them is the greater. In one the choir bursts out in resurrection faith: "Blessed is he who has set these accursed slaves against one another so that we can laugh at them as they laugh at us." The preacher then improves the occasion, "our laughing at them now, my brethren, is the pledge that we shall be enabled to laugh at them at the resurrection," and the congregation responds, "Praise to you, son of the Shepherd of all, who has saved his flock."[18]

A further reason for renewing the study of early Asian Christianity is the engagement that it reveals with other faiths and claimed paths to salvation. In the early history of Western Christianity, the gospel in conflict with the old nature religions pitted God against the gods, the One against the many, the White Christ against the Black Thor; and Western missionaries drew on the Greek philosophical critique of polytheism. In the Asian Christian documents, we see Christianity in engagement with Zoroastrianism, with the Chinese classical tradition, with Buddhism, with Indian traditions, and in due time with Islam also.[19]

We see something of the process of long engagement in materials from China in such documents as the great inscription of 781, which describes the first hundred and fifty years of Chinese church history. There are other aspects where our judgments must necessarily be tentative at present, but where further research could bring enlightenment. The tablet tells how the scholar emperor asked to study the Christian Scriptures; in a process lasting three years, some Christian writings were translated in the royal library,

---

[18] Translation from Sebastian Brock, *The Harp of the Spirit: Eighteen Poems of Saint Ephrem*, 2nd ed. (San Bernardino, CA: Borgo Press, 1984). See also another such dialogue in Sebastian P. Brock and George A. Kiraz, *Ephrem the Syrian: Select Poems* (Provo, UT: Brigham Young University Press, 2006), text 14.

[19] The best known example of the last named is the Apology for Christianity delivered by Patriarch Timothy I in a two-day dialogue with the Abbasid Caliph in Baghdad. See A. Mingana, "The Apology and Timothy the Patriarch before the Caliph Mahdi," *Bulletin of the John Rylands Library* 12 (1928): 137–227. A substantial section in English appears in John W. Coakley and Andrea Sterk, *Readings in World Christian History*, vol. 1 (Maryknoll, NY: Orbis Books, 2004), 231–42.

studied in the private apartments (that is, by the emperor in person), and as a result Christianity was allowed, nay encouraged, in China.[20]

Early in the twentieth century a cave in West China yielded a vast library of works in Syriac and Chinese, some of the latter being Christian, some Buddhist. Some of them are likely to have been among those translated in the royal library and approved by the emperor; others belong to a later stage of the Christian encounter with Chinese thought. The terms of the imperial edict suggest that the emperor saw Christian ethical teaching as compatible with Confucian and Jesus as the Sage. Confucian terminology, however, offered no way of presenting Christ as the savior and divine lord. It was Buddhist terminology that offered possibilities here, and the documents show how Syriac missionaries drew on titles of the Buddha such as "World-Honored One," and "Universal Lord," and interacted with Buddhist missionaries and Scriptures.[21]

There is much more work to do on these early Christian encounters with China, and a major area of church history to be illuminated by those willing to combine, as few can at present, the study of Syriac with that of ancient Chinese.

It is hard to think of anything approaching this sort of interfaith interaction in the story of the conversion of Europe. Had substantial contact between Asian and European Christians continued until the sixteenth century, European Christians might have been better prepared for their own encounter with Asia.

Another aspect of Asian Christian history offers a contrast with the Western model. The Persian Empire, the heartland of the Syriac church for centuries, had its Diocletian but it never had a Constantine.[22] Only in some smaller states such as Armenia, Georgia and, for a time, the Himyarite kingdom of Yemen, and among some nomadic and semisettled peoples, did the rulers become Christian. So, while Christianity was a substantial presence in Asia for centuries, it did not, as in Europe, triumph there. In most of Asia, Christianity was in a plural situation, usually in a minority, sometimes

---

[20] Text and commentary in John Foster, *The Church of the Tang Dynasty* (London: SPCK, 1939). Another translation appears in Coakley and Sterk, *Readings in World Christian History*, 243–46.

[21] For the documents, see P. Yoshiro Saeki, *The Nestorian Literature and Relics in China*, 2nd ed. (Tokyo: Maruzen, 1950). Extracts in English are given in Coakley and Sterk, *Readings in World Christian History*, 247–51. For discussion, see Gillman and Klimkeit, *Christians in Asia before 1500*, 275–83.

[22] An ill-advised initiative by Constantine designed to influence the Persian Emperor Sapor II toward favorable treatment of the Christians had precisely the opposite effect. A forty-year period of persecution followed; and between 344 and 367, a total of 16,000 names are listed as martyrs (Gillman and Klimkeit, *Christians in Asia before 1500*, 117). Despite periodic edicts of toleration there were also later outbursts of persecution.

a persecuted minority. In other words, the parallels are closer to the situation of large numbers of Asian Christians today than anything that the history of the West after Constantine can offer. Both Eastern and Western Christians need to study both heritages, for Christians today are joint-heirs to both.

How Early Global Christianity Fell Apart

Alas, a time came when the joint-heirs became strangers to one another, and a principal cause lay in the Christian possession of political power. In the early centuries the Greco-Roman Christian community, the Coptic Christian community, the Syriac-speaking Christian community, and the new centers of faith that had arisen through their work, all thought of themselves as part of a single great church. There were, from New Testament times onward, rubs and tensions when different culture groups lived together, and in the first three centuries Rome itself, with resident communities from across the Mediterranean world, was fertile soil for inter-Christian culture clashes. When Victor, an African Latin-speaking pope, insisted on what has become the Western date for Easter, his problem was probably not that the Eastern churches far away used a different calendar, but that Ephesian Christians in Rome were using the date for Easter that they used at home. As a result, some Roman Christians were still mourning at Passiontide when others were joyfully celebrating the Resurrection.[23]

And it is easy to see why another bishop of Rome decided that the highly charismatic Phrygian form of Christianity that came to be known as Montanism should not find a home in the capital.[24] But in general, the churches of East and West, in the Roman Empire and in the Persian Empire and outside both, saw themselves as a single body. When Constantine sought to bring an end to the Arian controversy, though he was facing an essentially imperial problem, he recognized that the church was wider than the empire; a small, but symbolically important group of representatives from outside the Roman Empire attended the Council of Nicaea in 325. In after years, other Christian emperors called councils; but, as the great Christological controversies of the fifth century tore the church of the Roman Empire apart, no one thought of consulting the Christians beyond the Roman Empire. The unity of the church was a priority for imperial domestic policy; no one considered the effect on the Christians of Iran or An-Iran, or the Armenians or the Ethiopians.

---

[23] Eusebius, *Ecclesiastical History* 5.23–25.
[24] As Tertullian complained, *Against Praxeas* I.

From one point of view, the Council of Chalcedon of 451 is a triumph, defining the safe areas for Christology while leaving room for maneuver; but in effect it represented a consensus between those who did their theological thinking in Greek and those who did it in Latin. Those whose theological vocabulary was in Coptic or Syriac, left outside, felt at liberty to be unconvinced by what the Chalcedonian Definition said, or seemed to them to say. Terms such as Nestorian, Monophysite, Melkite became theological swearwords to hurl at other Christians. The century after Chalcedon, as successive emperors sought imperial unity by imposing the formula as the final statement of Christology, brought disaster. The church split three ways, and broadly along cultural and linguistic lines: Greco-Latin, Syriac, Coptic.

It was the end of the shared consciousness that had constituted World Christianity. The sixth century is a neglected Christian watershed—the great ecumenical failure. Its effects were momentous. Speaking again broadly, it divided the Christians of Europe from those of Africa and Asia. African Christianity, a coherent whole comprising Coptic Egypt, Nubia, and Ethiopia, went its own way. Asian Christianity continued to spread for a time, reaching its height in the early ninth century.[25] But the arrival of the Arabs united in their newfound faith of Islam took over in Egypt and Syria (within the Roman Empire) and An-Iran (within the Persian) areas of immense significance for Christianity. Arab rule drove a wedge between these old Christian heartlands and those with whom they had once at shared in a single Christian community. The result was the slow eclipse of Christianity in Asia, its erosion in Africa, and the emergence of European Christianity as representative Christianity. European Christians came to think of themselves as, if not exactly the only Christians, at least the only authentic Christians. Any other Christian form being was readily seen as deviant, as the later encounters in India and Ethiopia, when the sixteenth century brought Europe's isolation to an end, abundantly illustrate. And in its isolation European Christianity developed features that impeded its later attempts to take the Christian faith to peoples beyond Europe.

There was a further result of the great ecumenical failure. The division of the church having once taken place along cultural and linguistic lines, it was all too easy for it to happen again. The relations of Greek-speaking and Latin-speaking Christians became increasingly acrimonious, until, by the eleventh century, the two had drifted hopelessly apart, each accusing

---

[25] The time of the patriarchate of Timothy I, mentioned above. See the map in Raymond Le Coz, *L'Église de l'Orient: chrétiens d'Irak, d'Iran et de Turquie* (Paris: Editions du Cerf, 1995).

the other of having altered the previously accepted creeds.[26] Once there had been a Christian consciousness that was as near global as knowledge of the world then available would permit. Now the defining European consciousness was that of Christendom, a word that simply means Christianity, but which in Europe acquired territorial significance. "Christendom" stood for contiguous territory from the Atlantic to the Carpathians, where Christianity was the basis of customary law; where populations were, in principle, subject to the Law of Christ, their rulers vassals of the King of kings, their Scriptures and their liturgy and their learning enshrined in the special Christian language, Latin. Europe was Christian territory over against heathen territory, Christendom over against heathendom. Christianity had become a geographical expression.

This is not the place to take the story further, to the emergence of vernacular expressions of Christianity in Northern and Western Europe in the sixteenth century; though one recalls the observation of Fernand Braudel that, to a surprising extent, the Protestant–Catholic divide in Europe follows the line of the Roman Empire.[27] After American Christianity came into being, the legacy of slavery introduced a further complication, as Black and White Christianity developed separately. Soon the division of the church on cultural and linguistic lines, in the sixth century a watershed, became routine until it became a matter of convenience.

The Remergence of World Christianity

Over a period of some four and a half centuries from around 1500, a great migration took Europeans in their millions to form vast new nations like those of the Americas, Australia, and New Zealand, which adopted the languages and cultural norms of Europe. The migration led to the setting up of maritime empires, which were largely dismantled in the twentieth century. (In the case of Russia, a land-based empire was reduced in the twentieth century.) They set up a world order and patterns of trade that in the mid-twentieth century began to unravel. That Great European Migration came to a halt in the mid-twentieth century (the state of Israel was perhaps

---

[26] The Western church had in fact done so, though without proper communication with its Greek-speaking partners.

[27] Fernand Braudel, *The Mediterranean and the Mediterranean World in the Age of Philip II,* English trans. (London: Collins, 1972), 2:771. Cf. ibid., 2:768: "What remained of the Roman Empire on the shores of the Latin sea put up more resistance in the sixteenth century than it had in the fifth."

its last major product), and then went into reverse as millions of Africans, Asians, and Latin Americans poured into Europe and North America, in a process that will no doubt continue.

These migrations were the background to a religious development that was to determine the shape of Christianity for the future: the reappearance of World Christianity in a magnified form. When the Great European Migration began, Christianity was a European religion and the religion of Europe; indeed Europe was Christendom, it was Christianity. Half a century after the end of that migration, Christianity in Europe was receding, and the majority of the world's Christians were Africans, Asians, Latin Americans, and the Great Reverse Migration was making many of them an organic part of Europe and North America. Once more, there is a church across the world, across the continents, across cultures, across languages, and once more there is just the glimmering of a world Christian consciousness, a recognition that we belong together. It is too late to restore the structures that collapsed in the sixth century, but there is, perhaps, time to develop that world Christian consciousness of mutual belonging and coinherence into a new and more effectual form.

The conditions of Pope Victor's third century Rome are now to be found not only in London and New York and Sydney, but in Nairobi and Singapore, with diverse and sometimes clashing forms, expressions, and customs of Christians from all over the world to be found side by side. The most pressing issues in twenty-first century Christianity are ecumenical. By its origin that word ought to refer to the inhabited world; but in earlier centuries people became used to thinking of the *oikumene* as the Roman Empire.[28] In the sixth century that habit proved disastrous, and all habits of thought that shut out large parts of the Christian world are similarly likely to be stultifying. The word "ecumenical" now has little to do with the relations of Lutherans and Baptists; ecumenical issues are about how African and Indian and Chinese and Korean and Hispanic and North American and East and West European expressions of Christian faith and life can live together and bring mutual enrichment and correction. The major ecumenical issues are about reversing the process of division of the church on cultural and linguistic lines, and returning to the multicultural model of the New Testament church.

Every aspect of church life—doctrine, worship, polity, ethics, social thinking, finance—is likely to be affected if we take that possibility seriously. And scholarship has its own part in the great drama that brings Christians

---

[28] Cf. Luke 2:1.

into true mutuality, with research and scholarship in Christian history having a part in a reconciliation that enables the New Temple of Ephesians to be built.

There are two Great Commissions in the New Testament. The Matthean Commission sends the apostles to disciple the nations—not to make some disciples in each nation, but to disciple the *nations,* discipling those distinctives that constitute and reflect nationality. Discipleship must reach the very roots of our identity, and the Matthean Great Commission, when fulfilled, brings distinctive forms of discipleship, reflecting the identity of the different nations. The Johannine Great Commission says simply, "As the Father sent me, so I am sending you." The disciple enters into the Lord's mission, which is his Father's mission. That mission was certainly to preach and teach; but it was also to heal and to suffer, to be and to do. All the distinctive discipleships of the different nations are taken up into Christ, in whom alone humanity is made complete. Can there be any more awesome scholarly task than to explore these in the history of the church in the inhabited world?

2

Origen, the Father of Mission Studies

Theological scholarship needs a renaissance of mission studies.[1] Christianity is now a non-Western religion. The majority of those who profess it live in Africa, Asia, Latin America, and the Pacific. The significant developments that determine what its shape will be in the twenty-first and twenty-second centuries will be those that take place in the southern continents, where Christian faith is in daily interaction with the cultures of these areas and daily developing in new ways as a result, and within the political and economic and social settings of those continents.

From the point of view of the traditional student of Christian history, the new situation requires profound rethinking. A Western Christian may enter into the feelings of the followers of Jesus who fled Jerusalem before the Roman War of AD 66–70. After the Roman victory, as the exiled believers remembered the now desolated temple that had once been their home, they could take comfort from the fact that Jesus now had more servants in Antioch and in Asia and in Greece and Rome—than Jerusalem had ever known. But in their hearts the survivors of the AD 70 holocaust must have known that the faith of Christ would now be carried on in a very different way. The new believers had no temple and, in the way a Jerusalem believer understood it, no Torah either. They would never hear the prophets read or the Psalms chanted in Hebrew, their children would be uncircumcised and would eat pork without revulsion. These Gentile disciples would continually raise questions about belief, social life, and moral choice that were not part of the great tradition—that is to say, the tradition of life in the

---

[1] For background to this statement, see A. F. Walls, "Structural Problems in Mission Studies," *International Bulletin of Missionary Research* 15 (1991): 146–55.

Messiah maintained by the Torah-keeping Jewish disciples when James the Just presided over the joyous company who held their property in common, shared their meals from house to house, and attended the temple prayers together.

We may now see a corresponding change in the way in which the story of the faith of Christ is carried on. For the student of the Christian faith, as for the student of the southern continents, the past century has provided materials enough to shatter the familiar frameworks of study. The pattern of assumptions behind a good deal of conventional discourse still seems to be something like this: centuries ago Christianity, the religion of the Roman Empire, became the religion of the West, helping to shape its culture. In the modern period, the Christian hold on Western culture has been loosened, to differing degrees in different areas. Insofar as the West still has a religion, it is Christianity, and Christianity has been important in its cultural development. The non-Western world, by contrast, has been shaped by Eastern religions. The colonial era, which established Western hegemony over much of the non-Western world, has come to an end, and with it the largely unsuccessful missionary attempt to replace the religions and cultures of the East with the Western cultural model. (It will be observed that this model of discourse has no effective space for Africa, or for the primal religions that cannot be identified as specifically Western or Eastern.) There are many variants of the model; some theological versions even stress the expansion of Christianity in the non-Western world without looking for anything much in Christian expression to change as a result—rather as if the Jerusalem church in AD 70 had assumed it would go on sending inspectors to approve new developments, as it had done in Samaria and Antioch in its early days.

New Understanding, Old Story

Such models of discourse simply cannot be sustained. The emergence of Christianity as a non-Western religion provides both a new story and new means of understanding the old story. The story of non-Western Christianity, with all its new elements, is continuous with earlier Christian history. It is also evident that Christian developments in different parts of the non-Western world have a certain coherence. In other words, the materials of mission studies, if we may use this term as a shorthand to cover all the studies arising from this new phase of Christian history, are not only relevant for the specific segments of social reality that they illuminate; they may also shed light on earlier Christian history, including specifically Western church history and the history of Western society. Even more, they may help to illuminate and explicate the Christian faith itself.

For a variety of reasons academic theology has often been rather slower to profit from the materials that have emerged from non-Western Christianity than have the historical and social and linguistic sciences; only now are the theological issues posed by the missionary movement beginning to make an impact on the academic theology of the West. It seems justifiable, therefore, to reflect further on the nature of mission studies; to seek analogies in earlier Christian history to the academic processes involved; to determine, in fact, when and where mission studies began. Is there any single figure who can be reasonably identified—not, indeed, as the founder or inventor of mission studies, for such titles are always invidious, but as a defining ancestor? Someone who embodies the nature of the task and points the way for successors? Who could be designated the father of mission studies in the way Eusebius is the father of church history?

I recognize that many candidates may be set forth as the defining ancestor of mission studies. The nominee that follows is offered because he illustrates so vividly the continued interaction of faith and culture that forms the raw material of mission studies and the dedicated and devout intellectual application to those issues that provides its processes. He was born in Alexandria in or about the year 185 of the Christian era. His name, Origen, is a compound of the name of the Egyptian god Horus, which suggests that his family may have had its roots in the Egyptian countryside.

The outline of Origen's life is well known and needs no detailed treatment here. The main sources for it, outside slight references in his own writings, are three in number. The most considerable is the account by Eusebius in his *Ecclesiastical History*.[2] Eusebius never knew Origen but revered him because his own revered teacher, Panphilus, who was Origen's student, did so. It is usual to allow a discount for the enthusiasms of Eusebius, but it is never wise to underrate him. His sources for the life of Origen were substantial, ranging from primary sources now lost (including an archive of more than a hundred letters) to gossip. In employing this material, he usually tells us which is which, and even if we ignore the gossip, there is plenty left. We know more with reasonable certainty about the life and worth of Origen than we do of most of his contemporaries.

The second source is Origen's student Gregory Thaumaturgus. Gregory came from a pagan family in northern Anatolia and became a major figure

---

[2] The main account is in Eusebius, *Ecclesiastical History*, book 6, between sections 16 and 39.

in the Christianization of his native Pontus. (The popular belief was that
when he began his work in Pontus there were only seventeen Christian
inhabitants, and when he died only seventeen who were not Christians.)
He met Origen through a strange set of circumstances: his brother-in-
law was appointed to a post in the Palestine administration, and it fell to
Gregory to escort his sister to join her husband in Caesarea. Origen had
recently begun to lecture there; Gregory attended the lectures, and they
changed the course of his life. In a rhetorical address to Origen he records
his indebtedness to his old teacher and gives a lively account of the latter's
teaching method and practice. We also have a letter written by Origen to
Gregory, probably some years before the address, urging him to bring his
studies and abilities, which could bring his pupil such wealth as a lawyer or
such prestige as an academic philosopher, to the basis of the study of Christianity.[3] To this theme we shall return.

Thoroughly Greek, Thoroughly Christian

A further source is more problematic but, as far as it takes us, fascinating.
It comes from the decidedly anti-Christian philosopher Porphyry, who, in
a work known to Eusebius, claims to have known Origen.[4] Porphyry notes
that Origen, like Porphyry's great hero Plotinus, was a pupil of Ammonius
Saccas, the most influential Alexandrian scholar of his time. But while
acknowledging Origen's great reputation, Porphyry complains that, as far as
rational behavior is concerned, he went in a totally different direction from
his master. He says,

> Origen, a Greek educated in Greek learning, drove straight toward
> barbarian recklessness. . . . He hawked himself and his literary skill
> about; and while his manner of life was Christian and contrary to
> the Law, in his opinions about foreign deities he played the Greek,
> and introduced Greek ideas into foreign fables. For he was always
> consorting with Plato, and was conversant with the writings of
> Numenius, and Cronius, Apollophanes, Longinus, and Moderatus,

---

[3] The two texts, with a French translation, are conveniently put together in H.
Crouzel, *Gregoire le Thaumaturge. Remerciment a Origene suivi de la lettre d'Origene a
Gregoire, Sources Chretiennes* (Paris: Editions du Cerf, 1969). An English translation of
both is given by W. Metcalfe, *Gregory Thaumaturgus: Address to Origen* (London: SPCK,
1920). Origen's letter itself is in chapter 13 of the *Philokalia*.
[4] Quoted extensively in *Ecclesiastical History*, 6:19.

Nicostratus and the distinguished men among the Pythagoreans; and he used the books of Chaeremon the Stoic and Cornutus, from whom he learned the figurative interpretation, as employed in the Greek mysteries, and applied it to the Jewish writings.[5]

This passage shows that Porphyry recognizes the considerable extent of Origen's learning and acknowledges that it was not superficial. Origen was, in fact, always "consorting with Plato" as well as regularly using the commentaries that, as he tells us elsewhere, Plotinus himself used (no doubt following their common teacher Ammonius Saccas). Porphyry, however, clearly believes that such activity is incongruous in a Christian because, by his definition, Christians are tied into "barbarian recklessness," with which such studies are incompatible. In other words, he takes for granted that Christians have turned their backs on the Greek intellectual heritage. By giving authority to Jewish writings, they have identified with the barbarian world; Greekness and Christianity do not belong together.

It will be noted that Porphyry says that Origen was brought up as a Greek (that is, as a pagan), and converted to Christianity. This cannot be the case; Eusebius's account of Origen's Christian home and upbringing is too circumstantial to be set aside. But Porphyry's mistake is a revealing one; he could not bring himself to believe that someone who had actually been brought up as a Christian could have the degree of Greek literary equipment that Origen obviously had. He knows that Origen lived as a Christian (and thus, from Porphyry's point of view, in an illegal and antisocial fashion); he knows also that intellectually he "played the Greek," even when talking of the Deity, applying Greek ideas to the Jewish Scriptures ("foreign fables") that Christians in general cultivated. Porphyry cannot divest himself of the idea that Greekness must involve some affirmation of the heritage of polytheism.[6]

It is precisely in this endeavor to be both thoroughly Greek and thoroughly Christian, in the conviction that this enterprise is possible, and in the massive scale of his attempt to implement it, that the enduring fascination of Origen lies. His is the most systematic attempt of early Christianity to employ the whole encyclopedia of Greek learning, as well as the categories of Greek intellectual discourse, to the exploration and elucidation of the Christian faith. Conversely, his is the most remarkable systematic attempt

---

[5] Ibid. The translation is that of H. J. Lawlor and J. E. L. Oulton, *Eusebius: The Ecclesiastical History* (London: SPCK, 1927), 1:192.

[6] For a full discussion of Origen's relations with Plotinus and Neoplatonism, and a full discussion of the issues raised by Porphyry, with bibliography, see Henri Crouzel, *Origene et Plotin. Comparaisons doctrinales* (Paris: Tequi, 1991).

to think the principle of Christ into the whole intellectual configuration of his time, to plot its significance on the intellectual map of his day. Into the different areas of the intellectual discourse of his day, he brings the implications of the statement that the one whom we meet in the gospels as Jesus the Christ is the Logos of God, the divine reason at the heart of the universe. The great themes of intellectual and scientific discussion—time, space, matter, the soul, the stars, the animal world, history, destiny—must surely be illuminated by that conviction. Origen ranges along all the major highways and over many of the subsidiary tracks of contemporary philosophy, ethics, physics, and linguistics, his guiding light the conviction of the ultimate significance of the Logos who is also Christ Jesus. He wades through waving cornfields of Greek learning and literature, and, while he rarely quotes authorities, handles the whole canon of Greek authors more effectively than even such a substantial representative of the Hellenic tradition as Celsus.[7] And into that body of traditional material he introduces the new literary source that Christianity brought to bear on the accepted contemporary corpus of writing, the prophetic and apostolic writings that Christians read in their meetings for worship.

Missionaries, Converts, and Christian Homes

Origen's parents were Christians; we do not know whether they were converts. Leonides, his father, gave him both a solid secular education and a thorough grounding in the Scriptures. This fact is worth a moment's reflection. The first major explorer of the significance of Christianity in the Hellenistic world is the apostle Paul. But Paul is a foreign missionary, and he thinks and writes as one. Deeply as he immersed himself in Greek thought, comfortable as he made himself in Greek culture (too comfortable for some of his colleagues, who would have liked him to identify more strongly with old and safe ways), he remained at heart a Jew. He knew where his background and identity lay. He never forgot that he was circumcised the eighth day, of the tribe of Benjamin, even if he could place those facts in proportion; and he knew exactly the difference between the cultivated olive tree, which represented Israel as his homeland, and the uncultivated graft that Gentile Christianity represented.[8] Though he enters Gentile culture, he does so as an outsider whose natural home is elsewhere, making the adventure for Christ's sake.

---

[7] On this range, see Henry Chadwick, *Origen: Contra Celsum*, translated with an Introduction and Notes (Cambridge: Cambridge University Press, 1954).

[8] See Romans 11:11–24.

The earliest Christian philosophers we know of—Justin, Athenagoras, Clement of Alexandria—were converts. Their writings reflect a consciousness that they now belong to Israel (Justin can do battle with Trypho the Jew over who owns the Scriptures), but they know they were not born there. They have been grafted in, grafts of the wild olive tree. The business of their life (and, since it is the question that their friends and neighbors raise, the center of their mission) is to establish the relationship of the Christ, who now claims their allegiance, to the Greek past. What was God doing in the Greek world over all those centuries when he was preparing Israel for the coming of the Christ?

This is not Paul's question. For Paul, the Jewish missionary, the astonishing revelation was that the Gentiles were to have such a significant place in God's salvation; it was the present and future, rather than the past, that gripped him.[9] Justin and his contemporaries, on the other hand, have to deal with the past of their people. The Greek worldview and its intellectual foundations were too comprehensive to be ignored; they had to be converted. And so the second-century generation of convert apologists develops principles for the critique of this Hellenic inheritance. Justin, still wearing the philosopher's short cloak that was the contemporary equivalent of the academic gown, introduced the Christian—and especially the prophetic—Scriptures into Greek intellectual discourse as a sourcebook of comparable, even superior, antiquity to that of the Greek literary tradition. All the time he is wrestling with the convert's question—how to turn an existing way of thought and life toward Christ, how to critique the Greek heritage: affirming, denying, discriminating.

Origen, with his dual education, Greek and Christian, takes the process a stage further—beyond critique to reconception, refiguring. He is not a convert; he has been born into a Christian tradition. In his day, Christianity was still a minority movement, even if a growing one, and could still attract hostility, both from state activity and from popular sentiment, but it was no longer foreign or alien; it was native. Origen does not sort out the Greek from the Christian elements in his upbringing; he has received both with his mother's milk. A careful Christian father—one who was ready to give his life for his faith—provided his children with a good Greek education without worrying too much whether all those authors were suitable for Christian reading, or pausing to cleanse Homer's mythology. Justin, the convert, is always afraid of the demons, always conscious of their presence in the Greek world. Origen, brought up as a Christian, is much more relaxed about such matters; in his consciousness, Christ has taken care of the demons.

---

[9] Ephesians 3:4–6.

Before he was seventeen, his father, Leonides, was imprisoned and then executed in an anti-Christian outburst in Alexandria. Origen tried to share his father's witness unto death; his mother frustrated him, it is said, by hiding his clothes. The experience left a permanent mark; Origen always associated Christian faith with the danger or expectation of suffering. The intellectual project that occupied his whole life was not maintained in unruffled academic calm but in an environment where visible Christianity was always insecure and often physically dangerous. The purpose of his teaching was to lead people to the point of potential martyrdom and to prepare them for the implications when they reached that point. It is common to stress the "realized" nature of Origen's eschatology; it should also be remembered that he and his pupils lived on the edge of time, in eschatological preparedness for death.

He was the eldest of seven children. The family property had been confiscated as part of his father's punishment, so Origen had to now support his mother and the family. He turned to teaching, qualified as he was to instruct in the standard Greek curriculum. This teaching was soon diversified in an unexpected way.

The outburst against the church that had claimed his father's life had disrupted the arrangements for meeting those who were inquiring about Christianity and for teaching those who had made this commitment and were preparing for baptism. Clement, the cultivated literary intelligence who had been in charge of both, had left Alexandria. Almost by default, Origen found himself in charge of the catechetical school, and eventually the bishop, making a virtue of necessity, formally appointed him to this task.

Origen as Christian Educator

We should not think of the catechetical school of Alexandria in terms of ideas about church membership classes. In some parts of the early church— Rome for instance—the parallels are closer, though a three-year period of instruction might seem long by modern standards. But Alexandria's school for Christian inquirers had taken account of modes of life in Alexandria. The city was a major intellectual center. It was home to the Musaeum, with its lecture halls and ambulatories (it was believed that philosophy was best done while walking), its great dining hall (intellectual conversation is stimulated by eating together), its magnificent library, restored by Claudius after earlier military damage, and its many professional chairs of philosophy, grammar, and literary criticism endowed by successive emperors. Alexandria's huge

Jewish community had already developed its own tradition of learning, which fused the Greek and Jewish traditions; the work of the greatest of the Jewish scholars of Alexandria, Philo, was to inspire and inform much of Origen's own work. The Christians of Alexandria had to work with people who had been influenced, at first or second hand, by the intellectual currents represented, on the one hand, by the Musaeum and, on the other, by the learned synagogue reflected in Philo. Those who approached Christianity as inquirers, whether sympathetic or critical, raised questions that came from the discourses of those institutions and had to be met in those terms. Nor was the choice before them simply between becoming Christians or remaining in a static inherited religious tradition. Christianity stood in a spectrum of religious options; those who were interested or concerned enough to investigate it might also be inquiring elsewhere. Nor was there any guarantee that if sufficiently attracted they would come into the church; Christianity itself shaded into other forms of religious philosophy, some of them less demanding or more accommodating. Part of the task of making Christianity thoroughly at home in the Alexandrian world was to develop the faculty of discrimination.

It was against this background that Origen's teaching career began. It went hand in hand with his own studies. He must have already been head of the catechetical school when, like Plotinus, he attended the lectures of Ammonius Saccas. He engaged in dialogue with learned Jews who knew Greek, so he learned Hebrew. We have already noted the outbreaks of violence, which meant that every so often one or more of his students was martyred. Origen acquired a reputation for staying with them to encourage and support them and several times was himself in danger of death. He is often called a speculative thinker, but his intellectual activity had severely practical implications, and his students' grasp of their subject might at any time be placed under empirical test.

This point leads us to a significant aspect of the process by which Origen implanted Christian thinking in Greek intellectual soil. Ideally, philosophy was not merely an academic discipline; it was a way of life. Plato taught that the end of philosophy was the vision of God. To turn to the philosophic life was in fact a form of conversion, a deliberate choice not to live in the way that most people do. The philosophical life required mental discipline, produced by the study of grammar, physics, and mathematics to prepare the mind for higher reaches of attainment; it also required moral discipline, the pursuit of virtue, the abandonment of vice.

By early Christian times, this ancient ideal had gone sour. Philosophy had become secularized, professionalized, trivialized; it had become a profession, a job, a career. The second-century Christian apologist Justin, who spent some time among the philosophers looking for the life-changing vision of which Plato spoke, rejected several as unworthy guides—one because he required too many propaedeutic subjects, and one because he wanted to settle the fee in advance (such a consideration indicated that the teacher was no true philosopher). The reaction on the part of the young inquirer Justin shows that the ideal of the philosophic life still had followers in the second century, even if the reality was often more sordid. There were still people looking for the vision of God in the philosophic life, expecting conversion thereby, and recognizing that this would imply a new lifestyle.

Origen's work starts at the point that Justin reached sometime after his Christian conversion. Christianity is true philosophy, leading humans not to the Platonic vision of God but to something even richer. They may become partakers of the divine nature through the Word. The Christian discipline embraces the whole universe of knowledge, for Christ is the Logos, the divine reason through whom all creation came into being. All that is in accordance with reason is his, and all sources of knowledge may be confidently explored by his light. It is the Christian confidence of Origen that impresses today; the convert's fear of the demons, so evident in Justin, has given way to assurance in the endlessly penetrative power of the Word who is Christ Jesus. His pupil Gregory reports that Origen excluded only the Epicureans from his philosophical curriculum; the practical atheism and the hedonism built into their system rendered them valueless in the search for truth. But all the other schools and all the academic disciplines could properly be laid under tribute by Christians. The old groundwork disciplines such as grammar and mathematics were still good for the mental discipline necessary for the study of philosophy, and helpful for the study of the Scriptures, which were the sourcebook of true philosophy. In a letter he tells Gregory, "I beg you to draw from the Greek philosophers such things as can be made curricular or preparatory studies to Christianity, for geometry and astronomy, such things as may be useful for expounding Holy Scripture. The philosophers say that geometry and music and grammar and rhetoric and astronomy are the handmaidens of philosophy. Let us say that philosophy itself is the handmaid of Christianity."[10]

Justin the convert had used the Scriptures to critique his intellectual heritage, enabling him to affirm part and abandon part and modify part. Origen, nurtured in the Christian faith, goes a step further. The Greek

---

[10] *Philokalia* 13.

intellectual inheritance is prolegomena to be put to use in opening up the understanding of life in Christ through the Scriptures. For Origen, the Greek inheritance is a means of appropriating the Christian one.

Christianity Annotated by Pre-Christian Learning

Gregory tells us that Origen engaged his students in dialectics to develop the faculty of discrimination, to avoid sloppiness and self-delusion. He adds that Origen did not think rhetoric particularly important, since it contributed to expression, rather than to substance; on the sciences, however, he discoursed until his students were amazed at the all-wise workmanship displayed in the created universe. From thence to philosophy. Origen was the first, says Gregory, to incline him to philosophize—by his words certainly, but also by his actions. Christian theology was annotated, as it were, by Greek writers— "So that we were taught to collate with all our powers all the writings of the ancients, whether philosophers or poets, rejecting nothing because we had not the necessary discrimination." They should not, in fact, reject out of hand any school of philosophy or any body of learning, Greek or barbarian, but bring them into critical relationship with the body of Christian theology until they form a commentary on it, not a substitute for it.

Moreover, in Christian studies, the moral disciplines are still vital, as they were in the Greek tradition. In their Christian form they were the disciplines of a godly life and the discipline of prayer. At the heart of Christian studies, the key to the vast encyclopedia of learning, are the Scriptures of the Old and the New Testaments. It is necessary to stress the two testaments, for there was a strong movement among Greek Christians to divorce the Old Testament from the New, to make Christianity more Greek by cutting it from its Jewish roots. Origen refuses to go this way; he insists that the two testaments belong together, with a unity found in Christ. The system of allegorical exegesis that he did so much to develop is entirely comprehensible in terms of contemporary Greek literary method. But underlying Origen's approach is the conviction that Christian philosophy cannot abandon the Old Testament or the rootedness of the gospel in Israel's history.

Origen, then, represents a Christian version of the Greek intellectual tradition in its goals, activities, and methods. In fact, the operation that he began rescued that tradition, gave it new meaning, depth, and energy when it had become stale and barren and professionalized. The Neoplatonist revival associated with Plotinus and Porphyry is another stream of reformation flowing at the same time and one that rejected the Christian version as "barbarian reck-lessness"; in the end, however, it was the application to Christian themes, the development of Christian theology, that restored vigor and purpose to the Greek intellectual tradition. With Christian theology, philosophy returned to big subjects and vital themes; once more it was a quest for truth, with an urgency in the quest. Christianity gave it a new sourcebook, new themes, and a new energy.

Yet in some respects the Christian appropriation of the Greek heritage was very traditional. It kept traditional methods, retained the old sources, gave them a new role, and restored something of the old motive and object. For Plato, as for the young Justin, the end of the philosophic quest was the vision of God. For Origen, the philosophic quest is the preparation for the Christian life. In this and many other respects he is most Greek when he is most Christian, and most Christian when he is most Greek. When Christianity came to the Greek world, it appeared at first to be incompatible with that world's essential Greekness. But it turned out to be a source of cultural preservation and renewal. It was not to be the last time in Christian history that this paradox occurred.

As Origen's catechetical school developed, he divided it, passing the elementary studies to Heraklas, the future bishop, and taking the more advanced students himself. He lived very simply—no wine, a minimum of food and sleep. He slept on the floor of his lecture room. It was the old ideal of the philosophic life actualized in Alexandria.

It seems to have been many years before the busy teacher wrote anything. The person who spurred him to write was a certain Ambrose. This man had come to Christian commitment through Origen, having previously been a Valentinian Gnostic (another reminder that Origen worked among people open to a whole spectrum of new religious movements). Posterity's debt to Ambrose is considerable; he provides the first known example of a creative initiative by a publisher. He provided Origen with a staff of seven shorthand writers who, because of Origen's crowded day of labor, worked shifts. In addition, Ambrose provided a staff of female copyists who tran-scribed what Origen dictated to the stenographers. From this initiative Origen's vast literary output emerged and began to be circulated. No one knows how much he wrote. Epiphanius, who thought him a bad influence, said Origen was responsible for six thousand rolls. "Who of us can read all he wrote?" asks a despairing Jerome. The *Commentary on John* alone had sixty-four rolls, and we have only nine of them.[11]

---

[11]   On the publication of Origen's works and his prolific output, see E. J. Goodspeed, *Christianity Goes to Press* (New York: Macmillan, 1940), 87ff.

A discerning publisher, Ambrose also commissioned works, some on matters that troubled him (the treatise *On Prayer* arose in this way), some on matters that he knew troubled other people. If Origen is the father of mission studies, Ambrose is the first mission studies publisher.

Throughout his service in Alexandria, Origen was a layman. Nor, despite his reputation as a teacher, was he ever invited to preach. It was on a trip abroad that this opportunity was offered, which did not please his bishop, who was still less delighted when the church of Caesarea ordained Origen. The result was that Origen was dismissed from his post in the catechetical school, and he had to leave the city where he had done such significant work. Caesarea readily offered him a home; as we have already seen, he settled into teaching there. His preaching developed, and when he was about sixty, he began to allow his sermons to be taken down in shorthand. We have some of them today. In the Decian persecution of 251 he was severely tortured. He died soon afterward, no doubt partly as a result of his ordeal.[12]

Building for God with Gold from Egypt

This account omits much that is relevant to Origen's mission studies career. One such aspect is his ecumenical vision. Few early Christian writers traveled so far; we find him not only on the beaten tracks but in Arabia and northern Anatolia. Another is his readiness to deal with religious eclectics, such as Julia Mamaea, the emperor's mother, and to put the Christian case to them.

But above all, he is a seminal figure in the story of Christian critical interaction with culture. Some of his profoundest insights in this area are to be found in his commentaries, or in those exegetical tropes that seem so foreign to the modern style of biblical interpretation based on the literary–historical method. He argues, for instance, that Heshbon, a Canaanite city destroyed by the Israelites, could be translated "the city of thoughts." He then points out that when the Israelites destroyed it, they did not leave it

---

[12] The literature on Origen is vast. See Henri Crouzel, *Bibliographie critique d'Origène* (Steenbrugge. Abbey of St. Peter, 1971, supp., The Hague. Nijhoff, 1982, 2d supp., Turnhout: Brepols, 1996). An excellent general presentation is Henri Crouzel, *Origene* (Paris: Lethielleux, 1984; English trans. Origen [San Francisco: Harper, 1989]). See also Jean Danielou, *Origen* (New York: Sheed & Ward, 1955). Two later specialist studies, Alan Scott, *Origen and the Life of the Stars: A History of an Idea* (Oxford: Clarendon Press, 1991), and J. Rebecca Lyman, *Christology and Cosmology: Models of Divine Activity in Origen, Eusebius, and Augustine* (Oxford: Clarendon Press, 1993), may be cited as examples of how Origen continues to provoke fresh thought and investigation.

in ruins but rebuilt it on the same site. It is a telling comment on the Christian cultural project as reflected in Origen's own work: the city of thoughts cannot be allowed to stand as it is, but equally it cannot be allowed to remain in ruins. It has to be rebuilt, but with the same materials. There is nothing wrong, nothing to be feared, in the materials from which Greek thought is constructed; they can be used in the Christian task of intellectual reconstruction.

Still more striking is a passage in his letter to Gregory Thaumaturgus, where he connects the construction of the tabernacle in the wilderness with the spoiling of the Egyptians. The gold cherubim that indicated the holy presence were made from Egyptian gold as were the pot that held the manna and the other vessels used in worship; and the curtains of the tabernacle were made from Egyptian cloth. Materials that were being misused in the heathen world were thus used, thanks to the wisdom of God, for the worship and glorification of God. The work to which he urges Gregory is to put Greek learning to the same sacred use.

Origen does not pretend that this is an easy matter; indeed he emphasizes the risks involved with another Old Testament allusion. Hadad the Edomite made no idols until he went to Egypt. But when he went there and married into the Egyptian aristocracy, he brought back the idea of setting up the golden heifer at Bethel and Dan. Origen tells Gregory, "I assure you, those who have taken what is useful in Egypt, left that country and made objects for divine worship, are rare. But many were the brothers of Hadad the Edomite."[13] Egyptian gold and Greek materials are to be used for the glorification of God, but it is necessary to watch out lest idols be manufactured in the process. For this reason Origen urged on Christians, learned and unlearned, the duty of discrimination and sought to provide them with tools for the purpose.

It has been a special feature of studies that arise from the exercise of Christian mission that they open up new fields of learning, establish new forms of inquiry, and gather new bodies of material. We cannot pause to consider Origen's astonishing achievement in the Hexapla, which, had he done nothing else, would have established him as a major pioneer scholar. In an age when few Greek Christians studied Hebrew and when tensions between church and synagogue were high, he collated the entire Hebrew text of the Old Testament with the texts of all four translations then known. For the Psalms, he collated two more texts, one of which he himself had

---

[13] *Philokalia* 13. Hadad must have here been confused with Jeroboam (cf. 1 Kings 11:14–25 with 1 Kings 12:26ff.)

·discovered in Palestine. Nor can we pause to consider how he developed the Bible commentary, taking the form over from the Gnostics who invented it and making it an instrument of reflection on Scripture. We cannot even pause for *Concerning First Principles*, the first work of systematic theology written for its own sake, rather than as an apology or a defense. Henri Crouzel designates Origen's work a "research theology." It is a happy phrase. Origen's theology is exploratory but open minded, reverent but not fearful. There is no merit in unreflective attachment to opinions. For Origen, only the Word, the Logos, deserved unconditional attachment.

The Greek intellectual inheritance, seized by Origen for the intellectual adornment of the Christian tabernacle, has shaped the whole theological tradition of the Western and Eastern churches. Other aspects of his legacy may yet remain to be exploited. One wonders whether his remarkable exploration of the meaning of time is among these. His view that time is a dimension of the world (it is not time that moves, but the world moves along time as a continuum) may one day attract Indian theologians, whose theology has to relate Christian expression to a metaphysic of time totally different from that with which the mainstreams of Christian theology have hitherto engaged.

This brings us to the point at which we began. The task that absorbed Origen's whole life is precisely the exercise before those who are now engaged in thinking the Christian faith into the fabric of thought of Africa and Asia and Pacific societies. These societies are as complex as the Hellenistic, and like that civilization they have inherited bodies of literature, wisdom, and tradition, written and oral frames of thinking that are as axiomatic for their peoples as the Hellenistic frame was for the likes of Celsus. The theological task has passed the stage where missionaries can be very significant; they already have contributed their part in the story; Paul has done his work. In many areas, perhaps most, it is not the task of the convert generation, relentlessly turning their ways of thinking toward Christ. They too have made their stand, and their contribution, like Justin's, has been vital. The weight of responsibility lies on a new generation of people, like Origen brought up in the Christian faith, confident in the Scriptures, and yet at home in the old cultural tradition—people who are heirs to both the Christian and that other tradition, who have taken in both with their mothers' milk. On such people depends, not only the future of African, Asian, and Pacific theology, but the future of Christian theology and of theological scholarship as a whole.

Those of us who cannot be part of that process can try to understand and interpret it; that too is a crucial dimension of mission studies. And for all of us, Origen may be an exemplar of the Christian scholar and of the role of mission studies. He does not provide a comfortable view of the scholarly vocation. He lived in utter simplicity, comparative poverty, and unremitting toil. His early years were full of danger, with narrow escapes from death; in his sixties he met imprisonment and torture. His church authorities restricted his scope and dismissed him from a teaching post. After his death he was often denounced without comprehension, pilloried as an arch-heretic by people who knew nothing of the setting in which his work was done and could only parrot in safety the established orthodoxies of a different time. He has never reached the calendar of saints.

His only earthly rewards seem to have been the love and eager loyalty of his students, the welcome and openheartedness offered by churches other than his own—and perhaps the unfailing confidence and resourcefulness of his publisher. But he saw the need to turn the learning of the Greek world to the worship and glorification of God. Let us salute Origen of Alexandria as the father of mission studies.

3

Worldviews and Christian Conversion

Worldviews are the mental maps of the universe that contain what we know, or think we know, about the universe and, how it operates, and about our own place in it. We use these maps to navigate our way through daily life. The maps are compiled from many sources: from our own observation and experience, from our family and our education, from the outlook and customs of our community, from the accumulation of sources we believe we have reason to trust. For certain purposes, we may borrow a map from a source that we do not regularly use, rather as one might consult an atlas for a specialized point of geography. We may, for instance, refer, if only occasionally, to the "atlas"—the detailed scheme of doctrine or and interpretation—of a religious system to which we give general recognition. In such cases we copy additional detail from the atlas on to our own maps. We are unlikely to copy all the maps that we find in the atlas of the religious system on to the maps we use for our own daily operations; while some things found in the atlas will seem to us to be crucial for those operations, others may appear to us unimportant, peripheral, or incomprehensible. The items we deem crucial will be copied on to our own map in detail; those that seem less important to us will be copied in sketchy outline, or simply ignored.

Our worldview maps cover not only the phenomenal world of what we can see and touch, but whatever we recognize as transcending that world, what one might call the sphere of religion. The maps also contain our ideas of morality and of obligation, the rights and duties that we recognize. They contain a sense of relationships, family and kin, clan and nation—those to whom we believe we belong. They also indicate those to whom we believe do not belong, and why that is the case. They indicate

our understanding of society, its ranks and hierarchies, and where we see
our place in them to be. The maps also show what we see as places of safety
where we may walk with confidence, and areas of danger, where we walk
warily or not at all.

The maps indicate the degree of contingency we feel, the degree of
certainty and predictability that we take to be normal, the degree of recognition we give to the activity of forces beyond our control. In this respect
in particular, worldview maps vary greatly. In so-called modern worldviews
the contingency factor is low; people expect to be in general control of their
environment, the electric light to come on at the pressing of a switch, clean
water to come from turning a tap. By contrast, for much of humanity, both
in earlier times and today, a high degree of contingency has been the norm,
with a lively consciousness of dependence on factors beyond one's control,
not only for light and clean water, but for the daily food supply. Along with
the degree of contingency, worldview maps also indicate places of power,
support, and protection. Where the places of danger are marked large on the
worldview map, and the degree of contingency is high, the places of power
and of protection, and the ways to them, will also be prominently plotted.

The items on the worldview map are plotted in relation to one other,
in two ways. The first way reflects their relative importance in the operations of life; just as a geographical map reflects the relative sizes of physical
features or populated areas, worldview maps show the relative importance of
different elements of belief or norms of conduct to the way life is conducted.
The second way in which the elements within a worldview are plotted in
relation to one another is that connections between different elements
are indicated: there are connecting mental pathways, rather like the roads
shown on a geographical map. Such mental pathways may link, for instance,
the area of rights and duties both to the area of religion and the area of kin
relationship; they may also link the places of danger to the sources of power
and protection.

Conceptual importance is not the same as operational importance.
Many peoples, for instance, have what we may call a "God component"
in their worldview maps; they have a concept of a Supreme Being, often
with a vernacular name, believed to be the creator and moral governor of
the universe. On a map of concepts such as a scheme of theology, this item
would be represented very large. But worldview maps are operational; and in
the operational religion of many peoples who possess such concepts of God,
far more attention is paid to territorial divinities who control the land, or to
ancestors who maintain the family and the clan, or to intermediary beings of

some kind, than to God. On such worldview maps, therefore, God appears relatively small in relation to the other entities who have more significance in the operations of life—even religious life.

Nor is this a feature of the worldviews only of so-called primal societies. We have already noted that worldview maps make selective use of the "atlases" of the great religious systems, copying in detail from the maps therein features that appear crucial for operational purposes, sketching others in broader outline, ignoring others altogether. This process occurs among Christians, Muslims and Buddhists alike—and in the construction of an infinite number of personal worldview maps.

For worldview maps are both personal and collective, the collective maps being identifiable where a community shares the same trusted sources, and thus makes use of broadly similar elements in broadly similar relationships. There may be oscillation and variation where some members of the community use trusted sources that other members do not. In this connection we may note that, except as an abstract concept, there is no such thing as *the* Christian worldview. There are elements from the sources that Christians in general trust, which will give a broad similarity to the operational maps of Christians across cultural divides; but the worldview maps of Christians from any given place or time will draw on other sources for their worldview that they do not share with fellow Christians of other cultures, but do share with people of their own culture who are not Christians. There are thus, in practice, a range of Christian worldviews, all sharing Christian elements, but each sharing other operational features with Muslim or Buddhist or primal traditionalist or modern agnostic neighbors.

With this in mind, we can proceed to consider how worldviews change.

Changing Worldviews

Worldviews, and the operational mapping process that produces them, are subject to change. They can be influenced by new ideas, outside events, emotional upheavals, the expansion of knowledge. Rarely, however, are worldviews entirely destroyed and replaced by completely different ones. What usually happens is that people modify their maps of reality, adding the new information correcting ideas they now see as wrong, altering the relationship of one set of ideas to another, making some bigger some smaller, crossing some out altogether. It is a process analogous to the way geographical maps are constructed and updated: marking a town that was not known to us before, or altering the shape of a stretch of coastline to indicate a bay or an inlet imperfectly explored previously, or showing a new road while deleting an old one no longer in use. Very rarely do people throw away the map altogether. Worldview maps, human operational systems, are usually revised and corrected, not abandoned and replaced.

It is important to remember this in relation to Christian conversion and to Christian nurture. We must not use New Testament passages that describe the new creation in Christ[1] and the moral renewal brought by the Holy Spirit as though they left no continuity with the past. Just as God made Adam from the dust of the earth and breathed into him the breath of life,[2] so the new creation takes place with preexisting materials. We are made by our past; it is our past that has shaped our identity; it is on the basis of the past that our operational maps have been constructed and are now open to revision. Our past cannot be abandoned; we cannot immediately draw a new map from scratch. Our past cannot be substituted by someone else's past, as happened when Gentile proselytes entered old Israel; nor can it be left as it is. Christian conversion involves the *conversion of the past*. In its simplest sense, conversion means turning—turning what is already there— including one's past—toward Christ. Conversion is not so much about new content as new direction.

When people become Christians they do not throw away their maps of reality; new elements are placed on the old maps. The old maps are modified to include new information, to delete wrong or outdated information, to alter the proportions of one element to another, as some components get bigger and some smaller. If God was on the map of reality before, that part of the map will almost certainly expand. Perhaps becoming Christian will mean that Christ is plotted on the operational map for the first time. But while some elements on the map may change drastically, others will change little, or not at all. For instance, Christian conversion may be slow to produce any major alteration in the ideas of relationship and belonging; the first changes in this area will probably bring recognition of kinship with other Christians belonging to communities other than the one constituted by biological kinship. Conversion may not alter the places of safety and danger that are marked on the map; the latter especially may remain exactly as they were before. Beliefs about witchcraft and sorcery may be in exactly the same place on the mental map of the universe as before, even if there

---

[1] E.g., 2 Corinthians 5:17.
[2] Genesis 2:7.

is now a more intense rejection of the actual employment of sorcery than previously.

People who become Christians do not in practice thereby throw away a worldview called "primal" or "Muslim" or "Buddhist" and take a new one called "Christian"; they amend their maps of reality to include new information and correct what they now see as errors. The new Christian elements will be placed on the old map; and elements that may seem characteristically "primal" or "Muslim" or "Buddhist" may still be on the operational map—and not necessarily in operational conflict with the Christian elements. Christian conversion involves turning what is already there—primal things, Islamic things, Buddhist things—toward Christ.

So Christians whose worldview has been shaped by one culture will have a somewhat different operational map of reality from Christians whose worldview has been shaped by another culture. There is thus no one single Christian worldview: all Christian worldviews share vital elements, and these shared elements make them quite different from the non-Christian worldviews of people from a similar cultural background; but they may still be sharply differentiated from some other Christian worldviews. For the same reason, they may contain important elements in common with non-Christian worldviews of the communities from which they come; and those features will differ from those on the worldview maps of their fellow Christians of another cultural background.

As Christian teaching proceeds, Christian ideas commonly penetrate more deeply; in other words, theology is introduced from the Christian atlas, and more information is added to the mental map. But there may still seem no reason to alter some areas on the map—for instance, the area where safe and dangerous places are marked. Beliefs about witchcraft and sorcery may remain very much the same. On the other hand, the way sources of power and protection are denoted may have been completely revised: the old protective mechanisms against evil deleted, and statements from the theological atlas about Christ as the source of power and protection introduced on the map. But the old pre-Christian map had shown a pathway that linked the place of danger to the source of protection. With the deletion of the old source of protection, that path has now disappeared from the map, and there may now be no clear pathway connecting the (still clearly marked) concrete danger of witchcraft to the newly entered theological statement about the love and power of Christ.

Early in the twentieth century, Donald Fraser, a sensitive Scottish missionary in what is now Malawi, described a common type of experience in the still young church in Livingstonia, where the mission schools and hospital were often held up as a model.[3] A young woman, a church member, suffers severe complications in the later stages of pregnancy. Why should this happen? She knows she has been faithful, and begins to wonder if the cause lies in her husband's misbehavior. He, sure of his own innocence, begins to wonder about his wife's. Family and neighbors differ in their guesses as to who is to blame. Those prepared to swear by the innocence of both parties suspect witchcraft or sorcery, and begin to calculate who among their acquaintance might have an interest in causing mischief, and have thus employed the psychic powers of witchcraft or the spiritual technology of sorcery. The woman is attending the antenatal clinic at the mission hospital. Her condition is identified, a healthy baby is triumphantly delivered in hospital, the mother is safe, the church receives both and thanks God.

And there, typically, the account in the missionary magazine will end. But Fraser was aware that for many in Livingstonia the story did not end there. Everyone remembers that something went wrong in the first place, and there must have been a reason for this. Husband and wife continue to have a niggling doubt at the back of their mind over what the other did; and there is a shadow over trust that no triumph of modern medicine can drive away. And the relatives continue to speculate about the part played by the putative secret enemy, and add this to the grievances they already have against the person they have identified as that enemy. And Fraser, writing in the 1920s, admits that there was nothing in the church's armory that could cope with this situation.

The problem is not a matter of faith: these are sincere, believing Christians. Nor is there anything necessarily wrong with the teaching they have received. The problem lies in the gap between the teaching and the mental maps of the universe. Our deepest operational beliefs are not necessarily those we state, but those we think we have no need to state—because we take them to be universal. And everyone in Livingstonia "knew" that a whole network of spiritual forces of diverse origin, some of them open to manipulation, were at work in the world. They also "knew" that in the way the world is constituted, moral (and for that matter ritual) misbehavior will reap its own reward. Complications in pregnancy could never be assumed to be a medical matter alone.

---

[3] See Donald Fraser, *African Idylls: Portraits and Impressions of Life on a Central African Mission Station* (London: Seeley, Service, 1923). On Fraser, see T. Jack Thompson, *Christianity in Northern Malawi: Donald Fraser's Missionary Methods and Ngoni Culture* (Leiden: Brill, 1995).

Missions and Modern Worldviews:
the Enlightenment Effect

Between the young couple and the mission hospital lies the European Enlightenment. For several centuries European Christians used maps of the universe in which Christian elements dominated. These included the theme of One God who created the world, redeemed it through the sacrifice of Christ and in the end would judge all humanity. But those maps still marked certain danger areas in the way that the pre-Christian European maps did. Witchcraft, for instance, was thought of as desperately dangerous as it had been before Christianity came to Europe. Accordingly, witchcraft remained on the European Christian mental map: indeed, it could now have a theological explanation that it had not before; witches were people who had made a pact with the devil. In European Christian countries witchcraft was a criminal offense, punishable by death—often by burning, to symbolize how important it was to destroy all trace of it.

Similarly European Christians continued to believe in supernatural interventions; just as evil such as witchcraft was attributed to the devil, so interventions for good were attributed to God. For centuries prayers to saints were held to produce miraculous healings: special holy places held to be charged with supernatural powers to help. In Protestant Europe this died down, because there was no place left for prayer to saints; but in Catholic Europe the idea of miracles continued.

In the seventeenth and eighteenth centuries the series of intellectual movements now collectively known as the Enlightenment took place in different parts of Europe. "Enlightenment" suggests illumination by new knowledge replacing the darkness of ignorance. Enlightenment took many forms; but among important common elements were the exaltation of reason, the development of science, and the heightening of the sense of autonomy of the individual self.

Christian Europe had taken for granted a foundation of divine revelation: Protestants tending to identify revelation with the Bible, Catholics with the authority of the church. Enlightenment principles challenged both. There is a strong argument for linking scientific investigation with the Protestant Reformation,[4] but the Enlightenment gave it a further boost. Science posited a uniform universe where the same process repeated under the same conditions produces the same result; laws of nature mean that the world works in a uniform way. But miracles represent a breach of natural order

---

[4] Cf. R. Hooykaas, *Religion and the Rise of Modern Science* (Leiden: Brill, 1973).

and cannot be routinely repeated. As for the autonomy of the self, Descartes set out the principle "I think, therefore I exist"—that is, the individual is defined by the individual's own mental activity, not by membership of a community. But Europe had long defined itself as a Christian community, indeed, as *the* Christian community, Christendom. People were Christians because they were born in a Christian country; they were baptized in infancy as Christians, since they had been born into the sphere of salvation. They lived under laws they thought Christian and from which they could not opt out. If Descartes was right, all this must be wrong, for religion must belong to the sphere of private judgment.

So the Enlightenment posed a challenge to the traditional European Christian worldview at key points: the primacy of reason in relation to revelation, the uniform laws of nature in relation to divine intervention through miracles, individual autonomy in relation to corporate identification with territorial Christendom.

Through the Enlightenment Christianity did lose some ground in Europe, and there was certainly a stream of Enlightenment thinking that was hostile to Christianity, and that stream worked toward the eventual secularization of Europe. But on the whole Christianity adjusted to Enlightenment thinking, and Christian worldviews were modified to reflect both Enlightenment and Christian ideas. There were both Christian and non-Christian Enlightenment worldviews. What they had in common was a firm distinction between natural and supernatural: a "natural" world roughly corresponding to what one can see and touch, where natural laws operate uniformly and the principle of repeatability can be used to verify statements. This natural or empirical world has a firm boundary. On the other side of that boundary with the natural world lies what one might call the world of spirit, the transcendent world. Many non-Christian Enlightenment thinkers said in effect that the spirit world does not exist, or if it does, we can know nothing certain about it. Christian thinkers insisted that the other side of the frontier was real and that God did intervene in the empirical to reveal Himself. Revelation occurred at defined crossing places on the frontier. In practice Christian Enlightenment thinkers held that these frontier crossings were limited. They argued, for instance, that miracles were a special dispensation belonging to the time of Christ and His apostles, and had now ceased. Likewise, dreams and visions belonged to biblical times; they were not reliable guides to the transcendent world now. Dreams, indeed, usually had a physical or psychological basis: nowadays guidance should come from Scripture and reason, informed of course by prayer; healing by means of scientific medicine, that is, by applying consecrated reason to the world that God had created. And witchcraft—that was a delusion. It was impossible to manipulate the natural world except in accordance with natural laws. The burning of witches had been a horrible mistake, cruel persecution of vulnerable or emotionally disturbed people. And witchcraft ceased to be a criminal offense and disappeared from the statute books of Europe.

The Enlightenment universe is the basis of "modern" worldviews. Enlightenment worldviews are maps of a universe smaller than that of most European Christians before the Enlightenment and smaller than those used by most people living in Africa or Asia, or for that matter, Latin America. Christian and non-Christian Enlightenment worldviews had in common that they left no place for witchcraft or sorcery, those danger signs marked on so many worldview maps across the globe. Christians and non-Christians might dispute whether miracles happened, but generally the question in dispute was whether they *had* happened in the past; no one was expecting the laws of nature to be suspended now. This meant reading the Bible, especially the Old Testament but also some parts of the New Testament, in a certain way, recognizing that God had used frontier crossings in the past that since the time of the apostles had been closed. Christians were now to exercise their ministry according to the way God had created the world, "thinking God's thoughts after Him" as the great astronomer Kepler put it. So education and medicine were areas to which Christians were especially called.

In this type of worldview the existence of the demonic was problematic. Many non-Christian Enlightenment thinkers tended to ignore it, or to attribute evil to ignorance; more enlightenment would banish it. Christians clearly had to face the issue of evil; but, now that they had accepted the autonomy of the self, they often tended to see evil in terms of individual guilt and sin. The phenomenon known as possession was, like most irrational behavior, perceived as a form of insanity.

All this meant putting brackets around parts of Scripture. The dreams, the visions, the healings, the prophecies, the works of power, belonged to an earlier stage of God's saving activity; such things had ceased with the apostolic age, and had little to do with contemporary Christian practice. They were genuine crossing places on the frontier between the transcendent and empirical worlds—but those crossing places were now boarded up.

Coping with the Enlightenment was not a matter of Christian retreat: it was a massive act of cultural adjustment, an act of contextualization. Nor did it fundamentally divide the more liberal from the more conservative Christians.

It is hard to think of a more powerful advocate of a Christian Enlightenment worldview than that staunch defender of biblical infallibility, B. B. Warfield.[5]

Enlightenment Christianity became the regular form in which the Christianity of the Protestant missionary movement was expressed. And the Enlightenment universe is the basis of modern Western theology, whether liberal or conservative.

The earliest Catholic missions took place before the Enlightenment; reading accounts of missions in the Congo in the sixteenth century one senses much in common in the outlook of the Catholic missionaries and the Congolese people that they met. Protestant missions did not start until the Enlightenment was well established, and it took firmer hold in Protestant Northern Europe than in Catholic Southern Europe. The missionary movement thus brought the Enlightenment with it. It brought Western education and health care. It brought modernity along with the gospel.

Christian Preaching and Traditional Maps of the Universe

Let us consider the worldviews of those hearing the gospel from Protestant missionaries with an Enlightenment worldview. Most of those societies had a larger, more populated universe than the modern one. Thus there were things on the worldview maps that no theology of the time could cope with, because the theology belonged to an Enlightenment modern universe and was thus too small to fit the larger universe of Africa.

Traditional African maps of the universe often had four components relating to the transcendent world: God, local divinities or territorial spirits, ancestors, and objects of power. Traditional systems varied as to which of these was the dominating element, that is, the biggest component on the map. In some systems God was the largest component; in many others, it was the local divinities—people believed in God, but their religious practice was determined much more by attention to the divinities, the lesser divine beings. Others had ancestor-dominated systems, where consultation of ancestral spirits played a larger part than activities directed to God or to divinities. Not all systems had all four components; if Okot p'Bitek is correct, the central Luo had no God component on their maps,[6] whereas

---

[5] See B. B. Warfield, *Miracles, Yesterday and Today, True and False* (Grand Rapids: Eerdmans, 1965; originally published as *Counterfeit Miracles*, 1918).

[6] See Okot p'Bitek, *The Religion of the Central Luo* (Nairobi: East Africa Literature Bureau, 1971).

peoples such as the Gikuyu had neither local divinities nor, for purposes of religion, ancestral spirits.

We have noted that all sorts of influences can modify worldview maps—dramatic or traumatic experiences undergone by a people, contacts with neighboring peoples, or internal movements of reformation or renewal. Sometimes indigenous prophets have arisen and altered the relative position of components on the map. In the nineteenth century the prophet Mohlomi arose in Southern Africa among the Sotho, and influenced the great Sotho leader Moshoeshoe and his people. They had an ancestor-dominated system; under Mohlomi's influence they moved to a system dominated by the God of heaven. It was not that they did not know about God before; but through the prophet movement the worship of God came to play a much greater part in Sotho life. In later years this helped to influence the Sotho toward Christianity, which almost invariably expands the God component on worldview maps; but in this case the expansion started well before the Sotho came into contact with Christianity. A similar event occurred in Southern Ethiopia among the Wolayta in the 1930s and 1940s, where a prophet movement shifted allegiance of some peoples from local divinities to the God of heaven and prepared the way for a movement toward the Christian faith.[7]

Let us now consider the effect of Christian proclamation on such traditional maps. If people respond at all to Christian preaching, they will add information to their map or alter the relative position of the components, expanding some, reducing some, perhaps erasing some. It is not likely that they will throw away the map altogether, replacing it by a totally new one. Many of the items will not move at all; there may seem for instance no reason to alter any of the perceptions about witchcraft or sorcery, especially among people who do not see themselves as witches or sorcerers. If dreams and visions were important before, they will continue to be so, but with a Christian content. If possession was important, it may continue in a new form, explained in biblical terms.

Enlightenment maps, that is, modern maps of the universe, have a sharp line between the phenomenal or empirical world and the world of spirit. The new maps leave that frontier open and allow for frequent traffic between the spirit world and the phenomenal world. There is, in fact, much more detail on these maps than on the maps used by Western people. They reflect a larger, more populated universe.

---

[7] Paul Balisky, *Wolaiita Evangelists: A Study of Religion in Southern Ethiopia, 1937–1975* (Eugene, OR: Pickwick, 2009).

The element on the worldview map that is first likely to show change under Christian impact is the God element. The God element is present to some extent in a majority of maps, conceptually, but is by no means operationally important in all of them. Under Christian impact, this often changes: the God element on the map is magnified, and expands over areas of the map that it did not cover before. The idea of God (usually known by a vernacular name) becomes invested with attributes from the Bible. We may note in passing that this is quite different from the experience of historic European Christianity: in Europe, God did not have a vernacular name; no one said that Zeus or Jupiter or Odin was the father of our Lord Jesus Christ. In Europe, the One God was proclaimed over against the old gods, the One against the many. In modern Africa, the God of the Bible was generally identified with the God element already on the worldview map. On that reset map, God becomes bigger, nearer; He is the one to whom the believer is taught to go for power and protection.

The God element may in the process expand into the space once occupied by the divinity element, that of the divine beings who in the traditional worldview were either rulers of a particular locality or of a particular department of life. In the traditional system they received recognition, perhaps with shrine offerings. As people turn to the Christian faith, the conviction grows that such honor belongs to God alone. But the divinity component does not necessarily disappear from the map altogether. For one thing, when Christians find themselves in difficulty for which they can see no help in the Christian system, they may make some recognition of the divinities, not permanently, not putting them back into their old places on the map, but as a one-off or occasional resort. This fact probably reinforces a tendency, very evident within the charismatic movement in Africa, to see the divinities as demons. They are the rivals, and thus the enemies of God, spiritual entities with real existence, but essentially evil. In this case the divinities do not drop off the map altogether: they take a new place on it but as demonic forces— a category clearly to be seen in the Bible, but absent from the operational maps of many "modern" post-Enlightenment Christians.

But on some African Christian maps, following the enlargement of the God component, the former divinities have been incorporated in other ways. After all, are the divinities always to be seen as the rivals of God, and not as His servants? There have been many interpretations of African indigenous religions that see the divinities as agents, even as refractions of God (for instance Idowu's interpretation of Yoruba belief in which the *orisas* are refractions of God's being[8]). Many have argued that Africa has a different picture

---

[8] E. Bolaji Idowu, *Olodumare: God in Yoruba Belief* (London: Longmans, 1962).

of the relations of God and the divinities from that reflected in the Semitic world of the Old Testament. In the Semitic world, the gods were rivals of Yahweh and thus had to be rejected; in traditional Africa, it is argued, the divinities are often to be seen as the servants of the God of heaven.[9]

But who are represented in Scripture as the spirit-servants of God? Surely it is the angels? Some of the African Independent Churches or "spiritual" churches stress the ministry of angels; and they draw attention to the importance of angels, sometimes named angels, in some parts of the New Testament; parts bracketed out in an Enlightenment worldview. Does the stress on angelic ministry in these churches arise in partial compensation for the loss of the activity of the divinities in traditional religion? One feature of contemporary African Christianity is the opposition between the radical charismatics and the "spirituals," whom the former accuse of occult activity. Perhaps both groups are using the same maps of the spiritual world, maps that were drawn in pre-Christian Africa, and have been revised in Christian response. They color the maps differently; what are colored as angels in one map are colored as demons in the other. But neither map corresponds to the Enlightenment version of the missionary period.

New Frontiers in Theology

We are in a period of theological ferment, when theological activity outside the West is needed to overcome major deficiencies in the Western theological tradition. Some of these arise from its long acculturation to a particular view of the world, not shared by the greater part of humanity. That worldview is now showing signs of losing its grip on the West itself: whatever "post-modernism" may mean it suggests a vision of reality beyond the modern. It is not that Western theology is wrong; it is simply too small for the operating systems of Africa (and indeed, of most of the world). A vast expansion of theological activity is needed as the interaction of the Christian faith with the cultures—that is, the operating systems—of Africa and Asia and Latin America throw up new issues for theology. Christian interaction with Hellenistic Roman culture led to the theological adventures that produced the classical doctrines of Trinity and Incarnation, using the intellectual materials derived from middle period Platonism. We now need an ecumenical theology of evil. At present we are too easily left stranded between the issues of personal guilt and atonement on the one hand and of

---

[9] P. J. Ryan, "'Arise, O God!' The Problem of 'Gods' in West Africa," *Journal of Religion in Africa* 11, no. 3 (1980): 161–71.

structural evil in society on the other. And when it is asserted that the gospel is addressed to both, we begin to quarrel about priorities. Perhaps we need to consider more deeply what Paul calls the principalities and powers in charge of the course of the world, yet defeated by the Resurrection of Christ and dragged behind the triumphal chariot of the cross.[10] And perhaps Christian worldviews with open frontiers between the phenomenal and transcendent worlds will give new vision to jaded theological activity. Perhaps a richer theology of the family, one that has a place for the ancestors, will come as a richer family reality of Africa and Asia than the atomized one of modernity. African Christianity may help us to reflect more on the implications of the Lord's words about Abraham, Isaac, and Jacob: "He is not the God of the dead, but of the living."[11] This could be the most productive era for theology since the early centuries.

---

[10] Cf. Colossians 1:13–15.
[11] Luke 20:37–38.

4

Toward a Theology of Migration

Two Great Migrations

Human history has often been determined by movements of peoples. The history of the modern world has been determined by a series of related movements that, taken together, can be seen as a single major migration, a massive movement of peoples. At the end of the fifteenth century Europeans began to move into areas of the world of which their knowledge had hitherto been scant and in some cases nonexistent. They continued to move into these spaces for some four and a half centuries, until roughly the middle of the twentieth century. People of European origin settled in the Americas, Australia, and elsewhere, producing new nations that used the languages and followed or developed the cultural models of Europe. So substantial was the movement that one of the new nations, the United States, came to outweigh all the European powers (with the partial exception of Russia), and a new cultural entity called (without much regard to geography) the West emerged, conceptually combining older nations and newer. This expansion of Europe was largely maritime, maintained by control of the seas; but one major empire, the Russian, expanded overland across Asia to reach the Pacific. Even where they did not settle, the children of Europe often established control, building up empires, dominating trade, and moving resident populations (in particular transplanting a sizeable part of Africa to the Americas). Those who left Europe for the wider world had many motives. Some came as conquerors, some as administrators, some as traders, some desiring to be benefactors; the majority, probably, sought a better life or a fairer society than they found in Europe.

The Great European Migration[1] made the modern world as we know

---

[1] I have sought to develop this theme in "Mission and Migration: The Diaspora Factor in Christian History," *Journal of African Christian Thought* 5, no. 2 (2002): 3–11,

it, establishing a world political and economic order that may now be in the process of implosion or supersession. The mid-twentieth century saw the virtual end of the migration beyond Europe,[2] the dismantling of the European empires, and the rise of Asian powers as possible successor states. It also saw the development of a new movement of population, created and fueled by the Great European Migration, but in some respects reversing it. Millions of people from the non-Western world began to move into Europe and the lands that Europeans had settled, above all the United States of America. Much early migration was a legacy of the old empires. Some arose from other Western international involvements. Many more people came to escape ruin at home. Still more were drawn in as a result of the economic order century by the Great European Migration.

Religious Effects of the
Great European Migration

The Great European Migration produced important effects in the sphere of religion. In India it created Hinduism as an entity as we know it today. In Sri Lanka it set on foot a Buddhist renaissance. In parts of Africa and Asia it produced a rapid spread and intensification of Islam (the main religious beneficiary of European colonialism). In Africa and some parts of Asia it brought prolonged interaction between the primal religions and Christianity or Islam or both. But the religious entity most changed by the Great European Migration was Christianity. When the migration began, Christianity was overwhelmingly a Western religion and indubitably the religion of the West, so much so that for centuries the term "Christendom"—which is simply another word for Christianity—was equated with Europe. Europe *was* Christianity, Christianity territorially expressed.

When the Great European Migration ended, however, Christianity was in marked recession in Europe and among the other peoples of European descent, and firmly established in many parts of the world where at the beginning of the migration it had no presence at all. Christianity has moved within a century or so from being a Western religion and the religion of the West to becoming a principally non-Western religion. The agents of this process are

---

and in "Christian Mission in a Five-hundred Year Context," in *Mission in the 21st Century*, ed. Andrew F. Walls and Cathy Ross, 193–204 (London: Darton, Longman & Todd and Maryknoll, NY: Orbis Books, 2008).

  [2] The issue of migration from one European country to another has by contrast become important in the twenty-first century.

many. For a time at the beginning of the migration, the Spanish employed the model of crusade, originally developed for reclamation of territory from Islam. The primary Christianization of Mexico and Peru was of this kind, together with that of some Pacific islands and, in part, the Philippines. But in Asia and most of Africa crusade was impracticable; and successive colonial powers lost enthusiasm for the extension of Christendom. Colonialism is the matrix of European secularization: it presented the choice between the political and economic interests of the European powers and their religious profession. It was the radicals of Christendom that produced the agency that was to count most in the transformation of Christianity from a Western to a non-Western religion. The missionary movement, foreshadowed by Ramon Llull and by Francis, was a model that differed in concept from the crusading, in that it depended on persuasion and demonstration, rather than on compulsion. This took missionaries into concerns that crusaders rarely had to worry about: learning a language, seeking to understand a society, looking for a place or niche within it, living—however unwillingly or uncomfortably—on terms set by others. The missionary movement from the West, Catholic in its first phase, Protestant in its second, Protestant and Catholic in its third, was a semidetached part of the Great European Migration—semidetached because its essential motor derived not from the economic, political, and strategic interests that produced the migration but from the nature of the Christian message itself. The missionary movement entered its old age as the Great European Migration came to a close. Under the conditions of the Great Reverse Migration, it is now in the process of transformation into something else, with the non-Western world increasingly assuming a sending role and producing the missionaries.

The religious effects of the Great Reverse Migration may prove to be as significant as those of the Great European Migration. Our immediate concern is with one aspect of the Great Reverse Migration. We have seen that it has made Africa part of the cultural landscape of the West. In the process it has brought African religion into that landscape; and the most noticeable dimension of African religion to be seen there is Christian. Not only is Africa now part of Western society, African Christianity is part of it too.

A Theology of Migration?

Tracing the place of the Christian faith in the migration that shaped the modern world and the migration that is helping to remake it raises the question of the theological significance of migration. For the beginnings of a theology of migration it is natural to begin with the book of Genesis, for that book is concerned with archetypes, with the recurring factors, the constants in human experience, and their divine ordination or regulation. The stories in the early chapters illustrate the themes of the origin of the universe,[3] the constitution of humanity,[4] gender relations,[5] the presence of evil and violence in society,[6] environmental catastrophe,[7] the principle of dependability in nature,[8] the emergence of the arts (or at least of music)[9] and technology,[10] and ethnicity and language differentiation.[11] The first section of the book contains archetypes for each of these themes, all of them fundamental to human experience, typically illustrated with a story. Migration receives no single, defining treatment in Genesis, but the book offers so many examples of migration that the reader is left in no doubt that it is one of the constants in human life.

But Genesis does not simply describe the human condition; its principal theme is the divine initiative in salvation, and its archetypes are set within a framework of divine providence and purpose. This becomes evident when we examine the collection of stories it offers about migration.

The first migration recorded in the book is the expulsion of Adam and Eve from paradise.[12] Humanity, that is, after forfeiting the original relationship with God, is shut out from an idyllic existence which depended on that relationship. The human lot is now a laborious one, outside the original homeland (though the longing for that homeland remains) in a challenging environment where it is necessary to contend with the soil for a livelihood. In the story of Adam and Eve we meet involuntary migration, migration that stands for loss: loss of home, loss of well-being, loss of expectations; migration that represents a transition from a desirable to a far less desirable way of life.

Other involuntary migrations soon follow. Cain introduces fratricidal violence into human society. He is aware he is likely to be repaid in kind (though a divine limitation is placed on this proceeding, thus rescuing society from total breakdown[13]). Cain is condemned to a wandering life

---

[3] Genesis 1:1–31.
[4] Genesis 2:1–3.
[5] Ibid.
[6] Genesis 3:1–16.
[7] Genesis 6:9–24.
[8] Genesis 9:8–17.
[9] Genesis 4:21.
[10] Genesis 4:22.
[11] Genesis 11:19.
[12] Genesis 3:4–19.
[13] Genesis 4:13–16.

of continual migration, away from the kinship group whose bonds he has violated. Soon the scene moves to that early story of attempted globalization, the construction of the Tower of Babel, where overweening human ambition leads to multiple and diffuse migrations and consequent differentiation of languages.[14]

In all these instances migration is represented as punitive, the result of wrongdoing, issuing in degradation and loss. But the second half of the book introduces another category of migration, illustrated in the course of the long saga of Abraham. When the story begins, Abraham is a settled city dweller, in Haran in Mesopotamia, participating in the "civilized" life that is only possible where cities are flourishing. He hears the divine voice calling him away to another, distant land, which will belong to his descendants.[15] He reverts to the life of a nomadic pastoralist, that is, a perennial migrant, and he remains in that condition all the rest of his days. One might have expected the story to reach its climax with Abraham's quest achieved, the divine promise fulfilled, the promised land occupied. But this does not happen. The only part of the land that Abraham receives is a burial plot for his wife, and he takes care to buy this at its market value, despite the fact that its Hittite owners are willing to give it to him.[16] And even then he does not settle; he returns to the nomadic life; the divine promise will be experienced by his children. But he has no children, and there now seems little prospect of their arrival. Desperate, he takes measures to secure a succession through a female slave; and a child comes, and receives his own divine promise; but Ishmael's inheritance is not Abraham's promised land.[17] Eventually the heir is born, though it is only after several generations that Abraham's descendants are in secure possession of the land.[18] Abraham undergoes the experiences common to pastoral migration: disputes over grazing lands, competition for scarce resources, consequent division of the clan. His junior, Lot, secedes from it.[19]

Abraham is the archetype of a category of migrants that differs from what one might call the Adamic. Adam leaves home from compulsion; migration means exile and deprivation. Abraham leaves in hope, with the expectation of a better life, if not for himself, then for his children. In Abraham's case, the stimulus to leave, and the only reason to hope the move will bring a better life than he already enjoys, is the divine call, the initiative of God; and the migrant life of a nomadic herdsman, taken up after

---

[14] Genesis 11:5–9.
[15] Genesis 12:1–4.
[16] Genesis 23:1–18.
[17] Genesis 16:1–10.
[18] Genesis 21:1–21.
[19] Genesis 13:1–18.

the experience of settled life in an urban setting, provides the background of his deepening relationship with God. For the promise to Abraham is not simply about land. It contains the words "all peoples on earth will be blessed" [or perhaps, "will bless themselves"].[20] Abraham's migration has a missionary aspect. It is to be a universal blessing, with benefits reaching people far beyond his kin.

Historians of religion from Wilhelm Schmidt and the Anthropos School to Åke Hultkrantz, with his ecological analysis of religions, have drawn attention to the differentiation to be observed in the apprehensions of the divine between peoples of nomadic or partly nomadic lifestyle, such as hunter-gatherers and pastoralists, on one hand, and those of settled cultivators, on the other. Cultivators, though they may recognize a God of heaven with ultimate supremacy, often have more urgent concern for their relations with lesser powers, the local owners of the land, the territorial spirits. If Abraham is to be the father of a nation in special relationship with the transcendent God of heaven, he must leave the settled city life of Haran in order to hear the voice of the God of heaven regularly. Had he stayed in Haran, no doubt the noise made by the gods of the land, the territorial spirits, would have drowned the divine whisper of the God of heaven.

The promise to Abraham passes to his descendants. The book of Genesis now picks up their story. It covers several generations, and involves a whole series of migrations. Isaac settles in the promised land,[21] but a dispute over inheritance in the next generation[22] forces Jacob to flee back to the old lands of his clan in Mesopotamia.[23] The move is temporary; he migrates back, and the relationship with the God of Abraham is renewed and deepened for a new generation.[24]

All Jacob's sons migrate to Egypt, Joseph transported as a slave, the others forced there by economic distress. With this migration the Book of Genesis comes to an end.

The central theme of the book of Exodus is the major movement of migration out of Egypt of the assemblage of ethnically related tribes that the children of Abraham have now become. The migration, again associated with the calling of the God of Abraham, Isaac, and Jacob, is sealed by dramatic events that cause the assemblage of tribes to find new identity as the nation of Israel, consciously the people of Yahweh, the God of Abraham,

---

[20] Genesis 12:1–3.
[21] Genesis 26:2–5.
[22] Genesis 27:1–28:5.
[23] Genesis 29:11–14.
[24] Genesis 32:22–32.

Isaac, and Jacob. Now, at last, Abraham's descendants are settled in the land promised to him, but not before another forty-year nomadic period[25] in marginal lands.

The story of Israelite migration does not, however, end with entry to the promised land. Once settled there, as the Book of Judges, the later Deuteronomic history, and the prophetic writings all bear witness, many Israelites reverted to the worship of their nature gods, the territorial spirits, the *Ba'alim,* the owners (if usurping owners) of the land. Some prophets speak of the forty years of wilderness wandering that preceded the entry to the land as the purest and most devoted period of Israel's history; settlement on the promised land brings with it social, religious, and moral decline.[26] The prophets denounce this collapse, and declare that it will lead to forced migration. National catastrophe follows: with mass deportations to Assyria and Babylon,[27] and the destruction of monarchy and temple, the symbols of national identity.

But another strain in the same prophets speaks of the exiles' ingathering and return. The second half of the book of Isaiah thrills with the good news of return from exile, as Israel's children remigrate to the promised land and set about reconstruction. It is a chastened people who return, conscious that they have been redeemed by God from slavery.[28] Yet another strain in the prophetic writings speaks of the developments among the nations, as Assyria and Egypt, where Israel's people had been slaves, exiles, or refugees, become devoted to God.[29]

The Old Testament record can in fact be presented as a story of successive migrations. Most of the migratory categories we know today are represented: traders, refugees, prisoners of war, deportees, returnees, asylum seekers, and economic migrants.

In Ruth there is even an asylum seeker with an unresolved claim for residence.[30] Ruth the Moabitess also represents another migratory category, that of aliens in Israelite communities. Israel, settled in the promised land, was taught in the Law to respect the immigrants living among them, the "stranger within the gates"; for the very good reason that the Israelites had once themselves been immigrants, living in someone else's land. Accordingly

---

[25] Cf. Numbers 33:1–40.

[26] E.g., Hosea 10:1–8, 11:1–7; Jeremiah 2:1–13.

[27] The northern kingdom of Israel was destroyed by the Assyrians; the southern kingdom of Judah by the Babylonians. In each case there were mass deportations by the conquerors.

[28] Cf. Isaiah 40:1–5, 9–11.

[29] Cf. Isaiah 19:18–25.

[30] Ruth 3:1–4:12.

the Law actually placed a curse on any Israelite who oppressed an alien settled among them.[31]

The Babylonian exile and the return from it, the enforced migration and the divinely led remigration, were climactic events for Israel; but they did not mark the end of migration. Over subsequent centuries thousands of Jews migrated all over the world. By the time of Jesus this "Diaspora"—the Greek word for it was regularly used—had planted vast numbers of Jews throughout the Roman Empire, and other vast numbers eastward of it. The early Jerusalem church was careful to count them among those who inherited the promise of the Messiah,[32] and the Acts of the Apostles demonstrates the importance of these dispersion communities to Paul and the other early Christian missionaries in reaching interested and concerned Gentiles who were ready for the news about Jesus.

A Biblical Theology of Migration: Two Categories

So far we have noted in the Old Testament two broad categories of migration. One is involuntary and punitive, the other voluntary and hope driven. Underlying both categories is the divine authority acting in judgment and mercy. One might call the first category Adamic and the second Abrahamic. Adamic migration is governed by "push" factors: the flaming swords of the angels prevent a return to Eden; the Assyrian and Babylonian warriors force people, weeping, from their homes. Adamic migration is a product of rejection and sin, a sign of divine judgment.

Abrahamic migration, on the other hand, is enforced by no flaming sword. Its stimulus is the divine word of promise. There is a cost entailed, the sacrifice of present sufficiency and security; but this is more than compensated by the hope that one's children will benefit. This is tellingly reflected in the thanksgiving ritual laid down in the Deuteronomic law for Israelite farmers. When the farmer harvested his crop, he brought the first fruits as an offering to God, and acknowledged that Abraham, the father of the nation, was a "wandering Aramean," a nomadic herdsman, who owned no land himself.[33]

But the distance between the two categories is not so great as may at first appear. Adamic and Abrahamic migrations are not wholly separate,

---

[31] Exodus 22:21; Deuteronomy 10:18–19.

[32] Note in Acts 2:39 Peter's call to those "far off." The speech, we should remember, is addressed to a crowd of Diaspora Jews.

[33] Deuteronomy 26:1–11.

mutually exclusive entities. The reason is that Adamic migration is itself redemptive in intention. The expulsion from Eden is not the final judgment, but the prelude to the story of God's salvation. Thus the prophetic word declares that the enforced migration of exiles must follow Israel's rejection of God's Word and purpose; but the same Word proclaims that the destruction will not be total; a remnant will remain,[34] and the day will come when his forgiven people will return rejoicing to their own land, purified from their disobedience, renewed through the fire of affliction.[35]

In the New Testament, Abrahamic migration is a key category, regularly used as a description of the Christian life. For Paul, Abraham is the archetypal Christian who responds in faith and obedience to the promise of God. This theme is worked out at length in the Letter to the Galatians,[36] and, more fully, in Romans.[37] For the writer to the Hebrews, Abraham heads the list of the heroes of faith[38] who died before reaching the better land that they were seeking for themselves and their descendants. For this writer, the Abrahamic promises are not exhausted by the occupation of Canaan[39]: "If Joshua had given them rest, he would not have spoken of another day."[40] The fulfillment of the promises will be to enjoy the "better country" that they will share with those who believe in Christ.[41] Abraham and the other old heroes of faith lived as migrants, longing for a better country; they will get permanent right of residence in a city God has designated for them.[42] The writer to the Hebrews constantly uses language applicable to migrants seeking a better life for their children.[43] The Epistle of James portrays Christians as Israel in diaspora;[44] all Jews were keenly aware of that huge Jewish population scattered among the nations. The First Letter of Peter also sees Christians as migrants, indeed as refugees in the world.[45] Clearly, Abrahamic migration is part of the self-understanding of the church of the apostolic age.

---

[34] Isaiah 10:20–29.
[35] Isaiah 49:8–21.
[36] Galatians 3:6–4:31.
[37] Romans 4:1–25.
[38] Hebrews 11:8–19.
[39] Hebrews 11:39–40.
[40] Hebrews 4:8.
[41] Hebrews 11:39–40, 12:22–24.
[42] Hebrews 11:15–16.
[43] Hebrews 11:13–14.
[44] James 1:1.
[45] 1 Peter 1:1.

Biblical Categories for Migration
and the African Diaspora

We have seen that migration is an essential, and not just an incidental, theme in the Christian Scriptures, and one that has attracted several layers of theological reflection there. It is now necessary to ask how far the biblical themes we have considered apply in the modern world, and in particular, how far can they be used to interpret the contemporary phenomenon that we have named the Great Reverse Migration?

Some features of the modern African diaspora readily suggest analogies with both the Adamic and the Abrahamic categories of migration. Forced, involuntary exile has become a feature of the African continent. Millions have fled ruin at home and found that migration only brings more misery. In calling this mode of migration Adamic, because it is associated with deprivation and loss, we dare not, even by implication, suggest that its origin lies in divine judgment. We can, however, with some confidence invoke the fact that in Israel's history Adamic migration, with all its misery and loss, is represented not as destructive but as redemptive. Thus the Adamic migration of the Babylonian exile issues in the message of comfort to God's people declared in Isaiah 40, the end of Israel's warfare, the pardon of her sins. Indeed, in the Servant Passages, which form part of this declaration, the servant vicariously absorbs the punishment of his people, wins back the freedom of many, and after much suffering and rejection sees his work finally vindicated.[46]

There are signs that this theme of redemptive migration has been appropriated by Christians in modern Africa. For instance, a paper by Dr. Falge shows how Nuer Christians appropriated Isaiah 18 (which is addressed to "Cush," and thus to the Sudan region) for themselves, reading the prophecy in the light of the events and experiences of decades of devastating war. They see themselves as having undergone in their homeland the dreadful disasters proclaimed by the prophet, but, again in accordance with the prophecy, the people "returned to the Lord" (as evidenced in the growth of the church). And when the remittances from those who had gone into exile in the West began to make an impact on those who stayed behind, another part of the prophecy seemed to be fulfilled. Disaster in the homeland had led to the exile of many (and, as in biblical times, the exiles tend to come from the most productive sectors of the community); but the gifts of the Nuer exiles eventually enabled the community at home to "make gifts to the Lord."[47]

---

[46] Isaiah 52:13–53:12.

[47] Christiane Falge, "Transnational Nuer Churches: Bringing Development to the Homeland and Morals to the United States," in *African Christian Presence in the West,*

The migration of the Nuer exiles, children of the biblical Cushites, had led the people from devastation to recovery, societal and spiritual renewal, and economic surpluses that could be shared by the migrants with those left behind. It is an interesting example of local theologizing that combines biblical reflection with reflection on the unspeakable horrors the community has undergone in recent years. In making sense of those experiences, this group of Christians has followed biblical precedent in identifying redemptive significance in the sufferings of Adamic migration.

Other recent studies reflect features of Abrahamic migration. Naturally, a large part of the constituency served by the African churches of the Great Reverse Migration reflects the Abrahamic characteristic of voluntary removal undertaken in hope of a better life for the migrants or their descendants. Some studies also share the characteristic essential to truly Abrahamic migration, a sense of divine calling. But there is yet another dimension of Abrahamic migration that raises particularly important issues. In the biblical model Abraham himself responds to the hope of a better future but experiences little of the promised blessing himself. His descendants eventually receive the land; but the fullest meaning and purpose of Abraham's migration, undertaken in response to the divine call, is that others receive benefit: ultimately "all families of the earth are blessed." The migrants, that is, have a mission to the host community and beyond that to the whole world. Some studies of African diaspora churches reflect such a consciousness, though in some cases the consciousness has developed over time. Commonly, consciousness of mission begins with awareness of the spiritual, pastoral, and often simply human needs of the migrant community itself; commonly also, that consciousness takes a new form with the realization that the "1.5 generation" (those born in the homeland but growing up in the West), and even more, those born in the diaspora, see the world in a different way from their parents, and are involved with the host community at a different level, Yet another dimension emerges with the realization of the spiritual poverty of the post-Christian West. In its most developed form what begins as service to the migrant community grows into mission to the world, the Abrahamic "all families of the earth" that are to be blessed through the migration.

The Great Reverse Migration may yet influence world history in the way that the Great European Migration did before it. However this may be, it seems certain that the Great Reverse Migration has the potential to influence the future of Christianity, not least through the interaction of the churches of the diaspora and the churches of the West.

ed. Frieder Ludwig and J. K. Asamoah-Gyadu, 300–313 (Trenton NJ: Africa World Press, 2011).

The events of the past century have restored Christianity in practice to what it always was in principle—a multicentric and global faith. Biculturalism is the norm of the New Testament Church. That church included within itself radically different ways of Christian living: on the one hand a converted form of Judaism that maintained food laws, Sabbath, circumcision, the ancient festivals of the Law; on the other a converted form of Hellenistic living that had none of these things. Yet these were not different churches; Paul insists that they are necessary to each other, building blocks of a new temple, necessary organs of a functioning body; only together can the full stature of Christ be reached.[48] This duopoly in the early church faded with the decline of Jewish Christianity; but multicultural Christianity returned in a new, more diffuse, form, spreading across the whole Eurasian land mass and down into East Africa, while consciously remaining one church, inside and outside the Roman Empire. This all came disastrously to an end in the sixth century when the church permanently split three ways along linguistic and cultural lines. When Christians who did their Christian thinking in Greek and Latin parted company with those who thought primarily in Syriac or Coptic, the way opened for centuries of further splits of the same sort. Then the eclipse of early Asian and African Christianity— undoubtedly hastened by the division—left Western Christianity as the representative Christianity of the world.

In the twentieth century the effect of the Great European Migration has brought back Christian multicentrism in a form larger and more diverse than ever before; the Christian faith has become more truly global than ever before. And the Great Reverse Migration has brought all these multiple centers of Christian life, African, Asian, Latin American, to the West. For the first time for many centuries there is the possibility of returning to something like the conditions of early Christianity with its different converted lifestyles equally essential to the welfare of the one culturally diverse church.

Will Christians, whether of the West or of the diasporas, follow the New Testament bicultural model, or even want to do so? Some current studies reflect negative indicators: grudging access to church premises, lack of understanding of immigrants' problems and traumas, a readiness on the part of both the old and the new Christian communities to live self-contained lives. But some others reflect visions of a church that does new things in the world: the possibility of a vast expansion of theology, as

---

[48] The Epistle to the Ephesians displays this theme in particular. See Andrew F. Walls, "The Ephesian Moment," in *The Cross-Cultural Process in Christian History* (Maryknoll, NY: Orbis Books, 2002), 72–81.

the little universe shaped by the Enlightenment categories gives way to a new model that faces African realities; of new dimensions of pastoral practice; of theological education transformed by liberation from Babylonian captivity; of Christian engagement with Muslims free from the burden of centuries of European history. Then the churches of the African diaspora may hear the pleading words that Paul heard when the Christian message first came to Europe from Asia: "Come over to Macedonia and help us."[49]

---

[49] Acts 17:9.

5

Globalization and the Study of Christian History

In Christian belief, salvation is a historical process. In some other religious traditions, notably those that have their origin in India, the historical process itself is the bondage from which humanity needs deliverance, and the insight that brings salvation is independent of the historical process. In the Christian understanding of the divine activity, salvation comes not only *in* history, but *through* history; history is, as it were, the stuff, the material in which salvation takes place. Salvation is centered in the Christ event; yet even in the simplest forms of Christian affirmation, that event does not stand alone. It takes place as the climax of a long period of preparation; it leads to a long sequel. Had human history been irrelevant to or insignificant in the saving process, the Incarnation might have immediately followed the fall. Instead, the story of the Incarnation is organically related to several millennia of human history.

The early focus of that story is on the westward migration of a clan resident in Mesopotamia, the expansion of that clan into a nation, the rise of that nation to local glory, and its decline into colonial servitude, with many vicissitudes in between. This part of the story encompasses the emergence and collapse of several major empires and takes in much of the Middle East, the Mediterranean, and North Africa. But it is only the prelude; the Christ event, when it comes, is a history in itself, a history datable, as the Gospel of Luke makes clear, by the reigns of Roman emperors and the incumbencies of legates and procurators and satellite kings and high priests. That history, lasting some thirty years or so, is rooted in the long preceding history of the nation and cannot be adequately understood without it.

But the Incarnation, though the climax of the redemptive process, does not mark its final act. It begins another phase of the history, which has so

63

far occupied two millennia, seen other empires rise and fade, and taken the story across Europe, Asia, Africa, the Americas, and the Pacific. The evangelist Luke adds a second volume to his account of what Jesus did and taught. The Acts of the Apostles is a carefully constructed book, providing an account of the spread of Christianity to the heart of the Roman Empire. Once, however, Luke interrupts the Romeward flow of his story to take his readers to another international highway leading into the heart of Africa (Acts 8:26–39). With the story we know as that of the Ethiopian eunuch, he shows us that with the gospel all roads do not lead to Rome, that the gospel travels on other highways too, and that one day the stories will join up. And Acts is a manifestly incomplete book. It ends with Paul, the outcome of his appeal to Caesar still unknown, teaching from temporary accommodation. The point is that the redemptive process does not end with Acts 28 or indeed with the apostolic age. It is an unfinished story, and we still have no sure means of knowing whether we are living in the very last days or still in the days of the early church.

Salvation as a Historical Process

God has been in no hurry over the process of redemption. Its record stretches from early historic times to the present day and has been part of the history of every continent and of vast numbers of peoples. This has important implications for the Christian study of history and especially of church history.

The first implication is that the redemptive purpose of God is cross-generational. It is not completed in one generation, only in the totality of the generations. It was not completed in the generation of the incarnate Lord or in that of his apostles. We should be wary, then, of using some later epoch—the Protestant Reformation, for instance, or the Evangelical revival—as though they were the defining description of the process. The redemptive process will not even be complete in the last generation of all, taking that generation in and of itself. What is only in germ, or even completely absent in one generation, may blossom in another and reach fruition in yet another. Prophets and psalmists kept this sense of generational continuity before Israel; and as a new age dawned at Pentecost, the first evangelistic appeal to go out from the church did not consider only the immediate hearers: "The promise is for you *and your children*," says Peter to the assembled crowds.[1] Modern Western Christianity has become self-

---

[1] Acts 2:39.

contained, and the potent sense of the ancestors has faded; we have lost the sense of "the God of Abraham, Isaac, and Jacob." Perhaps African Christianity will help to restore it as Africans increasingly assume leadership in the world church. Meanwhile, one of the vital tasks of the Christian historian is to convey the sense of salvation as a historical process. The great catalog of the ancestors of faith in Hebrews 11 closes with a remarkable statement. Neither Abraham nor any of the other heroes of faith have actually yet received what God promised them, because God has decided on a better plan—not for them but *for us*. Abraham,[2] the writer argues, and all the other Christian ancestors, will not be made perfect, that is, complete, until the Christians to whom the Letter to the Hebrews is addressed are gathered into their succession. Extending that argument further, Abraham is now waiting *for us*—the believers of the present age and their successors—before he and the other ancient exemplars of faith can enter into the fullness of their inheritance. The full significance of Abraham, the great archetype of saving faith, will be clear only when all the faithful are gathered in. The study of Christian history should therefore include display of the kinship of Christians across the generations, for this is how the process of salvation works.

Mission history as a genre has particularly suffered from one-generational focus. Much of the emphasis in mission history has been on the early period of evangelization, so that what passes for the church history of certain areas in Africa and elsewhere is merely a record of the establishment of churches. The attempt to obtain and record the testimony of the earliest converts is laudable and necessary, but it has often overshadowed what happened in later generations. The dimensions of Christian growth have often taken observers by surprise. When the members of Commission I made their report to the World Missionary Conference at Edinburgh in 1910 (and they included some of the best-informed and most-experienced people of their generation), they could think of the evangelization of inland Africa as hardly begun. They built their hopes for the Christian future on China, Japan, and India. How we need the history of those intermediate African Christian generations, comparative accounts of how people in different regions, areas and ethnic groups became Christians, and of what it meant to be Christian at different periods in each particular place.

A second implication of the cross-generational nature of Christianity concerns the record of the cross-cultural diffusion of Christianity. The progression of the generations also displays—as Paul Hiebert abundantly illustrated—the geographical, demographic, and cultural change in the composition of the Christian church. Cross-cultural diffusion is a recurring

---

[2] Hebrews 11:39–40.

factor in Christian history; indeed, it may be said that, historically, cross-cultural diffusion has been Christianity's lifeblood. At several crucial points in Christian history, it would have been reasonable to predict that Christianity would become a marginal faith in world terms (as has occurred with Zoroastrianism) or would die out altogether were it not that it had crossed a cultural frontier and taken root among a different people. These geographical, ethnic, and cultural developments, like the generational movements already referred to, belong together in the cosmic salvific process, the divine plan of redemption. The last recorded question of the disciples to the risen Lord is, "Are you at this time going to restore the kingdom to Israel?"[3] It was a natural enough question for Jewish people who had seen the triumphant rising of the Messiah from the grave. Nor does the Lord dismiss the question as entirely out of place or as reflecting a misunderstanding of his ministry; he merely tells them that times and seasons are in the Father's hands. The disciples, as Jewish people, naturally comprehended salvation in terms of the salvation of Israel. This was not wrong in itself, but the full salvation of Israel, involving as it did bringing into Israel huge numbers of those Israel called "the nations," was as yet a many-splendored thing beyond their imagining.

It was the emergence of Gentile Christianity—the first crossing of a cultural frontier in Christian history—that enabled the Christian faith to survive the fall of Jerusalem and the destruction of the Jewish state. In the meantime, the two forms of Christian life had to live side by side in one church. The Epistle to the Ephesians reflects two ethnic and cultural communities in the church. Each had its own converted lifestyle, one utterly Jewish and Torah based, the other reflecting the conditions of the Hellenistic world of the Eastern Mediterranean, but in converted form. There must have been many abrasive patches in churches made up of both groups, but the epistle makes it clear that the two communities belong together. They are each building blocks in the construction of the new temple; both are organs equally necessary to the functioning of the body of which Christ is the head. Indeed, as the epistle proceeds, we find that neither group can on its own realize the full stature of that body. We all come *together*, the apostle assures us, to the full stature of Christ.[4]

At that time there were only two communities in the church (or churches) being addressed. Since then Christian cross-cultural diffusion has brought many more into the church, and our own day has seen the greatest proliferation of all. Each is to have, like Jew and Greek in the early church,

---

[3] Acts 1:6.
[4] Ephesians 4:13.

its own converted lifestyle as the distinctive features of each culture are turned toward Christ. The representation of Christ by any one group can at best be only partial. At best it reflects the conversion of one small segment of reality, and it needs to be complemented and perhaps corrected by others. The fullness of humanity lies in Christ; the aggregate of converted lifestyles points toward his full stature.

The Cross-Cultural Dimension of Writing Christian History

The study of the past is always a cross-cultural exercise. Even when we share the ethnicity and language of the objects of our study, we do not share their world or their view of the world. They did not have options that are open to us; knowledge that we take for granted was hidden from them. Their minds were stored with things we have forgotten or never knew. They may have read our Scripture, but with different eyes, seeing different things as significant. If they shared the same theological tradition as we follow, it is unlikely that they understood or experienced it in the same way we do. The qualities needed in a historian are therefore the qualities needed for interpersonal crosscultural encounter—the qualities, in fact, of a good missionary. The historian needs the sort of empathy that makes it possible to enter the world of other people, the preparedness to labor to see the world as people of another day saw it, to understand their language and the way they used it. The historian also needs to explore the available options as they appeared to them.

This much is true for any attempt at historical investigation. In any attempt to interpret Christian history by taking account of the chronological and cultural generations as potential building blocks of the new temple, the need for such empathy is still greater. Church historians can benefit from the Hiebertian virtue of cultural sensitivity.

For instance, a culture-sensitive reading of the history of Christian doctrine might reveal how the crossing of cultural frontiers develops and enlarges theology. This happens because entry into a new culture at any depth may both pose questions previously unconsidered and provide intellectual materials for pursuing those questions. As the early church entered the Greek world at greater and greater depth, it came to a new, fuller understanding of who Christ is than Gentile believers could ever have attained simply from essentially Jewish categories such as Messiah. The great creeds are the product of the new questions posed by deeper penetration of the Greek world of thought. When today we recite the sonorous words "God from God, Light from Light, Very God from Very God, begotten, not made, being of one substance with the Father," we are drawn out in worship. Yes, we realize, this is who Christ, the Jesus we meet in the gospels, really is. But this discovery was the outcome of a long and painful process, attempting to think in Greek in a Christian way, asking Greek questions (questions that in Jewish culture might seem irreverent and presumptuous), using indigenous categories and terminology and conventions of debate, making and correcting indigenous mistakes. When the process was complete, it could be agreed that it was all to be found or implied in Scripture; but it was only following indigenous mental processes that made those discoveries in Scripture and in doing so brought classical Christian theology into being. Nor was there any loss, anything valuable to be given up; the word Messiah, for instance, still meant everything that it had always meant. But its translation and transposition into a new cultural setting had revealed new dimensions of who and what the Messiah is.

Similarly, Christian entry into the "barbarian" cultures of Northern and Western Europe following the collapse of the Western Roman Empire stimulated new thinking about Christ's atoning work. The practice of both Germanic customary law and codified Roman law raised issues such as the responsibility of kin for offenses committed by relatives and the relationship between compensation and offense that, when brought into interaction with the biblical material, made the theology of the atonement a major issue for Western Christian thinking, reaching classical expression in Anselm.

The Cultural Factor
in Contemporary Theology

Attention to the cultural factor in the history of doctrine, its persistent raising of new issues for theology, could make it much easier to recognize and cope with some important aspects of the contemporary theological situation. The determining factor in the contemporary Christian situation is the cross-cultural diffusion of the faith, especially during the past century, so that Christianity is now a principally non-Western religion. We must therefore increasingly expect modern theological issues to arise from Christian interaction, at a level wholly new, with the ancient cultures of Africa and Asia. It could prove to be a period, like that from the late second to the mid-fifth century, of immense theological ferment and creativity.

Africa is already revealing the limitations of theology as generally taught in the West. The truth is that Western models of theology are too small for

Africa. Most of them reflect the worldview of the Enlightenment, and that is a small-scale worldview, one cut and shaved to fit a small-scale universe. Since most Africans live in a larger, more populated universe, with entities that are outside the Enlightenment worldview, such models of theology cannot cope with some of the most urgent pastoral needs. They have no answers for some of the most desolating aspects of life—because they have no questions. They have nothing useful to say on issues involving such things as witchcraft or sorcery, since these do not exist in an Enlightenment universe. Nor can Western theology usefully discuss ancestors, since the West does not have the family structures that raise the questions. Western theology has difficulty coping with what Paul calls the principalities and powers, whether in relation to their grip on the universe or to Christ's triumph over them on the cross. The reason is that it is hard for Western consciousness to treat them as other than abstractions. So Western theology has difficulty in relating personal sin and guilt, on the one hand, and structural and systemic evil, on the other, and sometimes offers different gospels for dealing with each, or quarrels as to which has priority. Perhaps Africa, which knows so much about systemic evil, and where the principalities and powers are not a strange concept, may open the way to a more developed theology of evil, as the issues already appearing in African pastoral practice are threshed out.

The presentation of Christian history, therefore, must reveal not only the chronological movement of the generations but also the demographic movements in the constitution of the church. This will reveal the movement of the Christian heartlands as a feature of Christian history. At different times, different regions and cultures have provided the Christian mainstream, the representative Christians of that time. Were we able to assemble a group of representative Christians of the past, we might bring together Jerusalem apostles and elders with Nicene fathers, Irish monks, Victorian humanitarians, and African charismatics. We might reasonably claim that there is a relationship of historical continuity between such bodies of people, but we would have to acknowledge that these historically related groups of representative Christians often reflected quite different understandings of the Christian life. Each group would have practices and priorities that other groups would find strange, even repellent. By contrast, were we able to take five groups of representative Muslims from the centuries between the early Caliphate and the present day, there would be a good chance that they would at least be able to perform the Friday prayers together. Christian life and thought, taking as its norm the Incarnation of the divine Word, requires incarnation, embodiment in the cultural specifics of a particular time and place. Generations may be utterly diverse, therefore, in their understanding and experience of the grace of God and yet belong together in the ultimate purpose of God. The full significance of any one of them is not clear without the others. Abraham is waiting for us before he receives the fullness of what was promised to him. In the meantime, making sense of church history is a cross-cultural exercise.

Reflections on World Christianity and the Academy

In considering the present situation in the teaching of Christian history, I hope that some personal testimony may be forgiven. (Humility and charity are scholarly, as well as Christian, virtues, and I ask further forgiveness if they are found to be lacking in what follows.) I have spent more than half a century in academic life, holding posts in several African countries, in Britain and in the United States, and being privileged to be a visiting lecturer elsewhere in Europe and the Americas and in Asia and the Pacific. Some institutions where I have worked have had as their goal the good of the church and the preparation of the church's ministry; others have been public universities where religious and theological studies were conducted in the context of humanistic and scientific learning, with believer and nonbeliever working side by side. Many things have changed over the half century; some, perhaps, have not changed enough. What has changed most over the course of my lifetime is the demography of the Christian church, the southward movement of its center. Europe and, to a lesser extent, North America have seen recession, while Latin America, some parts of Asia–Pacific, and especially Africa have seen growth, and all present evidence suggests that these trends will continue. The corollary is that African, Asian, and Latin American Christianity will become more and more important within the church as a whole and Western Christianity less and less so. Neither the churches of the North nor those of the South have yet taken in the full implications of this major movement of the Christian heartland, the theological academy perhaps least of all.

Parts of the secular academy have been clearer eyed than the church or the theological academy. When I first joined the African Studies Association of the United Kingdom, I was one of only four members whose special field lay in religion. Among Africanists generally, religion meant African traditional religion (territory contested with the anthropologists) or Islam, though the study of African Independent Churches, as they were then beginning to be called, had also begun. My special concern, African Christianity in general, was widely thought of as "missions" and thus not really African at all, but rather a branch of Western activity within Africa.

The situation is different today. Historians, not theologians, opened the way. The leading British historian of Africa, Roland Oliver, first (as far as I have noticed) pointed out what was happening in African Christianity. He had already written *The Missionary Factor in East Africa* (1952—note the title) when, in 1956, he produced a pamphlet titled *How Christian Is Africa?* This pointed out that Christians in Africa appeared to be increasing in geometrical progression, having doubled their numbers every twelve years or so since the middle of the nineteenth century. Then the Ibadan School of History, led by K. O. Dike and his successors such as J. F. Ade Ajayi and E. A. Ayandele, began to produce their groundbreaking studies, with mission archives among their principal sources, their work revealing the immense scholarly value and significance of these collections. (Before their time it had even been solemnly stated, as regards one area of Africa, that mission sources did not exist.) The Ibadan School showed that mission archives were sources for African mainstream history. They showed that Christianity had on occasion played a determinative part in that history and that Africans were determinative figures in Christianity as far back as the 1840s. They showed that the history of such an important country as Nigeria cannot be understood without an understanding of its Christian history. The contribution made by the historical sciences to the study of religion in Africa has been vital. When theological studies cut themselves off from other branches of learning, they lose opportunities to renew their own streams with fresh, clear water. This point has been illustrated again more recently from the work of the historical sociologist the late John Peel.[5] His main sources—and they have been revelatory—are the records of nineteenth-century missionaries who were themselves Yoruba-speaking Africans.

By contrast with forty years ago, I now find that my colleagues in African studies, even if personally secular in outlook, fully recognize the importance of African Christianity. Social scientists, trained in participant observation, find themselves in Africa engaging in prayer, however little previous acquaintance they may have previously had with that activity. Political scientists see the importance of churches as viable forms of civil society and in some countries the only form that works. Specialists in popular literature have noted the phenomenon; I heard a learned paper that described the entire popular literature of Ghana as "religious fundamentalism." Where Africa is the focus of study in the secular academy

---

[5] See J. D. Y. Peel, *Christianity, Islam, and Orisa Religion: Three Traditions in Comparison and Interaction* (Oakland: University of California Press, 2015).

today, there is widespread acknowledgment that, if one wants to study modern Africa, it is necessary to know something about Christianity. In the theological academy, however, there appears much less recognition that, if one wishes to study modern Christianity, it is necessary to know something about Africa.

All over the Western world, ministers are being trained and future theological scholars are being identified and taken to doctoral level and beyond without any idea of what the church of today, in which they are called to serve, is really like. The way that Christian thought is presented to them often implies that it is a Western religion, or at least, if it did not start that way, it has now become one. Church history is a case in point. A common church history syllabus begins with what is called the early church. In fact, it usually deals only with the part of the early church that lay within the Roman Empire. By missing the early church beyond the Roman Empire, the syllabus also misses the significance in early Christianity of huge areas of Asia and Africa. It also loses the chance to compare the experience of Christians in the Persian Empire, who never had a Constantine, with the experience of Christians in the Roman Empire, who did. Students are led to identify the "Great Century of Missions" as the nineteenth, without noticing that there are other great centuries in the missionary history of the church, or instituting any comparison between the nineteenth and the ninth century. Even the Roman Empire in many a Western syllabus soon becomes in practice the Western Roman Empire. Yet in Protestant anxiety to ease the leap from Augustine (354–430) to Luther (1483–1546), the syllabus frequently omits a critical period of Western church history, the conversion period. So there is no study of the engagement between Christianity and the traditional religions of Europe, the very point where comparison of the experiences of African, Asian, and Western Christians can be most illuminating.

For the same reason, Western students often do not have the opportunity to reflect on how and why Western Christianity came to take the shape it did. They are left to assume that Western Christianity is a normative form of the faith, seamlessly connected with the church of the fathers. Even well-read, scholarly Western Christians are sometimes surprised at the statement that Africa has nearly two thousand years of continuous Christian history, or that nearly fifteen hundred years of Asian church history took place before Western missionaries arrived, or that the first preaching of the gospel before the king of northern England was roughly contemporary with that before the emperor of China. What Western scholars studied as the history of the church was in reality the history of the church in "our village." More seriously, nothing in their theological education has prepared them for intelligent participation in a church that is principally African, Asian, and Latin American in composition or enabled them to realize the changed place of Western believers within that church. Worse still, versions of such syllabi are, with the best intentions, exported to Africa and Asia. The impression they give there of the place of Christianity in history is utterly distorting; the picture of Christian history that they encourage among non-Christians is profoundly misleading. And the problems of relating this notional "general" history of the church to local church history are well-nigh insuperable.

Christianity has always been, in principle, global; this is not just a phenomenon of the twentieth century. It is arguable that the few centuries when Christianity was overwhelmingly Western actually represent an exception. A product of Western intellectual history has been translated into academic organization so that the history of missions has commonly been separated from the history of the church. There is no such division in reality; they are the same. We have seen that, in the purposes of God, the generations, cultural as well as chronological, belong together and complement one another. Surely they belong together in the study and teaching of church history.

Light is dawning in many places. The attempts at comprehensive church history writing are increasing. A shining example is the *History of the World Christian Movement* by Dale Irvin and Scott Sunquist, with the splendid accompanying book of documents.[6] There is a growing need for scholarly writing and teaching on African and Asian church history, for use not just in Africa and Asia but everywhere. Research in African and Asian Christianity is now a core requirement, belonging to the mainstream of Christian studies. The past forty years have seen these fields transformed through fundamental research work on primary sources. Whole forests of doctoral dissertations have grown up; thousands of academic articles of varying quality have appeared. There is still abundant fundamental work of this kind to be done, but there is also an enormous task of synthesis, as the dissertations gather dust and the very journals in which the articles appeared cease publication. It is work needed not in Africa and Asia alone but for the good health of Christian history everywhere.

This raises a final word about sources and resources for this renewal of the study of Christian history.

---

[6] Dale T. Irvin and Scott W. Sunquist, *History of the World Christian Movement*, vol. 1 (Maryknoll, NY: Orbis Books, 2001); John W. Coakley & Andrea Sterk, eds., *Readings in World Christian History*, vol. 1 (Maryknoll, NY: Orbis Books, 2004).

Sources and Resources for
Studying Christian History

In the early 1960s, I was involved in a program to collect church records in eastern Nigeria. We sought to persuade local churches to deposit whatever documents they held in a special archive. Many insisted that little would result, that these churches did not keep records, or that time and termite had destroyed them. In the event, hundreds of documents were brought forth and deposited in the archive: baptismal and marriage registers; records of services held, with a note of the preacher and text in each case; minute books of meetings; books recording decisions in disciplinary adjudications. Some of them went back to the 1890s. Here were records of seventy years of an African church, emerging, growing, worshiping, witnessing, sinning, repenting—and hardly a foreign missionary appearing anywhere. We made provision for the conservation of the documents and appointed an excellent young graduate (he later became Nigeria's first professor of church history) to record and catalog them. We talked of photocopying them, but such processes in those days were expensive—they could wait until next year. There was no next year. The Nigerian Civil War came. The building took a direct hit and was burnt to ashes. I walked in the ashes and saw not a leaf that could be recovered.

We cannot escape the possibility of catastrophe; that is the human condition. It is in the nature of civilizations—from the Assyrian to the American, from the tower of Babel to the skyscraper—to aim for permanence. It is of the nature of Christianity that we have no permanence, no abiding city, until the new Jerusalem comes down out of heaven at the last day. We have come to associate ideas of permanence with the normal conditions of theological scholarship. We have come to assume that scholarship will normally require comfortable, if not luxurious, surroundings and abundant, if not superabundant, resources. But there is no necessary connection between permanence or stability and research. The scholarship of Origen (185–ca. 254) was built up in an age of insecurity and persecution. The scholarship of Northern Europe in the age of its conversion was developed amid desolating wars, the literary conveniences of Augustine's day long vanished. Theology does not arise from the study or the library, even if it can be prosecuted there. It arises from Christian life and activity, from the need to make Christian choices, to think in a Christian way. The largest fields of Christian life and activity are now appearing in Africa, Asia, and Latin America, and we may expect, and indeed are already beginning to see, crucial theological issues arising there. This is where acute situations requiring Christian choice will be constantly arising, and new questions will be posed as the biblical materials interact at deeper and deeper levels with the cultures of Asia and Africa. Places in Europe and North America that we have come to regard as the leading centers of theological eminence may well retain large resources but become insignificant for the most critical tasks. After all, the greatest theological centers of the Christian world at one time lay in Syria and Egypt.

The new Christian heartlands have learned much about catastrophe: the wars, the natural disasters, the coups, the economic breakdowns, the International Monetary Fund, the world trade patterns. Many things conspire to divide the world between rich and poor. In countless African libraries, the journal subscriptions ran out long ago. Every year important books on Africa are published at prices no African institution can afford and that would swallow any African professor's salary for months ahead. Perhaps Africa, as happened elsewhere in the days of Isidore and Bede, will develop new and different structures for pursuing Christian scholarship. Africa and Asia have some unique resources, goldmines for Christian history. There are abundant records—printed, manuscript, and oral—that no one has yet collected or recorded. And there are human resources. The Christian world now has people who know what it is to live in a first-, a second-, or a third-century church. That could mean better resources for understanding the patristic period than the Bodleian or the Vatican libraries can supply.

That does not mean we should court catastrophe or sneer at the garnered resources in the older centers. Modern technology opens possibilities of sharing resources so that the Bodleian and Vatican libraries do not need to be replicated elsewhere. Perhaps the test of real sharing within the body of Christ may be whether new heartlands can get greater in substance.

The truth is that Christian history can now be satisfactorily studied neither in the Western world alone nor in the non-Western world alone, neither in the North nor in the South on their own. Even in scholarship, the cultural generations, like the chronological generations, belong together and need one another to carry out their respective parts in the construction of the new temple.

Part Two

AFRICA IN CHRISTIAN
THOUGHT AND HISTORY

6

The Cost of Discipleship

The Witness of the African Church

The Acts of the Apostles is a very carefully constructed book. Its subject is the progress of the gospel of Christ from Jerusalem, where Jesus died and rose again, to Rome, center of the great empire and civilization of the day. The author marks milestones on the journey: Samaria, Antioch, Cyprus, across Anatolia and Greece, until at the end of the book we are presented with Paul preaching in Rome. There is just one exception, one event where the book points in another direction. In chapter 8, the narrative is interrupted by the story of the Ethiopian eunuch. The story takes place on an international highway; but instead of describing, like the rest of the book, the westward spread of the gospel, we hear of its movement southward, into the heart of Africa. We are not told what happened when the "Ethiopian" got back; we are told rather that the Spirit took Philip away while the Ethiopian went joyfully home. It is as though the author is telling us "My own story is about how the gospel traveled the highway to the West; but there are other stories of the gospel's progress besides the one I am telling. One day we will see that the stories join up and the gospel is preached to the whole world."

The story of the gospel in Africa has so far lasted nearly two thousand years, but it has achieved particular importance in the course of the past century. In 1900 there were perhaps some ten million professing Christians in the whole of the African continent. No one knows how many there are today, but an educated guess might put the number at around 350 million. This explosive growth has made Africa one of the major Christian centers of the world. With the rapid de-Christianization of Europe over the same period, Africa has been steadily moving into the place once occupied by Europe in the Christian world. The implications of this change, not least for the intellectual and theological leadership of the church, have not yet been fully realized, either by the church in Africa or by the church in the West.

For the present, let us consider an issue that is foundational to any question of leadership: the quality of discipleship. One test of discipleship is suffering; and Africa, which has known so much suffering, has often been a furnace for the testing of Christian quality. Nor has this been only a development of recent years; the fires of testing have burned constantly over the many centuries that Christianity has been in Africa. We will follow a series of episodes in African Christian history where Christian discipleship was tested by fire—chapters in the history of Christian witness in Africa. The word "martyr" has come to mean one who dies for the sake of Christ, but the basic meaning is simply "witness." Our stories all concern African witness to Christ that has been tested by fire. They come from different centuries and from different parts of the continent; they show us some of the different ways in which the quality of Christian witness has been revealed in Africa's past.

Christian Witness and State Worship:
The Martyrs of Scilli

We begin in the second century, with one of the earliest pieces of African Christian literature to have survived from that time. It is an account of the trial of a group of Christians from the small town of Scilli in what is now Tunisia, held in Carthage, the provincial capital, on July 17, AD 180, before the provincial governor Saturninus. At that period Christians were subject to countless misrepresentations, including the charge that they regularly practiced ritual murder. One of the most common complaints made against Christians was that they were disloyal to their community, the imperial state of which the emperor was the head and symbol. That state took little interest in religion as such; people were free to choose from a huge range of religious options, and were equally free to ignore them; but there was an underlying civil religion concerning the state itself, symbolized by the spirit of the Caesars who had ruled and were ruling the state. And so a sort of patriot test was devised and applied to Christians. It involved sprinkling a few grains of incense into an altar fire as a sacrifice to the imperial genius or spirit. The act could be quite perfunctory, it need take only a few minutes, and the great majority of people would undertake it without hesitation. But Christians refused; they would make an offering only to God. As a result, they could be adjudged disloyal to the state, whereas their greatest fear was being disloyal to Christ.

The account of the trial makes clear that the governor, while wishing to deny Christians a platform for propaganda, is not anxious to put them to death. He does all he can to dissuade them from what seems to him obstinate self-destruction; he makes it as easy as possible for them to conform and thus escape death; he is even willing to adjourn the trial to give them time to think. But he allows no escape from the patriot test and there is no hesitation on the part of the Christians that worship should be reserved to God alone.

There are three men and three women in the Christian group, and one, Speratus, is the chief spokesman. The governor opens by making clear that they can be freed if they come back to "good sense." Speratus replies that they are not criminals, have done no evil, cursed no one, and accepted ill treatment thankfully out of respect to their emperor, Christ. The governor clearly takes this as a religious, not a political, statement. "We are religious too," he says, and describes its simple essence: an oath (which would involve sacrifice) to the emperor's spirit. Speratus asks for a hearing so that he can explain the Christian position, but the governor refuses, fearing a denunciation of state religion. Speratus insists that Christians serve God alone and in obedience to him live righteously and pay their taxes, and that their prosecution makes use of false witness and murder. Giving up on Speratus, the governor appeals to the others not to share this folly, but in vain. "We have nothing to fear but God in heaven," says one of the men. "Honor to Caesar as Caesar, but fear to God," says one of the women. The governor proposes they take time to think it over, but Speratus replies that in so straightforward a matter there is nothing to think over. The governor, perhaps remembering some of the horror stories circulating about Christians, then asks suspiciously what is in the box they carry; it turns out to be only their Scriptures, including letters of Paul, "a righteous man," as the Christians assert against the implied accusation of using evil books. The governor makes one last attempt to persuade them, offering them a month to consider. He then announces, "Whereas Speratus, Nartzalus, Cittinus, Donata, Vestia, Secunda, and the rest have confessed that they live in accordance with the religious rites of the Christians and, when an opportunity was given them of returning to the usage of the Romans, persevered in their obstinacy, the sentence is that they should be put to the sword." The response of the Christians was, "Thanks be to God—today we are martyrs in heaven." The writer of the account adds, "And so they were all crowned with martyrdom together, and they reign with the Father, the Son, and the Holy Spirit throughout all ages." It is significant that one of our earliest accounts of African Christianity should describe a martyrdom.[1]

Christian Witness and the Powers of Evil:
Antony of Egypt

Our second episode comes from the Nile Valley a century later—a pre-Arab Egypt where rural people, speaking a language related to ancient Egyptian, lived as other African villagers did and do, tilling the soil, dependent for their livelihood on the bountiful but capricious waters of the Nile. The earliest surviving literature in the Coptic language indicates something of their worldview; it consists of magical formulae intended to supply power and protection to people facing constant danger from forces seen and unseen. At an early date, and by means that are still unclear, the Christian faith began to spread among these Coptic-speaking cultivators. Most of what we know about early Christianity comes from urban settings; the Nile Valley offers a sight of rural people steadily coming to the faith. The early magical literature gives place to the Sahidic translation of the New Testament; evidently Coptic people had found a new source of power and protection in Christian faith.

An early Christian biography from this region gives the clear impression that the local community it describes was, by around AD 270, largely Christian. At that time the nearest large city, Alexandria, was still subject to the sort of state persecution that brought the martyrs of Scilli to their deaths. The biography in question is that of Antony, born in the village of Coma around AD 251. His family was prosperous in local terms, but Antony refused the Greek education that his family wealth could have bought him and that could have taken him into the urban cosmopolitan class. The biography speaks of his zealous attendance at church and careful attention to the Scripture reading. It is a reminder that in an oral society, where few would have access to written Scriptures of their own, the key aspect of the church service was neither sermon nor liturgy, but the reading of Scripture. From

---

[1] The account of the trial of the martyrs of Scilli occurs in many anthologies of early church texts. A convenient edition is E. C. E. Owen, *Some Authentic Acts of the Early Martyrs* (Oxford: Clarendon, 1927). In this essay, Owen's translation has been slightly revised. On the persecutions generally, and especially in North Africa, see W. H.C. Frend, *Martyrdom and Persecution in the Early Church* (New York: New York University Press, 1977).

the Scriptures read publicly, Antony heard the call to be a disciple of Christ and was increasingly convicted of how shallow his own discipleship was. His parents died—he was not yet twenty—and he inherited the small estate. It was the readings—the story of the rich young ruler and the Lord's charge to take no thought for the morrow—that caused him to give up his inheritance and leave his village in order to seek the life of a true disciple.

He was not the first to do this; there were already holy people living outside some Christian villages, but still in touch with their communities, so that villagers could consult them or seek their prayers. Antony visited these in turn to learn the special virtues or spiritual skills of each: learning gentleness from one, wakefulness in prayer from another, how to live with little food and little sleep, and above all learning to pray. He was preparing for a great spiritual encounter.

It is here that we can see how African was Antony's view of the world. As an African villager, he sees a universe packed with power—power that had potential for evil. As a Christian he identifies the evil powers known to all rural people with the devil. Satan himself leads the malign forces that obstruct his path to discipleship. And the natural habitat of such forces was the desert, the places where most people did not go, and above all in tombs and graveyards.

While Antony was visiting older disciples living beyond their villages, he was constantly assailed with what one might call ordinary temptations. He believed that Satan sought to discourage him by the difficulty of the disciple's life, to distract him with thoughts of his family, to seduce him by thoughts of the pleasures and especially the sexual delights that he was missing. In his accounts of these temptations, the demonic forces often take visible form, sometimes male, sometimes female. At length came a climactic experience in which he was assured that Christ had won the victory; he could say to Satan himself, "From now on I shall have no anxiety about you. The Lord is my helper, and I shall look upon my enemies."

Spiritual warfare had marked his whole life from the time he had embarked on the path of discipleship, but from now on the spiritual combat intensified. That experience of Christ's victory prepared him for the innovation he now undertook. He moved from the village environs into desert country—where the demons lived. He made his home in the graveyard of a village now abandoned to the desert, a natural haunt of evil forces. In the name of Christ, this disciple was about to challenge the demons on their own ground. Local people understood what he was undertaking, for, taking food and water for several days, he arranged for more to be brought to him later. In the tombs, evil resorted to frontal attack. A host of demons beat him and tortured him. The water carrier, concerned for him and hearing strange loud noises, came back before the time that had been arranged and found Antony mercilessly beaten and apparently dead. He carried him to the nearest village and laid him in the church, where the villagers came and stayed with him until nightfall, when one by one they fell asleep. Antony, regaining consciousness, insisted on being carried back to the tombs. The result was dramatic. In Antony's account, wild beasts—lions, wolves, scorpions—attacked him, but he refused to leave. The ferocity of the attack was due to Satan's well-founded fear that, were Antony to stay in territory acknowledged to be in the domain of evil forces, others would join him and demonic rule in the desert would be at an end. When Satan finally acknowledged defeat and conceded the tombs to Christian prayer, the good effects of the victory over evil were felt in the local community. Sick people received healing, bereaved people were comforted, long-standing feuds were settled. Antony's victory had blessed the neighborhood.

In Western histories of spirituality, Antony's importance is associated with the beginnings of monasticism, and his withdrawal to the desert is often portrayed as retreat from the world. If we read the story in its African context, it looks rather different. Antony sees the move to the desert not in terms of escape, but of conflict. Antony cannot be understood apart from his African Christian view of a powerpacked spiritual universe where Christ's victory must be displayed.

This was no emaciated ascetic; observers remarked on Antony's magnificent physique. His regimen as a disciple of Christ had brought him to that perfect balance and harmony with the environment for which humanity was created.

He was not long left on his own. Just as he had visited other experienced disciples, so people visited him. Often, as his fame spread, they came from far away, seeking his counsel, his prayers, his example. Many stayed; the enemy's fears were realized, for the desert, once left to the demons, became, as some said, a city where the praises of Christ were perpetually sung. The spiritual wisdom of Antony and the Desert Fathers who succeeded him was treasured in collections. They are perhaps the first written collections of African proverb literature, the first literary voice of the African peasant.

How shall we sum up Antony's witness to Christ? Antony represents perhaps the first revival movement that we know of in the early church. His conversion is not from paganism, but from ordinary Christianity. He lived when persecution still afflicted the church, and two of the only three visits he made to the great city were made to encourage its martyrs. The long arm of the state does not seem to have reached his rural area, but his call to radical discipleship and his witness to Christ were no less costly than those that led to death in the arena. The Christian life could not be an easygoing one; discipleship could not be combined with self-indulgence. Christian discipleship involves conflict with principalities and powers. The first stream of African Christian witness, as represented in the martyrs of Scilli, met the principalities and powers in the structures of society and paid with their blood. The second stream, represented in Antony, met them as spiritual forces deep in the constitution of the universe. They realized that those forces were impregnable to easygoing discipleship. Only when disciples took up the cross in order to be indeed Christ's disciples were they broken.[2]

The Witness That Transforms:
Takla Haymanot of Ethiopia

Antony lived to be 104. Somewhere around the time of his death in the middle of the fourth century, a peculiar chain of circumstances involving some shipwrecked Christians led to the foundation of a Christian church in the East African kingdom of Aksurn, and eventually its ruler and elders were converted. This was the nucleus of the church of Ethiopia. In the seventh century, as the whole world knows, a monotheistic prophet arose in Arabia whose uncompromising preaching made him unpopular in his idolatrous home city of Mecca. His followers were persecuted, and some of them fled across the water to Aksum, where they received shelter. It may be the kindness of African Christians to these first Muslims that lies behind these words of the Qur'an: "You will find those nearest in affection to you among those who are called Christians." The affection was, alas, to cool in later times.

Aksum and its Christian faith spread inland, on to the high plateau of Ethiopia. Christian migrants moved too, from Tigre, the old Aksumite heartland, into the interior. But would they carry their faith with them or retain it at all in their new surroundings? They were a minority, in unfamiliar surroundings, living among people who had never been Christians, and with very little pastoral care. Their indigenous neighbors worshiped the gods of the land, the local territorial spirits. One might well judge that,

---

[2] The early life of Antony referred to here is almost certainly by Athanasius; it occurs in most collections of that father's works, including that in the Nicene and Post-Nicene Fathers (ed. A. Robertson); see also Tim Vivian, ed., *The Coptic Life of Anthony* (San Francisco: International Scholars Publications, 1994). Of many studies of the outcome of Antony's movement, Derwas J. Chitty, *The Desert a City* (Oxford: Blackwell, 1962), may be found especially useful.

rather than becoming missionaries to their indigenous neighbors, it would be more likely that the Christian migrants would become assimilated to them and the recognition of the territorial spirits. What prevented this outcome was a series of revival movements in the Ethiopian Church that reflected the sort of discipleship that Antony had sought and that produced some outstanding witnesses to the power of Christ. The most famous of these is Takla Haymanot (ca. 1215–1313). It is difficult to separate the historical from the legendary in his remarkable career, but it is clear that, like Antony, he spent years developing a prayer life that would enable him both to confront evil powers and to sustain immense physical hardship and deprivation. Following this preparation he addressed himself first to the old Christians, the immigrants from Tigre, encouraging them, invigorating them, dragging them from compromise with the gods of the land. Then he turned to the indigenous communities, where the Christian presence was very weak, preaching Christ, confronting the territorial spirits in often dramatic power encounters, cutting down sacred trees. People said that the "satans," as the old sources call the territorial spirits who lived in those trees, fled in panic.

Takla Haymanot's next step was to collect young men from the Christian community and train them in the life of prayer that he knew. He chose as his training ground an area with very few Christians. The environment was harsh; his first disciples had to live on berries. They learned Christian scholarship the hard way; copying a gospel while seated on a narrow ledge above a precipice must have concentrated the mind wonderfully. People who had undergone this sort of spiritual training, learning to pray with Takla Haymanot, were not afraid of the low-grade territorial spirits at a local shrine. Nor did they fear the wrath of the most powerful chiefs or kings, pagan or Christian, but would rebuke them for their transgressions.

The Ethiopian Church has had a troubled history. Many times it has seemed likely that it would disappear; amazingly, it has survived. For centuries it was cut off from most of the Christian world. In the fifteenth century it was the target of a great jihad intended to wipe it out. Thousands of Ethiopian Christians were killed or forced to convert, hundreds of churches and monasteries were destroyed, multitudes of Scriptures and Christian books were burned in a period of cultural genocide. Christianity is not like Islam in the power to retain the allegiance of peoples century after century; Christianity often seems to wither in areas where it seems historically strong, and then find new life and strength elsewhere. In this respect the Church of Ethiopia, with all its many problems, is unusual. There are not many places in the world where a church has a continuous history of nearly 1,700 years. East Africa is one of them, and the witness of Takla Haymanot and his like is part of the reason. Once more the future was shaped by Christian disciples who refused the easy option and took up the Master's cross.[3]

Testing Time for Young Christians:
The Uganda Martyrs

In 1875 the explorer Henry Morton Stanley described to the Western world a populous, well-governed state in the heart of Africa, called Buganda. It was, he declared, open to Western influence and had already been penetrated by Muslim Arab influence. An almost instant response came from British Protestants and French Catholics, and their respective mission parties arrived at almost the same time.

Buganda was a sacred monarchy. When the Arabs had spoken to the Kabaka of Buganda about Allah, his first reply had been, "Where is there a God greater than I?" He was in sober earnest—no greater veneration was paid to anyone in Buganda than to the ancestral royal house. The Kabaka installed both missions at his court, and the two versions of Christianity went forth simultaneously. Initial response was slow, but in the early 1880s numbers of young men, members of the ruling class from which district chiefs were recruited, moved toward the Christian faith. The Kabaka soon found that their embrace of Christian teaching made them unwilling to cooperate with his sexual activities. Enraged, the Kabaka moved to damp down the Christian movement. Aware that the Protestants were expecting a bishop to come to the infant church, he ensured that the bishop was killed before he could arrive. Then he turned on the young converts. Some were tortured, some cut and sliced with knives, many were thrown on the fire and burned to death. These were very young Christians, with little teaching and limited knowledge of their faith, who reached martyrdom before they reached maturity. Some were Catholic, some Protestant, but the two missions were equally helpless; the word of the sacred monarch was law in Buganda.

But the infant church of Buganda stayed firm; there was no major departure from the faith. And after a few years, there came an extraordinary mass

---

[3] The source materials for Takla Haymanot are complex: see G. W. B. Huntingford, "The Lives of Saint Takla Haymanot," *Journal of Ethiopian Studies* 4 (1966): 35–40. A useful analysis is given by Taddesse Tamrat, *Church and State in Ethiopia 1270–1527* (Oxford: Clarendon, 1972).

movement, with hundreds declaring their allegiance to Christ. This movement had little to do directly with the missions; the Catholics had actually temporarily withdrawn from the area, and the Protestants were down to one man, and he died when the conversion movement was at its height. By 1890, Buganda could be described as a substantially Christian kingdom, where leaders in the state were often leaders in the church also. The slaughter of the young men bore a rich harvest among their peers and successors. Buganda produced its own missionaries who worked outside their area of cultural comfort as much as any Western missionary, and it produced not a few saints also. Apolo Kivebulaya, who was both missionary and saint, moved the Christian frontier deep into Congo. It was the custom of his people to be buried with the head pointing to home. The dying Apolo asked that he be buried with his head toward the Congo, toward the people with whom he wanted to share the gospel.

By the 1920s, Christianity had spread through vast areas of Uganda, and in many places Christianity could be taken for granted as the general custom of the neighborhood, as it had been in Antony's village many centuries earlier. Again as with Antony, there was a movement of revival, of renewal, that transformed whole communities. It began in a mission party, part English, part Ganda, that was opening work in Rwanda. The party became bogged down with racial tensions and bitterness. Then both groups confessed their sinfulness and were reconciled. The renewal movement spread back to Uganda and developed as a movement of radical Christianity, challenging cherished sins and long-standing compromises with territorial powers outside Christ, and the piling up of wealth. It opened unexpected ways for lay and for women's ministry. How the movement spread to other parts of East Africa—to Tanzania, Kenya, Sudan—taking different forms as it did so lies beyond the scope of this essay. For the present, it is enough to note that suffering, witness, and renewal have been recurrent themes of African Christian history from its earliest centuries to our own times.[4]

---

[4] On Buganda, see John V. Taylor, *The Growth of the Church in Buganda* (London: SCM, 1958); on the martyrs, see John Francis Faupel, *African Holocaust: The Story of the Uganda Martyrs* (London: Chapman, 1962). On the Ganda role in spreading the Christian faith, see M. Louise Pirouet, *Black Evangelists: The Spread of Christianity in Uganda* (London: Collins, 1978), and on Apolo Kivebulaya, see Anne Luck, *African Saint: The Story of Apolo Kivbulaya* (London: SCM, 1965). On the revival movement, see Kevin Ward and Emma Wild Wood, eds., *The East African Revival: History and Legacies* (Aldershot, UK: Ashgate, 2012).

Death Has Come to Reveal the Faith:
Sudan in Our Day

Colonial rule did more for the spread of Islam than all the jihads, and nowhere has this been more true than in the Sudan. Colonial rule, under the unusual guise of a condominium between Britain and Egypt, assisted a steady expansion of Islam and brought into being, at independence, a country where Arab Islamic rule was secured over peoples who were neither Arab nor Islamic. After independence, the cry "One nation, one faith" helped to consolidate that rule and to restrict or force out Christian missions.

Sudan has suffered more appalling violence than most countries could bear almost unremittingly from 1964 until the present. It has seen whole populations uprooted from their land and their way of life and the cattle that supported that way of life destroyed. Many of its Christian communities have been scattered—exiled to camps in Kenya and Ethiopia, or to shantytowns around Khartoum, driven from their towns to a countryside devastated by scorched-earth policies. There have been many martyrs and, as often in former times, their blood has been as seed. Areas that resisted the gospel for decades have responded to it. There are many stories about the *jak*, the traditional spirits of the land, now deserting that land, telling local people as they leave that they should no longer worship them but worship *Nhiliac*, God, instead. Soldiers in the early days of armed resistance "smoked the Bible," that is, tore out its leaves to roll cigarettes; the time came when they wanted Bibles to read.

The Dinka poet Mary Aluel Garang has a haunting line: "Death has come to reveal the faith." In the unspeakable suffering of Sudan, not only has the faith of Christ spread, but servants of the Christ who suffered have found new dimensions to their faith. Some further lines by this Christian poet of South Sudan may bring our survey of African Christian martyrs and witnesses to a conclusion in the present day:

God has come among us slowly,
And we didn't realize it.
He stands nearby, behind our hearts,
Shining his pure light upon us.
We ask you, our Father,
Great Lord of peace in heaven,
Who is calling us with a whisper.
Our Father knows the depths of the heart of humankind.

Our faith is weak; make us strong,
That we may stand firm with courage,
Until you reach us undeterred. . . .
Send us your power, O Lord,
The guiding Spirit of truth
To teach us the law which has been written.
We receive salvation slowly, slowly,
All of us together, with no one left behind.[5]

Our chosen chapters from the long history of Christ's church in Africa provide abundant testimony to the cost of discipleship, the processes that produce Christian quality.[6] In its witness to Christ the African church has had to withstand false gods, sometimes dressed up in patriotic garb. It has seen recurrent renewal movements when in danger of succumbing to easygoing Christianity. It has known what Paul calls the principalities and powers, and confronted them in the guise of both malign spiritual entities and malign political structures. In the light of events of our own day, is it not right to ask: Whom has God been preparing through the fires of affliction for leadership in his church at large?

---

[5] The recent (and earlier) Christian history of Sudan is explored in the monograph series *Faith in Sudan*, edited by Andrew C. Wheeler and William B. Anderson. Volume 11 in this series, Marc R. Nikkel, *Dinka Christianity: The Origin and Development of Christianity among the Dinka of Sudan with Special Reference to the Songs of Dinka Christians* (Nairobi: Paulines Publications, 2001), is the source of the poem quoted (in Nikkel's translation).

[6] The best general survey of African Christian history is Adrian Hastings, *The Church in Africa 1450–1950* (New York: Oxford University Press, 1994). Its restricted chronological scope is partly offset by a good introductory section and by the same author's *History of African Christianity 1950–1975* (New York: Cambridge University Press, 1971). Other useful general works are Elizabeth Isichei, *A History of Christianity in Africa from Antiquity to the Present* (Grand Rapids: Eerdmans, 1994); John Baur, *2000 Years of Christianity in Africa* (Nairobi: Paulines Publications, 1994); Bengt Sundkler and Christopher Steed, *History of the Church in Africa* (New York: Cambridge University Press, 2000); and Ogbu U. Kalu, ed., *African Christianity. An African Story* (Pretoria, South Africa: University of Pretoria, 2005). More discursive essays on African Christian history are offered by Kwame Bediako, *Christianity in Africa: The Renewal of a Non-Western Religion* (Maryknoll, NY: Orbis Books, 1995); and Andrew F. Walls, *The Missionary Movement in Christian History* (Maryknoll, NY: Orbis Books, 1996) and *The Cross-Cultural Movement in Christian History* (Maryknoll, NY: Orbis Books, 2002).

7

A Christian Experiment

The Early Sierra Leone Colony

Over the course of the past century the center of gravity of the Christian world has shifted completely. Europe, once the center, is now at best an outpost on the fringe of the Christian world, some would say an outpost likely to be overwhelmed. The great majority of Christians, and the overwhelming majority of practicing Christians are, and are clearly going to be, Africans, Americans, or Asians. And of these, the most startling expansion—the greatest Christian expansion since what were for Europe the Middle Ages—has been in Africa, where Christians have been increasing in geometrical progression, doubling their numbers every twelve years or so, for over a century. The greater part of African church history, however, has still to be written. Hagiography we have in abundance, and hagiography, like mythology, is a valid literary genre; but (again like mythology) it is a poetic, not a scholarly category. Of missionary history we have a little, though very little in proportion to the vast resources that the missionary society archives supply; but missionary history is only one specialized part of African church history; by far the greater part of African Christian life and African Christian expansion goes on, and has long gone on, without the presence, let alone the superintendence, of the European missionary.

The first modern church of tropical Africa with a continuous history to the present day is that of the Sierra Leone colony.[1] The colony was itself a sort of stepchild of the Evangelical revival, and in its early days

---

[1] This description is intended to distinguish it from those churches that derive directly from the ancient churches of Egypt and Ethiopia, or from Catholic Reformation missionary activity, and from the chaplaincies to European residents, which sometimes touched some Africans, in the forts and factories of Britain, Holland, Denmark and Brandenburg.

reflects the two ways in which the Evangelicals were to alter British attitudes to Africa: by institutionalizing and making respectable (and in a measure effective) opposition to the slave trade, and in the growth of the overseas missionary movement. In the creation of the Sierra Leone colony the humanitarian and missionary concerns of Clapham Evangelicalism, together with their economic theory and commercial interests, met together. This "Province of Freedom"—the phrase is Granville Sharp's[2]—on the west coast of Africa was to be a haven from the slave trade. Its orderly, industrious, and virtuous society was to be a pattern to the continent. Its prosperity—it was assumed that it would be prosperous—was to be the continent's envy, causing chiefs and peoples to abandon the slave trade as less profitable than an export trade in raw materials and agricultural produce. And its Christian character was to facilitate the evangelization of Africa, both by creating a Christian presence and by serving as a springboard for missionaries to the interior.

The first attempt to realize these visions, by means of a party of destitute Black people and Lascars from the British cities, leavened, probably accidentally, by London prostitutes, was an almost unmitigated failure.[3] The real founding fathers of the Sierra Leone colony were 1,131 men and women, Africans or of African descent, who arrived from Nova Scotia in 1792, and marched from the shore singing "Awake and sing the song of Moses and the Lamb."[4] Most of them had been slaves in North America; many, indeed, had been born in slavery. Now they were entering their promised land, and celebrated the crossing of the Red Sea with an appropriate song of Miriam. We may note in passing that the modern church of tropical Africa did not begin by missionary agency at all; it arrived, a ready-made African church.

The Nova Scotian settlers of 1792 were children of the Evangelical revival. Many knew of Evangelical experience and spoke Evangelical language as intimately as the Clapham philanthropists who planned and financed the settlement, though it was a more boisterous phase of Evangelical religion that most of them represented.[5] It is clear that they came as Christians, bringing their own churches, preachers, and church organization

---

[2] C. B. Wadstrom, *An Essay on Colonization* (London, 1794), 338.

[3] On the Sierra Leone colony as a whole, see the admirable *History of Sierra Leone* by Christopher Fyfe (Oxford, 1962). Cf. R. R. Kuczynski, *Demographic Survey of the British Colonial Empire*, vol. 1 (London, 1948).

[4] J. B. Elliott, *Lady Huntingdon's Connexion in Sierra Leone: A Narrative of Its History and Present State* (London: Society for the Spread of the Gospel at Home and Abroad, 1851), 14.

[5] Cf. A. F. Walls, "The Nova Scotian Settlers and Their Religion," *Sierra Leone Bulletin of Religion* 1, no. 1 (1959): 19–31.

and discipline with them; and all visitors to Freetown seem to have been struck by their religious activity. The directors of the Sierra Leone Company (or Company) reported in 1795:

> On that day [Sunday] they abstain entirely from work, dress them-
> selves in very good (and some even in very gay) attire, and repair
> together with their children to church, where their whole deport-
> ment during the service, and their whole appearance are represented
> to be such as form a very striking spectacle . . .
>
> The Nova Scotians are not only punctual at their worship, but
> many of them profess also in other respects much regard to religion.
> It is natural however to imagine that among such a body of men,
> almost all of them claiming to be thought Christians, there will be
> some who have imbibed very inadequate or enthusiastic notions
> of Christianity; a few perhaps who set up hypocritical pretensions
> to it; while there may be many others who, notwithstanding some
> defects in their religious knowledge, may be consistent and sincere
> Christians. There are five or six black preachers among them, raised
> up from their own body, who are not without a considerable influ-
> ence; and it is supposed that the discipline which they preserve in
> their little congregations has contributed materially to the mainte-
> nance of the general morals which have been spoken of.[6]

A visiting sea captain notes in his log: "They appear very Religious attending Service by 3 o'clock in the Morning and till Eleven at night, four, or five, times per week.[7] And an English lady, usually rather tart in her references to religion, remarked, "I never met with, heard, or read of, any set of people observing the same appearance of godliness; for I do not remember, since they first landed here, my ever awaking (and I have awoke at every hour of the night), without hearing preachings from some quarter or other."[8]

Thus did Sierra Leone appear indeed to be, in Wilberforce's phrase, the Morning Star of Africa. With a sober, prosperous, worshipping Chris-tian community settled on the west coast of Africa, surely the time was at hand when Ethiopia should stretch out her hands unto God.

A very few years brought disillusion and frustration. The settlers who had expected a land flowing with milk and honey, and in whose government

---

[6] *An Account of the Colony of Sierra Leone*, 2nd ed. (1795), 80.

[7] Samuel Gamble, captain of the Sandown; see A. P. Kup, "Freetown in 1794," *Sierra Leone Studies,* n.s., 11 (1958): 163.

[8] Anna Maria Falconbridge, *Two Voyages to Sierra Leone* (London, 1794), 201.

they would share as the elders of Israel, found in that green but barren land no milk, no honey, and not as much land as they expected; found government alien and grasping; and the Christian commonwealth, while it continued to sing and pray, became a community with a settled grievance and increasing mistrust of Europeans, however generous their professions. Besides the traumatic experience of slavery to European masters, they now felt they had three times been tricked and betrayed by authority, each time a European authority. They had originally enlisted in the British Army in the American War of Independence, on the promise of liberty and lands when the war ended. The promise of land had, of course, been made on the assumption of British victory; and the victory of the American rebels gave the British government the embarrassing problem of how to dispose of their loyal soldiers. Nova Scotia—at this time still a land with much virgin forest—was the expedient adopted for many; but in Nova Scotia there were also White loyalists, people who had given up estates in the revolted colonies in loyalty to the Crown. The Black ex-soldiers waited and shivered, but lands were desperately slow in coming; and, they complained it was Whites that were served first. When the proposal came of land of their own in Sierra Leone many leaped at the chance. Too many; the Sierra Leone Company had the embarrassment of having promised, through its agents, more than it could fulfill. With the introduction of a quit rent (regarded by the administration as a property tax, for overhead, but by the settlers as a deprivation of title) the breach became a gulf. Europeans, however fair their speech and loud their Christian profession, were untrustworthy, sharp practicers and, above all, always out to deny the Black people land.[9] Part of the settlement erupted in armed rebellion in 1800, and to add insult to injury, the rebellion was put down with the help of the then mainly pagan Maroons, newly arrived in the colony.

Nor were the Clapham philanthropists any better pleased. They had expected the settlers to be grateful and dutiful for all that had been done; instead, they were disgruntled and rebellious. Again, the economic theory on which the colony had been based was simply not working out in practice. Far from making a profit, the directors had steadily to record a loss. Each year's report informed shareholders with regret of the exceptional circumstances that had prevented a profit in the past year, and of the hopes for profit in the following year. Meanwhile the pro-slavery

---

[9] R. W. July, *The Origins of Modern Africa Thought* (London: Faber and Faber, 1968), 48–66. P. E. H. Hair, "Christianity at Freetown from 1792 as a Field for Research," in *Urbanisation in African Social Change*, 127–40 (Edinburgh: University of Edinburgh, 1963).

lobby was using the failure and discontent to pour ridicule on the whole cause of abolition.

Nor was there much to show for the other bright hope of Sierra Leone, its being the beacon light to Africa, the springboard of missionary enterprise. The Sierra Leone peninsula, a strip that had been acquired for the original settlement, and its neighborhood were not thickly populated. From the first, sporadic attempts were made by Nova Scotians and Company government alike to evangelize the neighboring peoples; but, under the pressing weight of the colony's own affairs, none of these was followed up with much drive. In the Sierra Leone River lay slave factories—neighbors of the colony with which, however distasteful it might be, the colony had to have neighborly relations. The factories depended on supplies of slaves from the lands beyond, and it was to these lands of the middlemen that much of the early missionary effort was directed. The area was partly, but not entirely, Islamized; and behind lay Muslim lands, ruled by the Fula builders of the empire in the Futa Jallon. With some of the nearer of these the colony had made contact. Islam and its book perhaps seemed less alien and more comprehensible than African traditional religion; and Timbuktu, though centuries past its prime, still had a fascination for the Western mind, which thought of it still as the center of a golden Islamic civilization. At any rate, missionary strategists of the period talk with obvious enthusiasm of anything that promised access to the Muslim heartlands of the West African savannahs, which have, as things have turned out, never been responsive to Christian preaching. For the early phase of the modern missionary movement, the Sierra Leone hinterland became a sort of rusk on which infant missionary societies cut their teeth. It need hardly be added that rusks are seldom anyone's favorite diet once the teeth are through.

These early missionary efforts do not make up a very inspiring story.[10] The Baptists sent two men. One was young and feeble, and had to be sent home quickly; the other got heavily involved in Freetown politics, and was extradited. The Methodists sent a whole party of local preachers as an agricultural mission to the Fula at Timbo; but, to the great relief of everyone who saw them in Freetown, they never got beyond the colony's borders. One of them began unpromisingly by shaking his fist in the face of the first Muslim he met and telling him Muhammad was a false prophet; and the wives, when they realized that it was a country where it would be difficult to do any regular shopping, decided to return to the ship, taking

---

[10] The outlines are in Charles P. Groves, *The Planting of Christianity in Africa* (London, 1948), 1:208ff.

their husbands with them.[11] Of the agents of the London and Glasgow Missionary Societies who survived beyond the first few months, one proved deficient physically and one morally; one left to become a lecturer in the cause of atheism[12] and one to be a slave dealer. The Edinburgh Missionary Society, after a shaky start (their two Presbyterians, with two Glasgow men, traveled on the same boat as the London Society's Independents, and by the time they reached Freetown the whole ship had been devastated by an outbreak of *rabies theologorum*), did rather better; but within a few years one had been murdered for his possessions and the other, Henry Brunton of Selkirk, left Africa to spend the remainder of his missionary service among the Tartar tribes of the Russian Empire.

Brunton's work was inherited by the Church Missionary Society (CMS), which, though founded in 1799, could not, because of the principles on which it recruited, get its missionaries on to the field until 1804, when it sent the first of a series of German Lutheran candidates to Sierra Leone to reopen Christian enterprise in the area known as the Rio Pongas, to the Susu, a people then less markedly Muslim than now.

The CMS provided the most considerable of the early missions that attempted to use Sierra Leone as a base for the interior.[13] The principal way of approach was by means of a school. The theory behind this seems to have been first, that very little could be done with adults; and second, that it should be easier to wean children away from pagan influences.[14] In any case, despite the grammar Brunton had prepared, the missionaries did not have enough Susu to preach in it. We have, therefore, the incongruous spectacle of a school for Susu children taught entirely in English, entirely by Germans. One or two of the boys did well; at least one came to England, piously lived, and soon succumbing to the climate, serenely died, and became the subject of an edifying tract;[15] but what was the prospect of the boys continuing to do well once they returned to take their place in the pagan or Muslim family and village? Others turned out less well, and the mission suffered from incendiarism. For twenty years the Sierra Leone colony had been used as the base for missionary operations in the interior. No less than six missionary

---

[11] Zachary Macaulay's mordant account is in his journals, in the Huntington Library, California. A version appears in Viscountess Knutsford, *Life and Letters of Zachary Macaulay* (London, 1901), 116ff.

[12] William Brown, *History of the Propagation of Christianity* (Edinburgh, 1854), 2:450.

[13] E. Stock, *History of the Church Missionary Society* (London, 1899), 1:82ff.

[14] CMS Archives, CAI \ E 5.

[15] E. Bickersteth, *A Memoir of Simeon Wilhelm, a Native of the Susoo Country in West Africa* (London, 1818(?), 6th ed., 1839).

societies had initiated operations there. Not one could be counted even a moderate success, and only one was being continued by the mission that had started it.

Meanwhile, both the government and population of the colony were being transformed. Close on the passing of the Act of 1807 that made the slave trade an illegal occupation for British citizens, Sierra Leone passed from the hands of the Sierra Leone Company to those of the British government, and the British Navy acquired the use of one of the two most magnificent natural harbors in Africa, enabling a naval squadron to be stationed in a position to intercept vessels carrying slaves. Though the British government for some years tended to consult the men of Clapham on matters relating to Sierra Leone, the "Province of Freedom" was no longer the responsibility of private Christian philanthropy. From 1808 it was a colony of the Crown.

The population likewise was diversified from several different sources. First, as we have mentioned, came the Maroons, formerly slaves in Jamaica, defeated heroes of a fierce guerrilla war and, like the settlers of 1792, unsuccessfully grafted into Nova Scotia. In Nova Scotia they had acquiesced in lectures on Christianity but their Christian veneer was of the thinnest.[16] There were disbanded soldiers and even convicts from the West Indies; above all, after 1808 there were the cargoes of the intercepted slave ships, brought into Freetown from every part of West Africa from Senegal to the Congo: at first a trickle, then a flood, till Nova Scotians and Maroons alike were overshadowed by the new population that had never known life across the Atlantic.

The Christianity of early Freetown deserves rather closer attention, particularly in its relations with European missionaries. As we have seen, the colony's oldest churches were not of missionary origin: congregations of Baptists, Methodists, and the Countess of Huntingdon's Connexion were present and active from the first day of the colony's establishment.[17] It was nearly twenty years after that before the first Methodist missionary arrived; and the Methodists were alone in Freetown having close relations with their colleagues in Britain.

---

[16] R. C. Dallas, *History of the Maroons* (London, 1803), 2:221ff.

[17] Elliott, *Lady Huntingdon's Connexion in Sierra Leone*; Thomas Coke, *An Interesting Narrative of a Mission Sent to Sierra Leone . . .* (London, 1812). Melvill Home, chaplain to the Company, estimated that 300 out of the 750 adults were "under a religious profession" (i.e., what Coke calls "serious characters"), two-thirds of them Methodists, the other third divided between the Baptists and Huntingdonians (letter to Thomas Haweis in the possession of Mr. Christopher Fyfe). On David George, the much-respected Baptist pastor, see A. H. M. Kirk-Greene, "David George: The Nova Scotian Experience," *Sierra Leone Studies*, n.s., 14 (1960): 93–120.

The origins of Freetown Methodism lie then in Nova Scotia. The minutes of the Methodist Conference (or Conference) of 1790 give the number in society in Nova Scotia as eight hundred, of whom a quarter are described as "Blacks." The colony was, to use the modern jargon, in a state of rapid social change. To the sparse colony-born population of principally English and Scottish origin—often liberal, even republican, in sentiment, and no great lovers of the Church of England—were added the White loyalists from the south, very self-consciously British and staunchly Anglican, as well as the Black population. As the latter received or renewed the impress of Evangelical religion from the colony's fervent preachers they saw the Church of England, as represented in the local chaplains appointed through the Society for the Propagation of the gospel, unsympathetic or hostile to the preaching and experience they knew; they would see it also as the church of the White Loyalists, the people whom government favored at their expense, the people who got grants of land while promises to Blacks remained unfulfilled. They would see also the Church of England becoming in effect the state church of the colony, though representing only a minority of its population. Unlike most British Methodists, the Methodists of Nova Scotia, Black or White, knew a Methodism that had never really been inside the Church of England. It is worth noting that when some time afterward the Methodist Conference came to send out a superintendent from Britain to Nova Scotia, he was a disastrous failure because he tried to impose a British pattern completely alien to the Nova Scotian experience.[18]

These things may help to explain the apparent touchiness and readiness to take offense, which the Nova Scotian community in Freetown seems so often to have demonstrated, and it is evident from the journal of Zachary Macaulay, first councillor and then governor of the colony, that some of the strongest opposition to the Company's government in the period before 1800 was centered in the Methodist society. To an extreme sensitivity on matters political was added a hardly veiled hostility to what the settlers called the "established church," that is, the colonial chaplaincy. Now the Company had guaranteed, and conscientiously observed, complete freedom of religion. The various congregations saw to their own affairs, and no one ever thought of the chaplaincy as superseding, or ever doing more than supplementing, them; nor were the chaplains always Anglican. The first two, Nathaniel Gilbert and Melvill Horne, though both in Anglican orders, had unimpeachable Methodist backgrounds and connections. But though

---

[18] M. W. Armstrong, *The Great Awakening in Nova Scotia, 1776–1809* (Hartford, CT, 1948); W. C. Barclay, *Early American Methodism* (New York, 1949); G. G. Findlay and W. W. Holdsworth, *History of the Wesleyan Missionary Society* (London, 1921).

Horne had itinerated with Wesley, he was a complete failure with the Freetown Methodists. His official position as chaplain identified him with the Company's government at a time when that government was becoming extremely unpopular; and it is probable that at any time few Freetown Methodists would have recognized in that rather scatterbrained English clergyman the Methodism they knew in Nova Scotia.

The years of frustration and bitterness took their toll. When the first Methodist missionary arrived in 1811, he found 110 members in society, about half the number on the books in 1792, though the population of the colony had quadrupled in the interim.[19] A certain fragmentation had also occurred, and we hear of various splinter churches.[20]

Nevertheless, the Freetown Methodists of this period and through the succeeding years began to exercise an influence on many of the essentially pagan Maroons, despite the fact that relations between settlers and Maroons as a whole were frequently bad and sometimes violent. The Maroon community, docile from the time of its landing as far as government was concerned, gradually assimilated to the established ways of the colony; and in most of those ways, including religion, the Nova Scotian settlers set the tone. Certainly well before the arrival of the first missionaries, Freetown Methodists had seen the conversion of the Maroons as part of their responsibility, and Maroons of the younger generation were attending society.[21]

This society preserved both the framework of Methodist organization and the principal elements of Methodist discipline. Both the early missionaries, George Warren in 1811 and William Davies in 1815, reported with surprise that this was so,[22] and Zachary Macaulay, who possessed a built-in resistance to most forms of human blandishment, confessed himself deeply impressed with the spirituality of a man like Joseph Brown, the senior local preacher.[23] The Wesleyan missionaries also found religious experience and a vocabulary describing it that they understood: "mourning for sin"—that

---

[19] George Warren in *Methodist Magazine* 25 (n.s., 9) (1812): 317. The originals of Warren's two letters in the *Methodist Magazine* appear to be missing.

[20] Ibid.; cf. Coke, *An Interesting Narrative*, 24ff.

[21] Cf. C. Marke, *Origins of Wesleyan Methodism in Sierra Leone* (London, 1913), 12–13. That recaptives were also in view is shown, for example, by *Methodist Magazine* 25 (n.s., 9) (1812): 639 (settler leaders introduce Warren to interested recaptives) and MMS Archives, James Wise and others to Wood, April 1816.

[22] Warren, *Methodist Magazine* 25 (n.s., 9) (1812): 637–39; W. Davies to Buckley, MMS Archives, February 20, 1815 (all references to MMS Archives are to Sierra Leone Box I).

[23] Macaulay, journals (above, 112 n. 2): "One of the most humble Christians I have ever met with."

is, the conviction of personal guilt; "enjoying the divine favor"—that is, possessing the sense of personal forgiveness, which might come sooner or later after this conviction; "groaning for full redemption," "seeking liberty," that is, looking for complete freedom from inbred sin. For example, Davies mentions one Prince Edward, who had been wild and trifling, but was convicted under one of Davies's earliest sermons. He thereafter attended both service and class meeting regularly, but always in evident gloom or distress. Then one day he confessed to Davies that he could not expect pardon from God unless he married the woman he was living with. This at length he did, and also made her, protesting, attend Mrs. Davies's class meeting. Within a week she was "groaning for deliverance," and a week later still appeared at the class meeting very cheerful, "with a clear testimony of acceptance with God and enjoyment of pardoning love." But her unfortunate husband, convinced of sin so long before, remained just where he was.

It was three months later, according to Davies's journal, that Prince Edward burst in while Davies was kneeling in prayer and picked him up in his arms shouting "I found him, I found him!"

Davies asked what he had found. "I found Christ. I feel his pardoning presence. His spirit says, go in peace, all thy sins are forgiven thee."[24]

This story, of course, could be paralleled in every detail of language a hundred times over in English or North American Methodism; and at least one celebrated preacher in England was capable of cavorting with a converted vicar in his arms.[25]

The insistence of classical Methodism on preparedness for death is paralleled in this story, related by Davies in a letter to the missionary society:

> [A certain young woman—a member of class, but without the assurance of salvation—had died.]
>
> About three nights before she died she was seeking the Lord continually . . . Upon [her] deathbed the Lord manifested himself. She called her grandmother (who is also a Methodist) in the night to tell her what God had done for her soul. Said she "Praise the Lord he hath pardoned my sins his sweet voice said to my soul, Arise shine thy light is come and the glory of the Lord is written upon thy heart go in peace and sin no more. I must see my class Mistress to tell her also what God hath done for my soul." In the morning Mrs.

---

[24] *Extracts from the Journal of the Rev. William Davies, 1st, When a Missionary at Sierra Leone, Western Africa* (Llanidloes, Wales, 1835), s.v. September 1815, February 4, 1816.

[25] Cf. F. W. Bourne, *The King's Son: a Memoir of Billy Bray* (London, 1871, many editions).

Davies went to see her and found her in great pain, yet enjoying
the liberty of God's children. About half an hour before she died,
she had a hard struggle with the enemy. She said I have just escaped
Hell, Satan would have me in, but the Lord delivered me and when
I escaped another soul dropt in.[26]

Not surprisingly, the last quaint touch was crossed out in London when
the letter was prepared for publication.

Nor need we think of the Freetown society as aping what they did not
understand. We have already seen that neither missionary had any serious
fault to find with discipline or organization.

Warren recorded his impressions of a sermon preached soon after his
arrival by the veteran blind preacher, Moses Wilkinson:

Moses Wilkinson preached this evening, from Isaiah iii, 11 and
12. He gave out his hymns and text from memory. His manner was
warm and animating. He seemed to strive at keeping close to his
text, and made, in the course of his sermon, several useful observations. While hearing him I was led to admire the goodness and
wisdom of God in the instruments which he frequently sees fit to
use, to advance the interests of his kingdom. Many of the wise and
learned in this world, if they were to see and hear such a man as
our brother, professedly engaging in endeavouring to lead their
fellow creatures from sin to holiness, would at once conclude it to
be impossible for them to effect the object which they have in view.
Experience, however, flatly contradicts such a conclusion. Numbers
have been led by their means to change their lives, and are induced
from day to day to pursue that conduct which conduces to their
own happiness and to the welfare of those that are around them.[27]

With this in mind we may consider the Freetown Methodist relationship with the missionaries from Britain; and here we are aware of a
strange ambivalence. On one hand, there was in the settler population, as
we have seen, a deep-seated resentment at and suspicion of Europeans; on
the other, the settler society was very self-consciously Methodist, proudly
if somewhat intermittently maintaining its contacts with the Methodist
Conference in England. It addressed a number of appeals to the Conference to send a preacher. One that attracted particular attention, written by

---

[26] MMS Archives, Davies to Buckley, August 10, 1815.
[27] *Methodist Magazine* 25 (n.s., 9) (1812): 637–39.

Joseph Brown, appeared in the *Methodist Magazine* in 1807; the Conference (or Dr. Coke) politely answered the various appeals, but it was not until
1811 that the preacher requested was actually sent.[28] George Warren, who
arrived that year, had the warmest possible reception—though the society
politely insisted on seeing his letter from the Conference. Moses Wilkinson,
now very old, blind, and lame, averred that "about two months since, it was
strongly impressed upon his mind that a person was coming to take charge
of them, and that he was already on his way."[29] The leader of a splinter society
offered to rejoin the main body and bring his flock with him. In the first few
months of Warren's ministry the congregation and the society increased, and
it was noted particularly that backsliders were returning.[30]

On his first Sunday, there was one signal from the society of what they
expected of their missionary. They inquired particularly if he were legally
qualified to administer the sacrament. On learning that he was, there was an
outburst of joy, and a clear indication that the society wished for the sacrament in its own chapel.[31]

In the early days of the Sierra Leone colony the Company chaplain
had administered the sacrament—in fact, Methodists were sometimes
apt to assert that this was his only function.[32] Long since, the society and
the chaplaincy had gone their separate ways; but, in accordance with old
custom and official Methodist discipline, members continued to attend the
communion service in the chaplaincy. For the sacrament to be regularly
administered in the Methodist chapel at the hands of an English minister
with the full authority of the Conference would be the final and most effective repudiation of contact between the society and the "established church"
of the government. Warren was very willing to accede; though caution and
a care for relations with the chaplain led him, like many of his brethren in
England under similar pressures, to stipulate that no administration should
occur when there was a communion service at "the church," and that those
who wished to receive communion at the chaplaincy were at liberty to do
so.[33] A major point, however, had been gained by the society: the arrival of
their missionary had sharpened their identity and their distinction from the
church of the government. They now lacked nothing.

---

[28] Brown's letter, dated 5 July 1806, indicates that he had made a similar request two
years earlier but had received no answer. Coke, *An Interesting Narrative*, 17ff., says "many"
letters were received on this topic over the years.

[29] Coke, *An Interesting Narrative*, 24ff.

[30] Ibid. 30ff.

[31] *Methodist Magazine*, 25 (n.s., 9) (1812): 638–39.

[32] Cf. Knutsford, *Life . . . of Zachary Macaulay*, 136ff.

[33] *Methodist Magazine*, 25 (n.s., 9) (1812): 638–39.

But within eight months, Warren was dead. More than three years elapsed before his successor appeared in Sierra Leone: an ardent young Welshman called William Davies with his wife Jane. He was welcomed by the Free-town Methodists with the cordiality they had extended to Warren, and large congregations came to hear him preach and "read the prayers of the Church of England."[34] He in his turn was deeply impressed as he talked to the leaders of the society. All the signs of spiritual awakening seemed present: the preaching, the prayer meetings, the class meetings, all seemed to evidence it, and Davies writes cheerfully "A prospect of seeing good days in this place."[35]

But clouds fell across these good days. First came the question of a school, which brought to the surface differing conceptions on the part of the missionary and the Methodist settler community. With Warren had come out three schoolmasters, and a school had been established in connec-tion with the chapel. The main expense of this was on the mission. Davies declared that the school was not touching the neediest class, the recaptives, but only the children of settlers and Maroons, many of whom were in a better position to pay than the Welsh poor. Accordingly he closed it, and opened a boys' school under his own direction and a girls' school under that of his wife. He administered these schools, not on behalf of the mission, but on behalf of the government. Governor MacCarthy applauded the fact that he undertook this duty without fee or reward; but the action would not commend itself in every part of the community.[36] Here was the missionary removing one of the props of settler Methodism, one of its distinctive insti-tutions, which had been initiated by agents of the Methodist Conference, supported by funds from England, and instead undertaking service on behalf of a government for which the settlers felt little sympathy.

A second, and recurrent, source of tension was finance, which had never really been set in order since the beginning of the mission.[37] English Meth-odism had been used to the preachers being supported by the circuits, and it had been assumed that a similar pattern would develop in Sierra Leone. It did not so develop. The society had been regulating its own affairs for years before the missionaries came; it welcomed the missionaries as consti-tuting assistance and recognition from the Conference, which had been regarded by the settlers with reverence from Nova Scotian days. The arrival

---

[34] MMS Archives, Davies to Buckley, February 20, 1815.

[35] Journal, s.v. February 26, 1815.

[36] Ibid., Introduction; cf. letter from Sir C. MacCarthy, printed as appendix; and MMS Archives, Davies to Buckley, 19 December 1815. The schools' daily orders are in MMS Archives, Sierra Leone Box I.

[37] Cf. MMS Archives, Hirst and Healey to Coke, April 21, 1812 (sic, though clearly a slip for 1813), and June 16, 1813; the same to Blanshard, July 20, 1814.

of missionaries and the institutions taken in hand by them vastly increased Methodist expenditure, for the cost of living in European fashion was extremely high; but it is very doubtful if the Freetown society ever seriously expected to be given responsibility for any considerable part of this new expenditure. Was it not the work of the Conference, which naturally wanted to assist a small outpost of Methodism? Why should a missionary of the Conference be on a different basis from the stipendiary missionaries of the CMS, who even got an allowance of cloth? This point is forcefully made in a letter in the name of the Freetown society leaders, apparently drafted by James Wise, the government printer, which reflects a literary competence equal to that of any of the early missionaries.[38] The fathers and brethren in London who received such letters, however, could only wonder at the large bills that continued to be sent in by the mission, and hope that the good Methodist principle of circuit support would at last, and before too long, be established in Freetown. Davies, caught between two firm-minded bodies, neither of whom saw any reason why they should substantially increase their contributions, effected a compromise; more and more he came to support himself on government emoluments.

This brings us to the greatest stumbling block of all, and one in which the attitudes and reflexes of official British Methodism were quite different from those of the Methodism of Nova Scotia or Freetown. British Methodism had been highly sensitive to any suggestion that it was a subversive movement, and very concerned to profess its essential loyalty, that the command to "honor the king" followed very naturally upon that to "fear God." Sidmouth's Bill of 1811, which demanded, *inter alia*, of each applicant for a preaching license the recommendation of six "substantial and reputable" householders in his own congregation, was partly inspired by the growing strength of Methodism, and partly conditioned by the belief that this growing strength was subversive of public order. The measure was killed, but the need to assert Methodist loyalty was increased by it. The affair of the Sidmouth bill also put Methodists into a position that they disliked and sought to avoid: of being classed as dissenters, and having, like other dissenters, to be watchful of their privileges and status in law. This was uncongenial to those who, as the Conference of 1812 said in its address to the societies, "considered themselves as belonging to the Church of England"—whether or not the Conference was justified in adding "of which class the great bulk of our Societies is composed."[39] Methodists of this

---

[38] MMS Archives, James Wise and others to Wood, April 1816.

[39] Cf. A. W. Harrison, *The Separation of Methodism from the Church of England* (London, 1945), 29ff.

stamp were quite unlike the older dissenting bodies, such as the Baptists and independents, in whom a long tradition of disabilities inflicted by church and state had produced a not unnatural tendency to political radicalism and republicanism, and a very sharp anti-Anglican feeling.

These features of the dissenting tradition were, however, as we have seen, established features of the life of Freetown Methodists. They were shared also by many Methodists in Nova Scotia, and also by at least one European who seems to have got on well with the Freetown Methodists, a Company schoolmaster called Garvin, back in Macaulay's time.[40] Probably to the Free-town society Garvin looked more like a "real Methodist" than any European they had met since Nova Scotian days.

William Davies, however, was no Garvin; he was very much a stan-dard-product Wesleyan minister of his own day, simplistic in his loyalty to the king and with no bitterness against the Church of England. While the leaders of Freetown Methodism were talking of the sloth and avarice of the "carnal merchant missionaries" of the CMS and even of their "church (so-called),"[41] Davies was establishing most cordial relations with the CMS missionary who was now colonial chaplain, Leopold Butscher. Butscher used to attend the Methodist chapel on Sunday evenings, sitting up in the pulpit behind Davies, and giving an additional sermon if, as Davies put it, "he thinks that I have not preached long enough, or well enough." And as for the communion service, which at one time seemed to be the symbol of the Methodists' self-sufficiency, not only did Butscher share in the administra-tion twice a quarter, once a quarter, Davies assisted him in the church, there was no morning service in the chapel, and the society once more attended service in the "established church."[42]

From one point of view, these developments were a pleasing expression of Christian unity; from another, they were imposing dangerous strains on unity. The hardness of attitudes must not be exaggerated; and after all, Butscher was no high church parson, but a German Lutheran whose wife was actually an English Methodist. There was always contact and fellowship between the Christian communities in Freetown, and the united missionary prayer meeting, in which Butscher joined, was held not only in the Meth-odist chapel but in the Baptist and Huntingdonian Churches, which had no European oversight.[43] But, given the history and suspicions of the Nova

---

[40] Fyfe, *History of Sierra Leone*, 69–70, 650.
[41] Wise and others to Wood, MMS Archives, April 1816.
[42] Davies, Journal, 37.
[43] Ibid. The building used for the chaplaincy had no lights, which made it unsuitable for evening use.

Scotian Methodists, anything that looked like an alliance of Europeans, government, and the established church was potentially explosive, and that the governor smiled upon the development of ecumenicity would do it but little service among them.

Governor MacCarthy smiled on Davies and all his works. Entirely dedicated to the ideal of a unified Christian civilization in Sierra Leone, to which the increasing numbers of recaptives would be assimilated, he found in Davies a very useful agent. That this cooperative European, a man with sensible ideas about the education of the recaptives and energy in attending to it, should have official charge of the Methodist society, hitherto one of the centers of Nova Scotian fractiousness, must have seemed great good fortune. He made Davies an alderman of Freetown;[44] later he was to make him mayor. Davies says MacCarthy was "like a father to me in all things."[45] Edward Bickersteth, visiting the CMS mission on behalf of the parent committee of CMS, was welcomed by Davies, whom he describes as having always shown himself friendly to the established church.[46] The credit of the Methodist society in the eyes of the small but influential body of Europeans began to rise: "European gentlemen of all persuasions" subscribed to the new Methodist chapel.[47] The time was not far distant when they wanted their subscriptions back.[48]

For relations between Davies and the society steadily deteriorated. How far his own tactlessness or worse may have contributed is hard to say. Certainly the Freetown society found him harsh and overbearing.[49] MacCarthy, on the other hand, speaks of his "eirenic actions and abilities," and his "anxious desire to avoid animosities";[50] but quite an ill-tempered man could pass for eirenic if compared with Governor Sir Charles MacCarthy in a bad mood. In any case it is certain that the Freetown Methodists, who had so long conducted their own affairs, were not ready to submit at once, completely, and forever to a pattern alien to their tradition and habits.

At any rate, before the end of 1816, hardly more than twenty months after Davies's arrival, he and the society had quarreled irremediably. The society called him to answer to a charge of immorality. The evidence was

---

[44] Davies, Journal, s.v. February 7, 1816.

[45] Ibid., 53.

[46] CMS Archives, CAI E 5.

[47] Cf. MMS Archives, Davies to Fleming, January 1817.

[48] MMS Archives, Brown to Entwistle, March 31, 1817.

[49] The missionary Samuel Brown speaks of Davies's "self-confident zeal" (MMS Archives, August 20, 1818), and says that the basic objection of the society was to his "temper" (ibid., February 24, 1817).

[50] MacCarthy to Davies, printed as an appendix to the Journal.

supplied by a lady of dubious reputation, and no one seems to have taken it very seriously—indeed the charge seems to have been almost as much a formality as such charges in Athanasian times. When it came to the point, the society did not press it; but they did object to the attitudes and intemperance he displayed when confronted with it. A crisis of authority was reached: the leaders declared Davies suspended pending investigations. The missionary was indignant; and while the leaders were, according to Methodist discipline, still conducting their investigations, Davies took the case to the civil magistrates and was cleared.[51] It was now the leaders' turn to be indignant, and they refused any further ministrations from their superintendent. The way in which Davies announces this is eloquent:

> The leaders of the Society in Free Town have declared against me and have refused me the pulpit. I am too plain for them, and truly I have found them a proud stiff-necked generation. I understand they are going to accuse me of lording it over them, of being too proud for a Methodist preacher, and of paying too much attention to Government; the truth in this respect is, when we arrived here, we found Methodism very low indeed in the esteem of Government and the European Gentlemen in the Colony. My dear departed Jane's and my own conduct some how or other pleased the most respectable part of the Community, in consequent thereof some got jealous. As far as I can judge, most of our Leaders are of the American Republic spirit and are strongly averse to Government, I am a loyal subject to my King, and wish to do the little I can for the support of that Government especially in a foreign part where there are not so many able advocates as at home.[52]

And so they parted, neither side understanding the other, each maintaining the Methodism they knew, yet each appearing in the other's eyes to be allied to things hateful to Methodism and pure religion.

Davies at once found employment under the government as superintendent of the new recaptive village of Leopold; and the new missionary intended by London to be Davies's assistant arrived to be his successor.

All this might pass for a storm in a small teacup were it not that it was repeated. The Freetown Methodists had no wish to break with the Conference:

---

[51] MMS Archives, Brown to Entwistle, March 31, 1817. The Anglican Government Chaplain, William Garnon, speaks of the groundlessness of the charge (CMS Archives, CA 0126, March 26, 1817).

[52] MMS Archives, Davies to Fleming, June 13, 1817.

they gloried in the Methodist name, they wanted the European preacher. When the preacher arrived, however, the old tensions reappeared. Traditions molded by Nova Scotia and Freetown marched uneasily with those molded by English Methodism. In 1821 the missionary superintendent of the day, John Huddleston, declared the society dissolved; and the Settler Methodist Church in Rawdon Street emerged as an entity independent of the mission.[53]

To the missionaries this must have been almost a relief, and certainly no restriction, for they had plenty to do in the colony; the new population of recaptives seemed, and were, far more important for the future than were the settlers. In Freetown and the villages vigorous new societies sprang up under missionary guidance and leadership. The Maroons, for their part, soon became restive under what they felt to be settler arrogance, and formed their own church, on Methodist lines, and leased it for a fixed period to the Wesleyan mission. Alas, they, too, found missionary assumptions different from their own; and eventually a British superintendent marched out of the Maroon church shouting "Your house is left unto you desolate," and the Maroon society, as the settler church had done, went its own way.[54]

The old societies, though small, and representing a declining community, made their own impact on the recaptives, who attended the settler churches just as they attended those of the missionaries. Here again, communal tensions appeared. A recaptive might be converted; he might have spiritual gifts; he might hold a government job, marry a Nova Scotian wife, buy a house from an impoverished family of the settler aristocracy. But all this could not make him a settler: and this was symbolized when the gifted recaptive preacher Anthony O'Connor was kept as an auxiliary, confined to the lectern, refused the sanctified eminence of the pulpit of the settler chapel, in practice reserved to settler preachers. In 1844, the West African Methodist Church—as thoroughly Methodist in doctrine and polity as its antecedents—emerged, under O'Connor's leadership, from the bosom of settler Methodism. As missionary and settler parted, settler and Maroon and settler and recaptive parted likewise—all without any abandonment of the Methodist name, polity, or practice.[55] Each community in Sierra Leone was radically affected by Christianity; the degree to which this transcended communal barriers should perhaps surprise us more than the frequency of ruptures.

---

[53] Fyfe, *History of Sierra Leone*, 139, 660.

[54] Ibid., 139–40, 201, 660, 669.

[55] See C. H. Fyfe, "The West African Methodists in the Nineteenth Century," *Sierra Leone Bulletin of Religion* 3 (1961): 22–28.

And yet despite all this, Sierra Leone was the Morning Star of Africa. The recaptives, uprooted from their own traditions, became in effect the first mass movement to Christianity in modern Africa. Furthermore, they became, in a matter of a generation, a large and highly mobile missionary force, with an effect right across West Africa and beyond it which passed anything Wilberforce could have envisaged.[56] All this was the fruit of the work of three agencies: first, of the European missionary force, which struggled through the appalling mortality of the era of the White Man's Grave; second, of the Christian settler community, which worked in its own way for the conversion of the newcomers,[57] and the extent of whose influence is hard to measure, for the new population adopted their ways and their revivalism entered the Christianity of the converted recaptives; third, the determination and energy of a most remarkable colonial servant, Sir Charles MacCarthy, a man often distrusted by settlers and suspected by missionaries. Into the story of this movement, which can be held to have abundantly justified this Christian experiment, we cannot go; and long before it reached its crest, the principal characters in our story had departed. Davies, back in Wales, overwhelmed with depression, broke down and committed suicide.[58] MacCarthy fell in battle against the Ashanti. As for the leaders of the settler Methodists, some people in Freetown believed that their indignant shades made a return to earth in 1861, when their successors at Rawdon Street reunited with the Wesleyan Methodist Mission.[59] It is at least unquestionable that in that year the chapel fell down.

---

[56] On the development of Colony society, see, for example, John Peterson, *Province of Freedom* (London: Faber and Faber, 1969); A. T. Porter, *Creoledom* (London, 1963). Its missionary contribution to West Africa has been both neglected and misread (e.g., Stephen Neill, *Christian Missions* (London, 1964), 305–306; R. S. Foster, *The Sierra Leone Church* (London, 1961); but see P. E. H. Hair, *The Early Study of Nigerian Languages* (Cambridge: Cambridge University Press, 1967); "CMS 'Native Clergy' in West Africa to 1900," *Sierra Leone Bulletin of Religion* 4 (1962): 71–72; "Freetown Christianity and Africa," *Sierra Leone Bulletin of Religion* 6 (1964): 13–21; "Niger Languages and Sierra Leone Missionary Linguists," *Bulletin of the Society for African Church History* 2 (1966): 127–38; cf. also J. H. Kopytoff, *A Preface to Modern Nigeria: The "Sierra Leonians" in Yoruba, 1830–1890* (Madison: University of Wisconsin Press, 1965).

[57] It is clear that early missionaries in the Colony saw Nova Scotian settler evangelists as effective rivals in recaptive villages: cf. of many, CMS Archives, CA 0126, Gamon to Pratt, March 26, 1817: "Now I see the need of your throwing all your strength into the Colony, so that each town may be possess'd by us, otherwise not only Mr Davies but a sad mongrel set of Baptists etc. will get there."

[58] See *Dictionary of Welsh Biography*, ad loc.

[59] For the reconciliation, collapse of the building, and the rationale offered by some, see Marke, *Origins of Wesleyan Methodism in Sierra Leone*, 113ff.

8

Christianity and the Language Issue

The Early Years of
Protestant Missions in West Africa

The association of Christian missions with the study of vernacular languages hardly needs emphasis; for Protestant missions in particular, with their traditional stress on the Bible as the authoritative guide to salvation, the translation of those Scriptures has often been a prime object. Lamin Sanneh has argued that the missionary stress on vernacular translation of the Bible played a major part in the inculturation of the Christian message, particularly in Africa.[1] But the story of translation is not always a straightforward one, as the early experience of Protestant missions in West Africa demonstrates.

The key to the history of language study and translation, as of so much else in the Christian history of West Africa, lies in Sierra Leone.[2] The founding of the Sierra Leone colony as a Province of Freedom in 1787, and still more, its refounding on a more secure basis in 1792, appeared to the leaders of the infant British missionary movement to open Africa to the gospel. From the beginning the colony had been a Christian enterprise. Its first designer, the philanthropic ironmonger Granville Sharp, conceived it as a Christian response to the satanic institution of the slave trade. The directors of the Sierra Leone Company, which took over after the collapse of the first settlement, were mostly Evangelicals associated with the activist group around

---

[1] Lamin Sanneh, *Translating the Message: The Missionary Impact on Culture* (Maryknoll, NY: Orbis Books, 1989).

[2] On the early history of the Sierra Leone colony, see Christopher Fyfe, *History of Sierra Leone* (London: Oxford University Press, 1962); John Peterson, *The Province of Freedom* (London: Faber and Faber, 1969).

111

Wilberforce and Thornton nicknamed the Clapham Sect.[3] And the Sierra Leone colony was reconstructed on the foundation provided by 1,131 people of African birth or descent who had been settled in Nova Scotia after the War of American Independence, deeply influenced by the Great Revival, who brought their own churches from America to Africa. Sierra Leone was intended as a demonstration model of African civilization and of a successful African economy that did not have recourse to slave labor or any toleration of slave trade or slavery. It was also conceived as a base for mission operations. Between 1796 and 1804 the London, Edinburgh, Glasgow, Baptist, and Church Missionary Societies all sent missionaries there, and Thomas Coke arranged for a party of Methodists, who would combine preaching with agricultural skills, to come as well.[4] These early missionary parties were not generally intended to work in the colony, which could be considered a Christian (and English-speaking) entity, but for the territories beyond it, usually in places where the Sierra Leone Company had commercial or other contacts.

For the most part these early missions were not so much failures as disasters. The longest lasting of them was begun by the Edinburgh (later called the Scottish) Missionary Society and taken up by the Church Missionary Society. Henry Brunton, a young minister of the Scottish Secession Church, and Peter Greig, a gardener accepted as a lay catechist,[5] were originally sent to the Susu, living to the north of the colony, on the Rio Pongas. It is with the Susu language that the story of West African translation begins.[6]

The Susu had been subject to Islamic influences, and had felt the impact of a Fula jihad; an eighteenth-century English visitor called them "a mixt people of pagans and Mundingoes [i.e., Mandinka, a people recognized as

---

[3] On the Clapham group, see especially Michael Hennell, *John Venn and the Clapham Sect* (London: Lutterworth, 1958); and on their involvement in the movement for the abolition of slavery, see Roger Anstey, *The Atlantic Slave Trade and British Abolition, 1760–1810* (Atlantic Heights, NJ: Humanities Press, 1982).

[4] See Chapter 7 above. The Sierra Leone journal of Zachary Macaulay is often revealing about the early missions; see Suzanne Schwarz, *Zachary Macaulay and the Development of the Sierra Leone Company* (Leipzig, Germany: Universitäts Verlag, 2003).

[5] Most of the records of the Scottish Missionary Society were destroyed after the dissolution of the Society in 1848; see John Kilpatrick, "The Records of the Scottish Missionary Society," *Records of the Scottish Church History Society* (3) 1950, 196–210. For the Society's work, see William Brown, *The History of the Propagation of the Gospel among the Heathen since the Reformation* (Edinburgh: Nelson, 1854). Brown was secretary of the Society for the last twenty-seven years of its life. On Brunton, see P. E. H. Hair, "Notes on the Early Study of Some West African Languages," *Bulletin de l'Institut Français de l'Afrique Noire* B 23, nos. 3–4 (1961): 683–95.

[6] This statement is not meant to discount the efforts at translation made by successive eighteenth-century chaplains to the Danish settlement at Accra.

Muslim]."[7] And their involvement in the slave trade kept them in touch with European traders and gave them some interest in the outside world. Of the earliest missionaries, with one anomalous exception to be noted later, only Brunton and Greig, the two Scots among the Susu, seem to have made much headway with any West African language. Their sojourn was not prolonged; Brunton was called to Sierra Leone to officiate as settlement chaplain, and Greig died through armed robbery. The Edinburgh mission to the Susu was abruptly terminated, and Brunton was eventually reassigned to a new mission to the Russian Empire. When he left, he took a number of young Susu to Britain with him (one even accompanied him to Russia) with a view to maintaining the study of Susu language. There were also Susu children among a group that Zachary Macaulay, governor of Sierra Leone, brought home with him in 1797.[8] The original plan, that they should be educated in Scotland at the expense of the radical and wealthy Evangelical Robert Haldane,[9] was abandoned in favor of placing them at Clapham, under the care of the rector, John Venn.

In 1799 the Church Missionary Society for Africa and the East, with John Venn among its leading lights, came into being, giving expression to the missionary enthusiasm of those Evangelicals within the Church of England who wished to maintain Anglican principles and ecclesiastical discipline.[10] But the society long had difficulty in obtaining missionary candidates who could meet the requirements for the ministry then laid down in that discipline.[11] In 1801 Zachary Macaulay, who as governor of Sierra Leone had stationed the early missionaries and was now closely identified with the Clapham group, introduced Brunton to the Church Mission Society (CMS) committee. The committee, who were at the time considering somewhat impractical projects such as a translation (in England) of the Bible into Chinese, were struck by Brunton's attainments in an African language. And they were charmed when he produced two Susu boys who translated back into English an epitome of the Bible that he had prepared. They pressed Brunton to publish the Susu grammar that he had been working on, and to compose Susu tracts.[12]

---

[7] Thomas Thompson, *An Account of Two Missionary Voyages . . . The One to New Jersey in North America, the Other from America to the Coast of Guinea* (London: Dodd, 1758).

[8] Fyfe, *History of Sierra Leone*, 77.

[9] On Haldane, see Timothy C. F. Stunt, *From Awakening to Secession: Radical Evangelicals in Switzerland and Britain, 1815–35* (Edinburgh: T & T Clark, 2000).

[10] On the process, see Hennell, *John Venn and the Clapham Sect*, chap. 5.

[11] See A. F. Walls, *The Missionary Movement in Christian History* (Maryknoll, NY: Orbis Books, 1996), 160–72.

[12] University of Birmingham, CMS Archives, Committee Minutes 1802. Charles

This was done, with the Susu children at Clapham evidently being used as a reference group for the tracts and Scripture portions. In 1802, *A Grammar and Vocabulary of the Susoo Language* appeared, the first work of such scope for any African language. The preface indicates an ambitious long-term aim behind this grappling with Susu. Drawing on the experience of the Gaelic schools in Scotland,[13] Brunton argued that missions must lay down a foundation of Christian knowledge before any significant response could be expected. In other words, he assumed that vernacular Christian education, beginning with the Susu, would be the means by which the Christian faith would grow in Africa. Scripture passages and tracts in Susu must accordingly go into circulation; the fruit, as in the Scottish Highlands, would appear in a later generation.[14]

The CMS committee seems to have shared this vision. The society's report for 1802 announces their publication of some tracts and Scripture portions in "the Susu dialect of Africa." "Never before has any book been written, much less published, in the native language of the western parts of Africa. The facility with which a missionary may now attain the knowledge of Susoo, which is understood through a vast extent of Africa, is obvious."[15]

The society may have been too sanguine about the number of speakers of Susu, about the serviceability of the translations, and above all about the ease with which the language might be learned from such materials; but Brunton's work effectively dictated mission policy for the immediate future. Quantities of the grammar and tracts were sent to Sierra Leone, and, using Macaulay's contacts, a corresponding committee was established there, charged with distributing the books and finding the teachers to use them.[16] Evidently the society, like Brunton himself, saw vernacular education, based on the Scriptures, as the foundation of mission work. And when, at about the same time, they at last identified missionary candidates, the society

---

Hole, *The Early History of the Church Missionary Society for Africa and the East to the End of 1814* (London: Church Missionary Society, 1896), provides what is virtually a calendar list of the attendance and proceedings at the early committees. On the matters discussed in this section, see Hole, *The Early History of the Church Missionary Society for Africa and the East to the End of 1814*, 63, 67–68, 74, 76.

[13] On this, and its later influence in Protestant missions, see Andrew F. Walls, "Three Hundred Years of Scottish Missions," in *Roots and Fruits: Retrieving Scotland's Missionary Story*, ed. Kenneth R. Ross, 4–37 (Eugene, OR: Wipf & Stock, 2014).

[14] H. Brunton, *Grammar of the Susoo Language . . .* (Edinburgh, 1802).

[15] *Report of The Church Missionary Society . . .* (London, 1802); cf. Hole, *The Early History of the Church Missionary Society for Africa and the East to the End of 1814*, 80.

[16] Cf. Hole, *The Early History of the Church Missionary Society for Africa and the East to the End of 1814*, 76.

determined to send them to the Susu people, restarting the enterprise that the Edinburgh Missionary Society had begun and in which Brunton had been engaged.

The new CMS candidates were German Pietists from the Berlin Seminary and came through an arrangement brokered by the pastor of a German immigrant church in London. In the early years of the CMS West Africa mission almost all the missionaries came from Germany. Most did not speak English and were assigned a period of preparatory study in England of the English language as well as theology. One of their tutors complained that his students were pious men but superficial theologians.[17] Brunton's Susu grammar became part of the staple of missionary training.

The first two missionaries, having completed their training, arrived in Sierra Leone in April 1804. The senior, Melchior Renner, was seized on, as Brunton had been, to act as colonial chaplain in Freetown; the other, Peter Hartwig, proceeded to the Susu country. He soon became a casualty, settling down as a trader, dealing in the principal local commodity, slaves.[18] Other German missionaries followed, and for most of them the path led to Susu country via Sierra Leone.

In 1807 the CMS asked Thomas Scott, the celebrated biblical commentator, to assume the theological tuition of the missionary candidates. The following year he was asked to teach them Susu and Arabic, neither of which he knew himself.[19] The reason for Arabic was the presence of Islam, and of literacy in Arabic among the Susu. After three months Scott wrote, "[Susu] we have mastered without difficulty, so far as the printed books go; and I hope to begin translating some chapters into the language."[20] He was finding Arabic more difficult. But the students, most of whom were of artisan or agricultural background, were struggling with English and Latin and Greek and Hebrew as well as Susu and Arabic. Scott took them through a liberal program as a prologue to the theology that he also taught them—Cicero, Horace, the Greek tragedies. Whether the prospective missionaries ever made, or could ever have made, much of an African language by studying it in this way as one more classical language, must be doubtful. It is clear that in practice few of them made much use of Susu, or greatly advanced its

[17] John Scott, *The Life of the Rev. Thomas Scott . . . Including a Narrative Drawn Up by Himself . . .* , 3rd ed. (London, 1822), 383.
[18] Renner and Hartwig appear as, respectively, no. 1 and no. 2 in *Church Missionary Society Register of Missionaries (Clerical, and Female) and Native Clergy* (London: CMS, 1904).
[19] Scott, *The Life of the Rev. Thomas Scott*, 380.
[20] Ibid., 381–82.

study. After a time the mission abandoned regular preaching to adults, and sought to lay the foundation of Christian knowledge by concentrating on a school. But the school did not provide the vernacular education of Brunton's and the committee's earlier vision with its inspiration in the story of Scottish Highland Christianity; the German missionaries conducted it in English. The local slave trade ensured a demand for the English language; it also ensured that there were Susu speakers with enough English to act as interpreters. The mission had the patronage of one prominent local chief who had himself been educated in England, and even been baptized there.[21] The missionary who gained most fluency in Susu was probably the early renegade Hartwig, and he acquired his competence while a slave trader. In 1814, penitent and very sick, Hartwig made contact with the society once more, and his last months were spent in translating the Gospel of John into Susu.[22]

Around the time of Hartwig's reappearance in the mission, the first signs appear of new and enthusiastic application to the vernacular. Two missionaries, J. G. Wilhelm and J. S. Klein, who had been among the most promising of Scott's students, planned a new Susu grammar that could be used by translators and vernacular tract writers. Klein was married to Scott's niece, who kept her uncle informed. Scott was delighted; this was, he said, exactly how he had envisaged developments. "Wonders" were being done in Asia through translation; it should be the same in Africa. In his view Wilhelm and Klein were the first of the missionaries to have the ability to translate directly from the biblical languages; now at last they could put their training to good use.[23] The vision of a foundation of Christian knowledge laid through vernacular literature is thus revived. But it is noticeable that Scott took for granted the missionaries' competence in Susu, "an imperfect African dialect," as his son calls it; it was their competence in Greek and Hebrew, not in the African language, that gave him confidence in their program of translation.

There was one other missionary, who had not been Scott's pupil, who had independently taken up language study. Gustav Nylander, a Baltic German, sent to Sierra Leone in 1806, spent his first six years there with some frustration as chaplain in Freetown. In 1812 he shook free, and crossed to the shore opposite to the colony, where the Bulam language was spoken.

---

[21] On William Fernandez, see Hole, *The Early History of the Church Missionary Society for Africa and the East to the End of 1814*, 598. Edward Bickersteth, to be mentioned below, also mentions him and his protection of the mission.

[22] See Eugene Stock, *History of the Church Missionary Society: Its Environment, Its Men and Its Work* (London: CMS, 1899), 1:88.

[23] Hole, *The Early History of the Church Missionary Society for Africa and the East to the End of 1814*, 599.

Circumstances had cut off these Bulam speakers from those to the south of the Sierra Leone peninsula, generally designated Sherbro. Nylander stayed on the Bulam shore until 1818. He translated two gospels, the Johannine epistles, parts of the liturgy and a catechism, and conducted services making use of them; they seem to have been printed in Sierra Leone.[24]

Between them, Nylander, Wilhelm, and Klein, with the returned prodigal Hartwig, might be seen as signaling, if not a breakthrough, then at least a new stage in the Christian engagement with West African languages. But it all came too late; time was running out for the Susu and Bulam missions and, with them, for the study of African vernaculars. In 1807 came the act making the slave trade illegal for British subjects; most other nations soon concurred. To police the act's provisions, Sierra Leone was taken away from Sierra Leone Company administration and became a crown colony. A naval squadron patrolled the coast, intercepting ships suspected of carrying slaves, and bringing them into Freetown. There was no way to repatriate the unfortunate people aboard them; henceforth the Sierra Leone peninsula became their home.

The initial expedient was to "apprentice" the recaptives, or Liberated Africans, as they came to be called, to the earlier members of the Province of Freedom, the settlers, so that they might learn the customs and arts of civilization. This soon broke down, the Liberated far outnumbering the original settlers. The architect of change was Colonel Sir Charles MacCarthy, who became governor of Sierra Leone in 1816. MacCarthy wanted to transform the miserable recaptive settlements into model English villages, each centered on its church and its school. He early concluded that the best agents of change would be missionaries, and set about persuading the CMS that their staff would be better employed in the colony than among the Susu.[25] He found an ally in Edward Bickersteth, who in 1816 was deputed by the CMS to visit West Africa and make recommendations about the rather disappointing mission there. Even before he got to Susu country Bickersteth was confiding to his journal his view that the move to the colony was to be followed:

It appears very important to mark the indications of a providential leading. Among these I consider the protection of an established government, the facility and safety of intercourse with the people,

[24] On Nylander, see *Church Missionary Society Register of Missionaries*, no. 3.
[25] See A. F. Walls, "A Colonial Concordat: Two Views of Christianity and Civilisation," in *Church, Society and Politics*. Studies in Church History, ed. Derek Baker 293–302 (Oxford: Blackwell, 1975).

the economy attending a mission, and the number that may easily be gathered together. In the absence of supernatural inspiration, such circumstances may be considered as the call "Come over and help us," and all these things speak strongly in favour of our exertions in the colony.[26]

Arrived in the Susu mission, he tried to preach through an interpreter; but the interpreter did not understand such key phrases as "forever," and was quite prepared to translate nonsense, apparently hearing "written in a book" as "written with his foot."[27]

Bickersteth recommended that the society concentrate its work on the Liberated Africans in the Sierra Leone colony. The Methodists were already directing their work to the recaptives in Freetown. The demands of the colony were such that the Susu mission could not be sustained. Its missionaries, and their accumulated experience, were transferred to Sierra Leone. (The Freetown Corresponding Committee and its stocks of Brunton's books in Susu had long been forgotten.) In 1818 Nylander, the sole representative of mission among the Bulam, followed the others to the colony.

This marks the fading of the vision that opened with Brunton's grammar, of vernacular education laying a foundation of Christian knowledge in the languages of Africa. Nylander's hope, of churches that preached and worshiped in those languages, faded too. Mission work in the Sierra Leone villages was conducted in English. There was little alternative. The intercepted ships carried people who might come from anywhere between Senegal and the Congo, and sometimes beyond either. Though collected at the coast, victims of the slave trade often came from territories far inland. A single ship might have picked up people from many locations, speaking a variety of languages. A single colony village might contain a range of communities originating in different places across West Africa. There was no single language that could be regarded as dominant, not at least before the 1820s brought increasing numbers of Yoruba; and by that time the pattern was set. English, acquired in North America, was the language of the original settlers, the natural role models of the newcomers. It was the language of the colonial administration. It became the language of evangelism, worship, and education—the language, that is, of Christianity. This took place despite the fact that for most of the missionaries, who were the people responsible for evangelism, worship, and education, English was a second language. They were much too busy to learn a third. One of them writes,

---

[26] T. R. Birks, *Memoir of the Rev. Edward Bickersteth* (London: Seeley, 1851), chap. 11.
[27] Ibid.

Sometimes I have not an hour to myself from Monday to Saturday, as I have to attend to brickmakers, masons, carpenters, storekeepers, cultivation, landsurveying, etc., beside our schools, which contain 409 scholars.[28]

Missionaries were superintendents of the English-model villages, which bore names drawn from the names or titles of British royalty (Regent, Leopold, Charlotte, Kent) and other eminent British figures (Bathurst, Wellington, Wilberforce), or in one case, from an event significant in British life (Waterloo). The missionary superintendents were responsible for feeding their populations, and leading them to economic self-sufficiency. They were responsible for civil order, and for the conduct of schools. However, they had not set out to be builders of a community; they had responded to a missionary vocation to preach the gospel. The missionary just quoted, W. A. B. Johnson,[29] was at the time seeing in the largest of the villages, Regent, a large-scale Christian movement, and was lamenting that his secular duties prevented his carrying out house-to-house visitation as he wished. But such visitation and his regular preaching were in English. Many of his hearers had been on the slave ships only a few months before, and before that speaking their mother tongues in their homelands; now they were attending service according to the Book of Common Prayer, and hearing Johnson preaching and teaching in English. Johnson himself describes his first sight of the miserable, disorientated new arrivals, many very ill after the ordeal of the voyage, and notes that "there are a very few of these poor people who can speak broken English."[30] Only months later tumultuous scenes occurred in a prayer meeting as young men, falling under conviction of sin, began to cry out "Oh, Jesus, Massa, have mercy." Leaving the meeting, Johnson found a house full of people "crying aloud 'Oh, Jesus have mercy' etc . . . weeping and trembling, and others singing praises to Jesus as well as they could, in their broken language." The movement spread, and led to a vigorous Christian community at Regent that every visitor seems to have described in glowing terms.

---

[28] From an entry under 1817 in Johnson's journal. See Robert Benton Seeley, *Memoir of the Rev. W.A. B. Johnson* (London, 1852).

[29] Johnson was an Anglicization of Jantzon. Unlike most of the early German missionaries of CMS, he did not have a seminary or mission background. Born in Hanover, he had moved to Britain, the other Hanoverian domain, for work, before his Evangelical conversion and missionary call. For the same reason, his English is more fluent and easy than that of some of his colleagues. See *Church Missionary Society Register of Missionaries*, no. 25.

[30] An 1816 journal item, preserved in Seeley, *Memoir of the Rev. W.A. B. Johnson.*

These are scenes reminiscent of the Great Revival in America. That such scenes should occur at all at so early a stage in the growth of a church is remarkable; revival of this nature is a feature of established Christian communities, not of those hearing the Christian message for the first time. It is still more remarkable that the phenomena should occur in English, albeit fractured, among people just beginning to use the language. Further study of Johnson's correspondence points to two features of Regent that throw light on the process of evangelization there. One is the high value Johnson places on a number of African assistants. Some of these clearly acted as vernacular evangelists, gathering and teaching people from their own ethnic group. No doubt there were similar developments in other villages, which would suggest that some, at least, of the early communication of the Christian message in Sierra Leone was in African vernaculars. The other factor of interest is the activity of representatives of the congregations of the original Nova Scotian settler community, which strongly maintained the traditions and institutions of the American Great Revival and expressed them in (sometimes fractured) English. Johnson and other missionaries complained of this activity, but may sometimes have benefited from it.

What is undeniable is that the colony of Sierra Leone gradually emerged as a Christian community, the most substantial early success of Protestant missions in Africa. And its Christianity was English-speaking, with literacy in English, and its people enthusiastically participated in the British cultural and literary inheritance. By the mid-nineteenth century it had a higher literacy rate and a proportionately larger school population than many European countries,[31] and a comfortable middle class who wanted grammar school education for their children.[32] Sierra Leone, reassuringly, appeared to be reproducing the "civilization" that many expected to be the fruit of the gospel. In this respect it resembled the only larger body of African Protestant Christians, those living in the Americas, and especially those in the Caribbean. Writers who combined the Evangelical concern for missions with the humanitarian hatred of slavery regularly contrasted the piety, orderly conduct, and steady advance in civilization of the converted slaves and former slaves of the West Indies with the barbarity of their European masters and oppressors.[33]

---

[31] Cf. Henry Venn, *West African Colonies: Notices of the British Colonies on the West Coast of Africa* (London: Dalton and Lucy, 1865).

[32] See the portrait of the colony and its church in Jehu J. Hanciles, *Euthanasia of a Mission: Church Autonomy in a Colonial Context* (Westport, CT: Praeger, 2002).

[33] It is a regular theme of Thomas Fowell Buxton, *The African Slave Trade and Its Remedy* (London: Murray, 1840), and of disciples such as the Baptist writer David Jonathan East.

Before about 1840, the most noticeable and substantial African Christian communities appeared to be English speaking, and to be following the cultural models of English-speaking countries. And this sometimes led to an assumption that future Christian expansion in Africa would follow a similar course. The issue of African vernacular languages, so prominent in the early days of missions, had apparently, as far as Africa was concerned, receded in importance. It could even be argued that, as civilization spread in Africa, the African languages would die out. The loss of such imperfect vehicles of meaning need not be regretted; after all, the whole treasury of classical and European literature would be available to African Christians.[34]

There were dissident voices, and none more unconventional, or more trenchant, than that of Hannah Kilham.[35] This Sheffield lady, once a Methodist, was the widow (following a very brief marriage) of Alexander Kilham, founder of the Methodist New Connexion. After her husband's death she became a Quaker, active in such Quakerly concerns as the abolition of slavery and the education of the poor. These interests combined to turn her attention to Sierra Leone. Hearing Bickersteth's account of the colony and its challenges, she wrote to him to ask what language was used in the schools there. She was told that it was English, and her dissatisfaction grew into a conviction that she should go to Sierra Leone herself. She negotiated with CMS about going there with W. A. B. Johnson and his wife, who were in Britain at the time. And she pressed upon anyone who would listen the importance of African languages. She had little success; to most of those people in Britain who were well disposed to Africa, the best possible outcome seemed to be that Africans would learn English. Her Quaker friends, such as the philanthropist William Allen, were supporting projects that brought African children, especially the sons of chiefs, to Britain for education in English. This seems to have turned Hannah Kilham's thoughts to promoting the study of African languages through Africans resident in Britain rather than going to Africa herself. Allen and others joined a small Committee for African Instruction[36] set up in 1819 to give backing to the proposals. Hannah Kilham's vision was of a purpose-built institution in London, heated by steam "as in Russia," to help Africans cope with the cold,

---

[34] Cf. J. F. Schön and S. Crowther, *Journal of an Expedition up the Niger* (London: CMS, 1842), 358.

[35] On Hannah Kilham, see Sarah Biller, *Memoir of the Late Hannah Kilham; Chiefly Compiled from Her Journals* (London: Darton & Harvey, 1837); Mora Dickson, *The Powerful Bond: Hannah Kilham 1774–1832* (London: Denis Dobson, 1980).

[36] The committee was noticed outside the Society of Friends; see *Missionary Register*: J 820, 332–33; ibid., 1822, 13H34.

where two speakers of each of the ten most important African languages could live. (She was aware of the problems of reliance on a single informant.) The residents would not only get an English education; they would be encouraged to write their own languages and compile vocabularies. By such means it would be possible to produce elementary books in those languages before the residents returned to Africa to use them as teachers among their own people.

Before this ambitious program could be set on foot, an opportunity appeared of starting on a more modest basis. A ship arrived in London with two sailors from the area of The Gambia, who might afford access to Wolof and perhaps Mandinka languages. The committee arranged to buy the freedom of Mahmadee and Sandanee and to secure them appropriate accommodation in London. William Singleton, another Methodist turned Quaker,[37] superintended their general education and Hannah Kilham ensured that they learned to write Wolof. Wolof and Mandinka vocabularies were duly produced and Hannah Kilham composed primers for teaching and some Scripture passages and other materials in Wolof.

The next stage was to attempt to apply these in Africa. Singleton made a reconnaissance visit to both The Gambia and Sierra Leone. His visit, though not uniformly successful, was judged to be sufficient to justify a venture to The Gambia, under Hannah Kilham's leadership, in 1823.[38] Generally speaking, the Society of Friends had not yet shared in the missionary movement; Hannah Kilham had been able to persuade her friends that an educational and agricultural mission could be entirely in accord with their principles. And Mahmadee and Sandanee would return home at the same time as the mission, and be able to start their careers of teaching.

The Gambia mission did not thrive; its decline set in when Hannah Kilham left it to investigate the situation in Sierra Leone. There, the colony confirmed all her fears about the limitations of working entirely in English and her belief in Christian education in the vernacular. She met Nylander, who shared her views, but had ceased to campaign for them. She noted the vast array of languages to be found in Freetown among recaptives and the peoples bordering the colony, and worked at vocabularies for Fante and Mandinka among the former group, Susu and Bulam among the latter.

---

[37] A. F. Walls, "William Singleton," *Proceedings of the Wesley Historical Society* 34 (1963): 23.

[38] See the account in J. Ormerod Greenwood, *Sierra Leone Bulletin of Religion* 4, no. 1 (1962): 9–22; J. Ormerod Greenwood, *Sierra Leone Bulletin of Religion* 4, no. 2 (1962): 61–71.

After the collapse of The Gambia mission, Mrs. Kilham made two further visits to Sierra Leone. In the course of them she met a missionary, John Raban,[39] who, noting the increasing number of Yoruba recaptives now coming into Sierra Leone, was working at Yoruba as a means of evangelization. He was much impressed by a young Yoruba recaptive that he had baptized, one Ajayi (Adjai), who had received the name of Samuel Crowther.[40] Crowther was almost certainly the language informant who introduced Hannah Kilham to Yoruba.

She continued to advocate vernacular literacy—which for her was inseparable from Scriptural teaching—and study of African languages. Her manifesto, *The Claims of West Africa to Christian Instruction in the Native Languages*, appeared in 1830.[41] The same year she determined to put her principles into practice in a school of her own that would operate in the vernacular. She left for Sierra Leone with a group of CMS missionaries, including Raban. She established her school in the village of Charlotte, which the CMS had vacated, and commenced perhaps the most fulfilling period of her life. She concentrated on two languages, Yoruba and Mende (then commonly called Kossoh). Her school was still expanding when, following a brief reconnaissance of Liberia, she died at sea on March 31, 1832, in her fifty-eighth year. Her school was taken over by the Wesleyan mission, but did not last long without her.[42]

Hannah Kilham's great dreams—the acceptance by the missions of the option for the vernacular, and the establishment of the African language institute—were never realized in her lifetime. What she achieved, she had to do herself, or with a few like-minded friends and helpers. Perhaps she had too many dreams, too many good ideas, too many burdens on her conscience. When in Africa she could not help wondering whether her duty lay in feeding the hungry in Ireland; when occupied in Irish famine relief, her thoughts turned readily to the claims of Africa. She never wavered, however, in asserting those claims. In a letter to Joseph Rowntree, who shared her views on the importance of vernaculars, she bursts out,

> how long have the attempts of missionaries been baffled, whilst they have wished to force the English language upon the people, despising their own as not worth cultivation. Is this not like

[39] On Raban, see *Church Missionary Society Register of Missionaries*, no. 95.

[40] On Crowther, see J. F. Ade Ajayi, *Christian Missions in Nigeria 1841–1891. The Making of a New Elite* (London: Longmans, 1965).

[41] On Mrs. Kilham's linguistic work, see P. E. H. Hair, "Bibliographical Note on Hannah Kilham's Linguistic Work," *Journal of the Friends Historical Society* 49 (1960): 165–68.

[42] Dickson, *The Powerful Bond*, 241.

expecting the people to profit by an unknown tongue? . . . And how
can instruction be in anything else but through the medium of that
which is already known?[43]

The same letter mentions her predecessors in West African languages:

Some attempts were made many years ago in two languages, the
Bullom and the Susu; but whether from want of some individuals
being set apart to this work exclusively, or from any other cause,
there did not appear to be that practical use of the books when
prepared which the translators had no doubt designed for them.
They are both deceased; and one or both being Germans might
render it less easy for English missionaries to prosecute the plans.[44]

The Bulam translator was, of course, Nylander, whom she knew, and
who had died in 1825. It is striking that she did not even know the nationality of Brunton, on whose pioneer work three decades earlier mission policy
makers had placed such hope.

In the event, Sierra Leone produced a new community, rejoicing in the
English language and English literary culture as part of its own inheritance. It
also produced a new language, though this took much longer to gain recognition. As it developed, Sierra Leone Krio was called broken English, or even,
with a dig at the German missionaries held responsible for the fractures,
German English. Because of this, it long held inferior status, as a form of English
manqué. The British declaration in 1896 of a protectorate covering much of the
hinterland united the fortunes of colony and interior, ensuring in the process
that Krio would become the lingua franca of modern Sierra Leone.[45]

Hannah Kilham died without success or successor. And yet in a way she
never could have guessed she pointed to the future. Administrative changes
in Sierra Leone, beginning in her own time there, closed the MacCarthy era
and took the missionaries out of community superintendence. They turned
to other things. Raban's enthusiasm for Yoruba is symptomatic of this, as is
the initiative of his young protégé Crowther in preaching in this, his native
language. In the year that Mrs. Kilham died, Jakob Friedrich Schön[46] arrived

---

[43] Hannah Kilham to Joseph Rowntree [1829], Kilham Papers, Friends House,
London.

[44] Ibid.

[45] See Clifford N. Fyle and Eldred D. Jones, *A Krio-English Dictionary* (Oxford:
Oxford University Press, 1989). The New Testament in Krio was published in 1992.

[46] On Schön, see *Church Missionary Society Register of Missionaries*, no. 181. The

in Sierra Leone in the service of the CMS. He took to African languages with vigor, studying Igbo and especially Hausa, languages from the Niger basin, that had many speakers in Sierra Leone. In after years he was to be the regular consultant of the CMS in matters concerning African languages. More importantly, he, with Crowther, set forth a new vision of the place of West African languages in the Christian story, which took up all that Brunton and Nylander and Mrs. Kilham had attempted. The general acceptance of that vision transformed missionary enterprise in West Africa. Its barest outline must form the conclusion of this study.

In 1841 the British government accepted a proposal by the Evangelical humanitarian and antislavery campaigner Thomas Fowell Buxton for an exploratory mission to the Niger. It was meant as a large-scale feasibility study for a "New Africa Policy" designed to stifle the slave trade, foster the development of agriculture in Africa, and open the way for Africa to enter the economic comity of nations freely and on equitable terms. The expedition included scientists of every description; it also conveyed two representatives of the CMS: Schön and Crowther. The latter, now in his thirties, was still a lay teacher–catechist with the society. They joined the expedition in Freetown, along with interpreters for the various languages of the Niger region—all drawn from Sierra Leone recaptives who had originated in those areas. After a few months the expedition was abandoned as a disaster. Forty of its European members had died; most of the others had been seriously ill. It was the end of any public support for a new Africa policy, or for humanitarian schemes in Africa generally. Buxton never recovered.[47]

But the reports of Schön and Crowther on the expedition have a very different tone from other assessments at the time. Conventional wisdom deduced from the disaster that Europeans could not long survive in inland Africa. Schön and Crowther concluded that the evangelization of inland Africa would have to be carried out by African missionaries. They also held that the expedition had proved the importance of African languages, which should now become a special branch of missions, with specially designated workers. Furthermore the Christian community in Sierra Leone would provide both a source of supply of missionaries and a gigantic language laboratory in which all the languages of West Africa were already spoken. Contrary to the expectation of many, the homeland languages had not died out among those who had arrived in Sierra Leone. The children of Liber-

---

French scholar Delafosse described him as the "discoverer" of Hausa, in the sense of indicating its importance as a language and the huge numbers speaking it.

[47] On the expedition, see Anstey, *The Atlantic Slave Trade and British Abolition*.

ated Africans, though learning English at school and using it in church, also spoke the languages of their parents with fluency. This had enormous implications, and enormous promise, for the Christian future in West Africa.[48]

This vision showed the way to that future; not precisely, or smoothly, or without pitfalls, but in convincing outline. Yoruba recaptives in Sierra Leone, now sea-going traders on their own account, found their way back to their homelands. They settled, but wanted the church life they had known in Sierra Leone. The principal mission that went there in response to such appeals, that of the CMS, included many Yoruba-speaking Christians from Sierra Leone led by the newly ordained Crowther. The ensuing Yoruba translation of the Bible marked a new epoch, as being the first in which a mother tongue speaker—Crowther himself—played a determining, not just an ancillary role. In Sierra Leone itself the arrival of S. W. Koelle[49] in 1847 brought unprecedented exploration of the Freetown language laboratory; his massive *Polyglotta Africana*[50] laid the foundations of comparative African linguistics. Eventually Crowther was leading a mission with an all-African staff, many of them with a background in Sierra Leone. Ironically by then the passing of a generation was bringing about the long-predicted demise of the homeland vernaculars of the Liberated Africans in the Sierra Leone colony, and the new African missionaries had to learn from the beginning the languages of the people amongst whom they worked.

It was one more twist in the story of Christian mission and West African languages:[51] a story of interplay between classical Protestant convictions about Scripture, the apparently remorseless pressure of events, and a succession of visionary nonconformists.

---

[48] Schön and Crowther, *Journal of an Expedition up the Niger*, 347–70.

[49] On Koelle (*Church Missionary Society Register of Missionaries*, no. 379), see P. E. H. Hair, *The Early Study of Nigerian Languages* (Cambridge: Cambridge University Press, 1967); and the commemorative issues of *Sierra Leone Language Review* 3 (1963), 4 (1964), and 5 (1966).

[50] S. W. Koelle, *Polyglotta Africana* (London: CMS, 1854); reprinted with historical introduction by P. E. H. Hair and word index by David Dalby, Graz: Akademische Druck und Verlagsanstalt, 1963.

[51] This account, concentrating on the earliest developments, with Sierra Leone and the neighboring territories at its center and important consequences for the Niger area, omits important developments in Gambia and Ghana.

9

The Discovery of African Traditional Religion and Its Impact on Religious Studies

Brookes' General Gazetteer or Comprehensive Geographical Dictionary[1] is a pocket-sized reference book of the late eighteenth century. It claims to describe the "Empires, Kingdoms, States, Provinces, Cities, Towns, Forts, Seas, Harbours, Rivers, Lakes, Mountains, Capes etc., in the known world, with the government, customs, manners, and religion" of the inhabitants. It is full of facts and figures providing, for instance, the dimensions of the roof of the Great Hall of the old Scottish Parliament Building in Edinburgh and the figures for sail cloth manufacture in Dundee. Information on Africa, however, is sparse. We learn from it that Africa is one of the four principal parts of the world; but beyond that the feature most fully described is the variety of wildlife:

> There are more wild beasts in Africa than in any other part of the world . . . as the hippopotamus, or river horse, the rhinoceros, with two horns upon its nose, and the beautiful striped zebra. They have crocodiles, ostriches, camels and many the other animals not to be met with in Europe.[2]

Information on the human inhabitants of the continent is hard to find in the book. The map that accompanies the article on Africa divides it into regions with names such as "Sarra, or the Desert," "Monomatapa,"

---

[1] Richard Brookes, *The General Gazetteer or, Compendious Geographical Dictionary in Miniature*, 3rd ed. (London: W. Palmer, 1806).
[2] Ibid., 5.

"Monoemugi," "Nigritia or Negroland" and "Guinea." The article on Guinea may stand as a specimen of the information the book conveys about Africa.

> *Guinea,* a country of Africa of which little is known except the coast.... It is very unhealthy for Europeans, though the Negroes live a considerable time. The natives in general go about almost naked, and there seems to be little religion or honesty among them. The commodities purchased here, are gum senega, at Senegal; grain, upon the Grain Coast; elephant's teeth, upon the Tooth Coast; the greatest plenty of gold, upon the Gold Coast; and all, in general, furnish slaves.[3]

A work of reference at the height of the European Enlightenment was thus for all practical purposes useless when it came to information about Africa. People who could eloquently discuss the nature of liberty and the anatomy of human society were without any way of conceiving Africa and its peoples in human terms. Africa was Never-Never Land, the home of the crocodile and the two-horned rhino. In terms of human society, the only generally comprehended fact about Africa, the one fact that everybody knew, was that Africa furnished slaves.

It was the issue of slavery that gave rise to a major development in Western intellectual discourse about Africa. In the early nineteenth century slavery came to dominate the discourse as a result of two movements that played into each other; the movement for the abolition of the slave trade (and, later, of slavery itself), and the new developments in thought and action about Christian missions. Both developments linked thought about Africa with thought about America.

The Protestant missionary movement and the movement for the abolition of slavery grew up together. Both grew up in the eighteenth century, took shape in the 1790s, and both had achieved general recognition and a good measure of acceptance by 1840. And it is among writers on missions, for the most part heart-felt opponents of slavery, that we find the first widespread development of a discourse about Africa in human terms.

A good representative of this discourse is the Methodist theologian Richard Watson[4] (1781–1833), one of the first secretaries of the Wesleyan Methodist Missionary Society, and an active member of the Anti-Slavery

---

[3] Ibid., 127–28.
[4] On Watson, see Andrew F. Walls, "Wesleyan Missiological Theories: The Case of Richard Watson," in *The Global Impact of the Wesleyan Traditions and Their Related Movements*, ed. Charles Yrigoven, 27–47 (Lanham, MD: Scarecrow Press, 2002).

Society. He was author of a textbook of theology that was used in the training of Methodist ministers until the beginning of the nineteenth century.[5]

Typically for his period, Watson sees Africa and the African population of the Americas as part of the same picture. The latter were, for him, in effect a part of Africa that had been broken off. As secretary of the Missionary Society, Watson had to think both of infant missions in West and South Africa and of the crowded congregations and large church buildings of the Caribbean.

The Caribbean missions had deeper roots than the earliest Methodist missions in Africa. The first Methodist contacts with Africans had occurred in the Caribbean; Antigua had a Methodist Society from 1760, and there was a Methodist presence in other islands too. The Methodist presence in West Africa had itself been originated by Black Methodists moving from the American colonies after the Revolutionary War, first to Nova Scotia, and then, in 1792, to Sierra Leone, the colony inspired by the philanthropic campaigners against the slave trade. In comparison with those in the Caribbean, Methodist missions on the African continent, while showing encouraging results, were at an early stage. It is not surprising, therefore, that in the 1820s Watson should view the churches of the Caribbean as the earnest of what Africa as a whole would be when the long-hidden God of Africa was revealed. Afro-America contained the germ of the Christian Africa of the future.[6]

The principal materials available to Watson for the study of African religion came from Afro-America. Watson's theology, as we shall see, allowed for the presence of elements of divine revelation outside the Christian, but he lamented that the experience of slavery had broken up the original patterns of African religion. This loss was part of the uniquely harsh suffering that Africans had endured in America.[7]

The literary sources for Watson's view of Africa were the Bible and the works on world history then generally available. He identified modern-day Africans as the descendants of the people named in the Old Testament as Cush, Mizraim, and Put, not as descendants of Canaan. The curse of Genesis 9:25–27, so often used to justify African slavery, Watson sees as irrelevant to Africa. (Though he adds that, in any case, all curses are lifted by the all-embracing atonement of Christ.)[8]

---

[5] Richard Watson, *Theological Institutes: Or, a View of the Evidences, Doctrines, Morals, and Institutions of Christianity* (London: John Mason, 1829).

[6] *The Works of the Rev. Richard Watson, Vol. II* (London: John Mason, 1834), 126.

[7] See his sermon on the text "Honour All Men," in ibid., 88–130.

[8] Ibid., 94ff.

From general history Watson draws a picture of a glorious African past. Africans produced the great Nilotic civilizations and introduced writing to the world. African leaders were prominent in early Christianity. Africa at one time had been a nursery of civilizations; even contemporary African states such as Ashanti and Dahomey reflected the remnants of this.[9] But alas, population movements had brought such things to a standstill, and the slave trade had made contemporary Africans the most cruelly treated peoples in the world. They were misrepresented by pseudoscholarship and false interpretations of Scripture as well as mistreated; as the glorious past of Africa proved, its people did not lack capacity, but opportunity. With the coming of the gospel, opportunity was restored and Africa could look forward to a glorious future in the kingdom of God.

Watson took for granted the moral bankruptcy of humanity apart from Christ, and believed that the most recent studies provided proof that heathenism was full of superstition, immorality, and, above all, fear. In the 1820s there was little to point to by way of serious studies of Africa, but contemporary conventions made it easy to group all forms of "heathenism" together, and it seems probable that the studies that Watson had in mind were those emanating from missionaries in Bengal. In the eighteenth century European scholarship had generally diffused a benign picture of Indian society, based on the Sanskrit classics; the reports of the missionaries brought together by such writers as William Ward and Claudius Buchanan described social and religious practices in Bengal at a popular level: the immolation of widows on the funeral pyres of their husbands, the Car Festival of Jagannath, devotees swinging from hooks in their flesh, temple prostitution. These pictures stirred Christian opinion deeply, and Watson would have been well aware of this body of writing.[10]

Nevertheless, Watson acknowledged that not everything in heathenism was evil, and that glimpses of truth came from the primeval revelation (remains, he would say, of the greater knowledge of God that the world's peoples had in patriarchal times[11]).

However, he identifies the dominant aspect in the heathenism of his own day as fear and insecurity in dealing with the spirit world and saw fear at its starkest in the Caribbean, where transportation and slavery had broken up traditional religious patterns, causing the loss of the intellectual stimulus that

---

[9] Ibid., 92–95.

[10] See, e.g., Allan K. Davidson, *Evangelicals and Attitudes to India: Missionary Publicity and Claudius Buchanan* (Abingdon, UK: Sutton Courtenay Press 1990).

[11] Cf. *Works IV,* 212; Watson, *Theological Institutes,* 42–53.

religious systems provide. "Some of the milder forms of Paganism" might well have been preferable to this.[12]

Watson's picture of Africa, past, present and future, is characteristic of the new discourse constructed from the confluence of the visions of the missionaries and the humanitarians. This discourse continued to be fed by journals and letters from the mission field printed in missionary magazines—a genre that created a new reading public with an active interest in Africa. Some missionaries wrote books, and some of these were widely read. The descriptions of the kingdom of Ashanti by the Wesleyan missionary Thomas Birch Freeman[13] opened new visions; and Sir Thomas Fowell Buxton used them extensively in the book that so abundantly reflects the confluence of the missionary and humanitarian views: *The African Slave Trade and Its Remedy*.[14]

Buxton's book is both an analysis of the existing woes of Africa (induced by the European imposition of the slave trade) and a presentation of a proactive economic program of Western reparations to Africa. Two biblical texts adorn its title page to indicate its two themes: the present suffering of Africa and the possibility of a glorious future. One is "This is a people robbed and spoiled; they are all of them snared in holes, and they are hid in prison houses; they are for a prey, and none delivereth; for a spoil, and none saith, Restore."[15] The other is "The desert shall rejoice and blossom as the rose."[16] Richard Watson would have understood and approved.

A few years later David Livingstone published his book *Missionary Travels and Researches in South Africa*,[17] containing substantial accounts of the areas through which he had traveled. The term "researches" is significant; the book is intended to contribute to current knowledge. Early in the book comes an account of a conversation between a missionary doctor and a Kwena traditional doctor, a man much in demand for healing the land of drought in a region of low rainfall.[18] The conversation covers points of

---

[12] *Works II*, 112.

[13] Notably Thomas Birch Freeman, *Journals of Various Visits to the Kingdoms of Ashanti, Aku and Dahomi in Western Africa*, 2nd ed. 1844 (reissued London: Frank Cass, 1968).

[14] Thomas Fowell Buxton, *The African Slave Trade and Its Remedy*, 2nd ed. (London: John Murray, 1840). Some journals by Freeman were seen by Buxton before their publication and are among the "fresh sources of information" mentioned in Buxton's preface.

[15] Isaiah 42:22.

[16] Isaiah 35:1.

[17] David Livingstone, *Missionary Travels and Researches in South Africa* (London: John Murray, 1857).

[18] Ibid., 23–25.

difference between the worldview of traditional African society and that of a Western Christianity infused by the Enlightenment. Livingstone's evident purpose is to demonstrate African intelligence and dialectical skill; there is no rhetorical triumph and no knock-down argument on the part of the missionary, no conviction and conversion on the part of the traditionalist. When the missionary doctor speaks of what God says in his Book, the rain doctor does not dispute it or deny the divine origin of the Christian Book; he merely says that God told his people differently, just as he has given Europeans many desirable things that he had withheld from the Kwena. But he had given the Kwena the gift of rain making, which outsiders who do not understand should not despise.[19] Livingstone does not locate the Kwena in some remote alien world of thought; he believes them to resemble the people of the Scottish Highlands a few generations back (and his grandfather was a Highlander).

Livingstone was one of a significant group of missionaries with informed scientific interests, who recorded detailed observations on topography, flora, and fauna, as well as about the peoples they encountered and the development of the work of their missions. This produced a distinctive genre of literature that I have ventured elsewhere[20] to call "missiography": a mixture of materials designed both to widen general knowledge and to develop understanding of missionary operations in their context. By the eighteenth century missiography was merging into ethnography as missionaries, especially as their linguistic skills deepened, gave more and more detailed accounts of the life and thought of the peoples they lived with.

A good example of the new development is the work on the Zulu by the Anglican missionary Henry Callaway,[21] an associate, though not a disciple, of Bishop Colenso, in which the study of religion is integrated with every aspect of Zulu society. This is in accord with Callaway's theology, which sought not to replace Zulu tradition by Christianity but to graft Christianity on to Zulu tradition, changing only what was clearly incompatible with Christian belief. Somewhat later the Church of Scotland missionary Duff Macdonald published a two-volume work entitled *Africana, or the*

---

[19] Livingstone adds, "These arguments are well-known, and I never succeeded in convincing a single individual of their fallacy."

[20] A. F. Walls, "The Nineteenth Century Missionary as Scholar," in *Misjonskall og Forskerglede: festskrift till Pofessor Olav Guttorm Myklebust*, 209–21 (Oslo: Universitetsforlaget, 1975); reprinted in Andrew F. Walls, *The Missionary Movement in Christian History: Studies in the Transmission of Faith* (Maryknoll, NY: Orbis Books, 1996), 187–98.

[21] Most notably in Henry Callaway, *The Religious System of the AmaZulu* (Springvale, South Africa: Natal, 1870).

Heart of Heathen Africa,[22] devoting one volume to a wide-ranging study of society in what is now Malawi, and another to an account of the early days of the Blantyre Mission there. Macdonald clearly enjoys surprising his Western readership by disturbing their preconceptions about traditional Africa. He has, for instance, a chapter about initiation rites headed "The Heathen University," and one on religious beliefs is "African theology." There is also a striking passage where Macdonald pictures a crowd of pale, overstretched British workers hurrying in response to the factory bell passing the lodgings of harassed students who have been trying to do without sleep, and contrasts this with the confidence and quiet poise to be seen in African society. He concludes that an attempt to rank Africans in classes, on the models recognized in British society, might place most in the category of "gentlemen in easy circumstances." Western civilization, he continues, has not noticeably increased the sum of human happiness; it has merely moved the deficit into another column. The gospel, accordingly, is not about the civilization of the heart of heathen Africa.

An Irish missionary of the Church Missionary Society, John Roscoe, provides another example. In 1911 he published a major study of the Baganda.[23] Roscoe had little conventional academic background; his work flowed from his quarter of a century of living with the Baganda and of speaking with them in Luganda. His book deals with every aspect of Ganda life, thought, and society.

When Callaway, Macdonald, Roscoe, and other missionary authors like them write at length on the religious beliefs and practices of the Zulu, Chewa, or Baganda, they do so in the context of the social organization and life of these people as a whole. Their books are essays in understanding, and the motivation for the essays arises from their missionary activity. They had come to Africa to communicate the gospel and had found it necessary to understand in order to communicate. The studies can in one sense be described as anthropological or sociological, but their source and origin is essentially missionary. They were pioneers of a new branch of scholarship that was developing out of Christian missions and impacting the academic world by a curious route.

During the second half of the nineteenth century the social sciences had received new impetus from the natural sciences. Darwin's *Origin of Species*, published in 1859, set out the principle of biological evolution. In subsequent decades the principle was introduced into a range of studies outside

---

[22] Duff MacDonald, *Africana, or the Heart of Heathen Africa* (London: Simpkin Marshall, 1882).

[23] John Roscoe, *The Baganda: An Account of Their Native Customs and Beliefs* (London: Macmillan, 1911).

that of biology and heavily influenced emerging branches of study (hardly yet "disciplines") such as sociology and anthropology. In many quarters the principle of evolution began to be seen as the key to understanding human history and the development of human institutions.

It was argued that across the world there were human societies at different stages of evolution, as reflected in their intellectual and technological development. In other words, there were higher races, where intellectual and technological progress had developed, and lower races, where it had not yet progressed so far. As regards religion, the same principle could be observed; there were "higher" religions, where philosophical and ethical systems were highly developed, with great historically identifiable teachers and a body of literary texts; there were "lower" religions with no developed philosophy or literature. Hinduism, Buddhism, Zoroastrianism, Judaism, Christianity, and Islam were representatives of the first group; the religious manifestations to be seen in Africa, in the Pacific Islands, and among the forest and mountain peoples in Asia and the Americas belonged to the second, reflecting the effects of the evolutionary principle at its "lower" end. The new branch of study known as Comparative Religion which took shape in the late nineteenth century made Hindu and Buddhist Scriptures and ancient Chinese texts objects of academic study in the West, and of some popular attention also. The religion of African and of other societies thought of as "primitive" or "undeveloped," sometimes misleadingly labeled "animism," was of less interest in itself; but it was seen as useful as illustrating the evolutionary history of religion, and thus contributing to the history of the evolution of humanity.

Various stages in this evolutionary history were identified: "animism," the belief in spirits, animatism, polydaemonism, were all precursors of polytheism. Some societies, of which ancient Israel was the prime example, developed to henotheism, and thence to ethical monotheism. One main source of evidence lay in ancient literature, the Greek classics and the Old Testament being the literatures most readily accessible. The Old Testament thus became a quarry for evidences of the various "stages" of evolutionary development, and some Christian interpreters used this in conjunction with a theology of "progressive revelation."[24]

The other main source for understanding the past history of religion was the religion of contemporary "primitive" societies. The founders of the new science of anthropology had been educated in the classics and were

---

[24] A good representative that became a standard theological textbook is W. O. E. Oesterley and T. H. Robinson, *Hebrew Religion: Its Origin and Development* (London: SPCK, 1930, 2nd ed. 1937). The influence is clearest in the early sections, by Oesterley.

well read in the Bible, even if they had departed from orthodox Christian faith. Early anthropologists such as E. B. Tylor and J. G. Frazer were essentially generalists, constructing general theories of society and religion; and Frazer in particular devoured accounts from all over the world of "survivals" from the past. They were not themselves fieldworkers[25]; and most of the people in a position to provide evidence of "primitive" belief were missionaries. As a result, missionaries became providers of data for the anthropological generalists.[26] African (and indeed Pacific and Native American) religion began to be studied for what it might say about the history of human society.

In this way the study of African religion passed from missionaries to academic anthropologists and became a field within the social sciences. In time the anthropologists left the library for fieldwork of their own and ceased to be dependent on the missionaries, becoming in the process the principal providers of detailed local studies of African religion.[27]

Edwin W. Smith, perhaps the first significant writer to generalize about African religion as a whole, rather than providing detailed accounts of the religion of specific peoples, combined missionary concern with the concerns of the academic anthropologists.[28] Born in South Africa where his father was a Primitive Methodist missionary, he, too, became a missionary, in what is now Zambia, and principal translator of the Ila Bible. In collaboration with an official of the administration, he wrote a substantial study of the Ila-speaking peoples.[29] After illness interrupted his missionary service he

---

[25] This statement is in general true, but a period spent in Mexico, with an opportunity to view monuments of Mayan culture, was important in the development of Tylor's thinking.

[26] The case of Roscoe is especially striking. He left the mission to become lecturer in anthropology at Cambridge, working with Frazer. As he did not hold a university degree, the University of Cambridge awarded him the honorary degree of MA. It is perhaps unfair to compare the books on East African peoples directed by him as a fruit of Cambridge "anthropological expeditions" with his book on the Baganda, written after twenty-five years of close study.

[27] In the field of African religion, the influence of Edward Evans-Pritchard (1902–73) is particularly notable. Evans-Pritchard began his fieldwork in Sudan in 1926; his work *Witchcraft, Oracles and Magic among the Azande* (Oxford: Clarendon Press, 1937) provided models for the study of such themes in relation to other African ethnic groups, as did his more wide-ranging studies of the Nuer, notably *Nuer Religion* (Oxford: Clarendon Press, 1956).

[28] On Smith, see W. John Young, *The Quiet Wise Spirit: Edwin W Smith 1896–1957 and Africa* (Peterborough, UK: Epworth Press, 2002).

[29] Edwin W. Smith and Andrew Murray Dale, *The Ila-Speaking Peoples of Northern Rhodesia* (London: Macmillan, 1920).

joined the staff of the British and Foreign Bible Society. In this capacity he was responsible for a flood of books, some learned, some popular, on a wide range of topics. He remains the only missionary to have become president of the Royal Anthropological Institute. He was also one of the founders of the International African Institute, and of its journal *Africa*.

Several of Smith's works explore African religion with a missiological bent. In *The Golden Stool*[30] (the reference is of course to the sacred monarchy of Ashanti), he seeks to understand the transcendent element of African social institutions. In *The Shrine of a People's Soul*[31] the former Bible translator argues that the African vernaculars house the most sacred items of African consciousness (Smith is an early prophet of mother tongue theology) and stresses the need for vernacular Christian literature.

Smith broadly accepted the evolutionary approach to religion characteristic of his time; he even wrote a book called *The Religion of Lower Races*,[32] though the preface indicates that this title was not his choice, but that of the publishers. But he is one of the earliest writers to link the study of African pre-Christian religion with that of African Christianity. Whereas many in the missionary movement assumed that as Africans became Christians, they would become in effect Western Christians, Smith argued that the already emergent African Christianity was likely to have more life and color than its Western counterpart.

Smith's last major literary contribution appeared in 1950: a symposium edited by him, with the title *African Ideas of God*.[33] The contributors were mostly field missionaries, and together they demonstrated how widespread and how significant was belief in God in the pre-Christian religions of African peoples—one of Smith's regular themes.

The chapter on Yoruba ideas of God was contributed by Geoffrey Parrinder.[34] He had become a missionary of the then newly formed Methodist

---

[30]   Edwin W. Smith, *The Golden Stool* (London: Holborn, 1926).

[31]   Edwin W. Smith, *The Shrine of a People's Soul* (London: Edinburgh House Press, 1929).

[32]   Edwin W. Smith, *The Religion of Lower Races, As Illustrated by the African Bantu* (New York: Macmillan, 1923).

[33]   Edwin W. Smith, *African Ideas of God* (London: Edinburgh House Press, 1950). A second edition, revised by Geoffrey Parrinder, appeared in 1961.

[34]   Late in life Parrinder wrote an account of his years in Dahomey, which includes some other biographical information: Geoffrey Parrinder, *In the Belly of the Snake; West Africa over Sixty Years Ago* (Peterborough, UK: Epworth Press, 2000). See also Ursula King, ed., *Turning Points in Religious Studies: Essays in Honour of Geoffrey Parrinder* (Edinburgh: T & T Clark, 1990); Martin Forward, *A Bag of Needments: Geoffrey Parrinder and the Study of Religion* (Bern: Peter Lang, 1998); Andrew F. Walls, "Geoffrey

Missionary Society in 1933. His only higher education had been his ministerial training at Richmond College.[35] This had included a course on comparative religion, centered, as the custom of the day was, on the great Asian religious traditions; African religion did not figure in it.

Parrinder was appointed to what was then denominated French West Africa, where he moved between Dahomey (now the Republic of Benin) and Côte d'Ivoire. He was influenced by inheriting from a missionary colleague a small library of works on Africa that he devoured. Like many other missionaries, he began the study of the religion of the peoples where he was living; and the move between Côte d'Ivoire and Dahomey made such studies comparative. In Dahomey the major ethnic group where he worked was Ewe, but there was strong historic influence there from Yoruba. In Côte d'Ivoire the main ethnic group was Akan. Accordingly, the Akan, Ewe, and Yoruba religions became the components of an exercise in comparison, as Parrinder noted the broad similarities and the differences of emphasis.

By following the logic of his missionary experience, which had taken him to African locations far distant from each other, Parrinder went beyond most of his predecessors in instituting comparison between the manifestations of religion among different African peoples. By the time he was writing the article for *African Ideas of God*, he had already completed the manuscript of a book entitled *West African Religion,* published in 1949.[36] It brought together descriptions of the religious systems of the Yoruba, the Akan, and the Ewe, showing how much they had in common but indicating the structural differences also.

The book was published by the Methodist Church publishing house in Britain: a brave act, since it was not clear that there was any market for books on African religion. Certainly there was no academic market; outside specialist studies in anthropology, African religion played little or no part in university courses. In the preface Parrinder expresses a hope that the book would be of use to missionaries and to government (i.e., colonial government) officers. As a published work, it was addressed primarily to expatriates in Africa, intended, perhaps, to persuade them that there was more significance

---

Parrinder (1910) and the Study of Religion in West Africa," in *European Traditions in the Study of Religion in Africa*, ed. Frieder Ludwig and Afe Adogame, 207–15 (Wiesbaden: Otto Harrassowitz, 2004).

[35] He had studied for a year at the University of Montpellier, primarily to improve his French.

[36] Geoffrey Parrinder, *West African Religion Illustrated from the Beliefs and Practices of the Yoruba, Ewe, Akan, and Kindred Peoples* (London: Epworth Press, 1949). It was substantially a doctoral thesis for the University of London. Parrinder, who had left school at sixteen, had also completed a BA, a BD, and two master's degrees since his arrival in Africa.

in how Africans understood their relations with the transcendent world than most expatriates of the time realized.

But new developments were afoot, though few realized their significance. Africa was about to enter the academic world established by the West.

Higher education in tropical Africa had begun in Sierra Leone, with the Fourah Bay Institution, later called Fourah Bay College, founded by the Church Missionary Society in 1827. It was intended to provide a standard of education beyond the capacity of the ordinary schools of the colony, and directed toward the best products of those schools. A primary, but not the sole, aim of the college was the provision of an educated ministry for the church.[37] A new dimension was added in the 1840s with the vision of the evangelization of Africa by African missionaries,[38] and the college, which had fallen into decline, was effectively relaunched to that end. Arabic was one of the subjects taught, and one of its teachers, S. W. Koelle, became the pioneer of comparative African linguistics.[39] By the 1870s the college was affiliated to the University of Durham in England, and was presenting students for degrees in arts and divinity. From that time until the Second World War, this essentially missionary and church institution acted as the university of Anglophone colonial West Africa, drawing its students from far beyond Sierra Leone.[40]

At the end of World War II, the British government set up a commission to examine the development of university education in the British colonies. The commission's first assumption was that one university would suffice for Anglophone West Africa, but it eventually decided on two: the University College of the Gold Coast, conceived as an African Oxbridge, and University College, Idaban in Nigeria, offering a more modern type of curriculum, on the lines of the newer English universities. In keeping with its Oxbridge ethos, the Gold Coast University received a Department of

---

[37] The first name on the register of the Fourah Bay Institution was that of Samuel Adjai Crowther, later to become a missionary bishop and perhaps the most widely known African Christian of the nineteenth century.

[38] See *Journals of the Rev. James Frederick Schön and Mr Samuel Crowther who accompanied the Expedition up the Niger in 1841. . . .* (London: Hatchard, 1842), especially Schön's concluding report.

[39] On Koelle, see P. E. H. Hair, *The Early Study of Nigerian Languages* (Cambridge: Cambridge University Press, 1967).

[40] It is appropriate to mention here the substantial publication by a Fourah Bay graduate, the Anglican clergyman J. Olumide Lucas, *The Religion of the Yorubas, Being an Account of the Religious Beliefs and Practices of the Yoruba Peoples of Southern Nigeria, Especially in Relation to the Religion of Ancient Egypt* (Lagos, Nigeria: CMS Bookshops, 1948). Lucas received a doctorate in divinity from the University of Durham.

Divinity; at Ibadan, where the first university head was a British scientist, there was initially no intention to provide for the study of theology or religion. But in 1947, when the time came for the college to open, there was such demand from Nigerian students and potential students that a Department of Religious Studies was created.

Though in general the academic arrangements for the new universities followed British models, no precedent for such a department existed in Britain, where the terms in use were "Divinity" or "Theology" (meaning Christian theology) or occasionally, where there had been fear of denominational strife, "Biblical Studies." (As we have seen, the University College of the Gold Coast followed a British model in this respect.) The first member of staff to be appointed to the pioneer Department of Religious Studies at Ibadan was Geoffrey Parrinder, the scholarly missionary who had been studying and writing on West African religion (his recently published book was on the table at his interview for the post[41]), and it was Parrinder who drew up the department's first syllabus with three subject areas: Old Testament, New Testament, and African traditional religion.

The term "African traditional religion" was coined by Parrinder himself, extending the principle by which he had given the title "West African Religion" to the Yoruba, Akan, and Ewe religious systems. He later wrote,

> My understanding of African Traditional Religion (a term that I may claim to have invented, and that others have used) was partly shaped by study of the historical and literary religions. It seemed important to consider African religion in the manner of the study of World Religions, and there were many parallels, for example with the gods and customs of ancient Egypt or Greece, or with modern Hinduism. There are problems with this approach but also advantages in that African religion is not taken as isolated from the rest of the world or scorned as mere fetishism or superstition, but as having its own traditions and history, even where unwritten, and with its social and personal characteristics.[42]

Parrinder's *West African Religion* inevitably became the textbook for the new subject. Many of the students at Ibadan were Igbo from Eastern Nigeria, and the results of interaction with them became clear when a new edition of the book appeared,[43] in which Igbo became a fourth pillar of the

---

[41] Parrinder, *In the Belly of the Snake,* 156.
[42] Ibid., 5.
[43] Geoffrey Parrinder, *West African Religion: A Study of the Beliefs and Prac-*

edifice of West African Religion. Aspects of the religion of other Nigerian ethnic groups represented among the students, such as Nupe and Bini, were also included. The new material did not fundamentally alter the picture that Parrinder had originally drawn; rather, it confirmed and extended his concept of a broadly similar body of religion extending across West Africa.

In 1954 Parrinder published another book, with the title *African Traditional Religion*,[44] informed by the reading of much anthropological literature, which extended the principles underlying his *West African Religion* to the whole of sub-Saharan Africa. The book was published in Hutchinson's University Library, a series intended as textbooks. The Ibadan experiment had made African traditional religion an academic subject. And though the impact on Western academic structures came slowly, what had begun in Nigeria spread rapidly to many of the other universities springing up across the African continent. These universities frequently followed the Ibadan model by establishing Departments of Religious Studies. Of the earlier foundations, Fourah Bay College in Sierra Leone maintained its Faculty of Theology; the University of Ghana converted its Department of Divinity into a Department for the Study of Religions, where the professor, who in England had been a patristic scholar, came to write books on the three major religions of Africa: Christianity, Islam and African traditional religion.[45] His successor, a distinguished Ghanaian churchman, wrote on prophet movements in Ghanaian Christianity.[46] Nigeria's second university, the University of Nigeria, Nsukka, was established in 1961 by Nnamdi Azikiwe, governor general and a leading figure in the movement for independence. The intention was to draw on diverse traditions of university education, not only on the British, and to address specifically Nigerian topics and needs. The university had from the beginning a Department (originally designated a college) of Religion that established parallel courses in Christian and Islamic Studies, with African traditional religion a required component of both. The majority of the new universities in East and Central Africa, and

---

tices of the Akan, Ewe, Yoruba, Ibo and Kindred Peoples, 2nd ed. (London: Epworth Press, 1961).

[44] Geoffrey Parrinder, *African Traditional Religion* (London: Hutchinson's University Library, 1954, rev. ed. 1962; London: Sheldon Press 3rd ed., 1974).

[45] See, e.g., Noel Q King, *Christian and Muslim in Africa* (New York: Harper and Row, 1971).

[46] C. G. Baeta, *Prophetism in Ghana: A Study of Some Spiritual Churches* (London: SCM Press, 1961). In 1968 Professor Baeta edited *Christianity in Tropical Africa* (London: Oxford University Press, 1968), in some sense a landmark in that it embodied proceedings of a conference of the International African Institute on African Christianity.

most of the later universities in Nigeria, also established Religious Studies departments. In these the study of African religions and the term African traditional religion (with "ATR" as a familiar abbreviation) became part of the staple fare.

The idea of a single body of religious thought and practice, to be found, with some variations, across sub-Saharan Africa, was increasingly taken for granted. Such an idea fitted well into the new sense of African cultural identity and respect for the African past that accompanied political and intellectual decolonization. There was ample incentive to study the traditions of Africa and few reasons to question whether some of these were unique to Africa.

As African scholars began to take leadership in the new Departments of Religious Studies, the study of African traditional religion developed in new and interesting directions. Among the most influential scholars in this regard were the late Bolaji Idowu at the University of Idaban and John S. Mbiti of Makerere University and later the University of Nairobi.

Parrinder had seen a fourfold division of the transcendent world in African traditional religion: God, divinities, ancestors, and manifestations of power. In different religious systems, different components dominated, so that, while most African peoples recognized God as supreme, in many African religious systems lesser divinities or ancestors received more attention. Idowu[47] argued that Yoruba religion, often seen as polytheistic, with the *orisas,* lesser divinities receiving more attention than the Supreme God, was in principle monotheistic; the *orisas* were not to be seen as "lesser divinities" but as emanations, indeed refractions, of Olòdumare, who is God.

Mbiti's book, *African Religions and Philosophy,*[48] modified the concept of African traditional religion by arguing that the differences to be found across the continent justified speaking of African religions in the plural, but that a common African philosophy underlay them. Like Idowu, he emphasized the importance of the God component in African religions, demonstrating its centrality in many, and making collections of traditional prayers.[49]

Idowu and Mbiti were Christians and active churchmen, trained in Christian theology, and they saw more of that theology within African religion than most European writers, whether missionaries or anthropologists,

---

[47] E. Bolaji Idowu, *Olodumare: God in Yoruba Belief* (London: Longmans, 1962); E. Bolaji Idowu, *African Traditional Religion: A Definition* (London: SCM Press and Maryknoll, NY: Orbis Books, 1973).

[48] John S. Mbiti, *African Religions and Philosophy*, 2nd ed. (London: Heinemann, 1990).

[49] John S. Mbiti, *Concepts of God in Africa* (London: SPCK, 1970); John S Mbiti, *The Prayers of African Religion* (London: SPCK, 1975).

had done. African Christians were now studying the pre-Christian religion of Africa, not simply denouncing it, but seeing God there.[50] Mbiti's type of argument, indeed, drew protests from the Ugandan poet Okot p'Bitek, who insisted that not all African peoples—his own Central Luo were a case in point—had a concept of God at all, and that African scholars were now presenting African traditional religion reconstructed along Christian lines.[51]

The issues between the old religion(s) of Africa and the new Christian faith being embraced by so many Africans were taken to a new level by Kwame Bediako, who produced a critique of the contributions of Idowu, Mbiti, and Okot, among others, in the course of his major work *Theology and Identity*.[52] In Idowu and Mbiti, and in many other African Christians writing about "African traditional religion," Bediako sees close parallels to Christian writers of Greco-Roman background in the early Christian centuries. Idowu and Mbiti are seeing the God of Israel, the God of the Scriptures, the God and Father of the Lord Jesus Christ present and at work in pre-Christian Africa, just as Justin and Clement of Alexandria had seen him at work in the pre-Christian Greek world, despite its demonic elements. The study of the old pre-Christian religion of Africa cannot ultimately be detached from the study of African Christianity.

From one point of view African Christianity is ancient, with a continuous history since early Christian times. From another it is part of a huge ongoing demographic and cultural transformation of Christianity. After many centuries of dominance among the peoples of Europe and their descendants elsewhere, the Christian faith is increasingly more characteristic of peoples of the non-Western world. This phenomenon, often called "World Christianity," engaged much of the later energies of Kwame Bediako.

We have seen that the concept of what came to be called "African traditional religion" was forwarded by developments in academic organization. These made the indigenous religions of Africa a topic in their own right. Nor is it accidental that these developments took place amid the rising consciousness of common African identity that followed decolonization and the emergence of the African nations.

---

[50] We should not overlook the work published as far back as 1944 by one of the architects of Ghana, J. B. Danquah, *The Akan Doctrine of God* (London: Lutterworth Press, 1944), which presented Akan belief in terms of the philosophy of religion familiar to Western Christian theologians.

[51] Okot p'Bitek, *African Religions in Western Scholarship* (Nairobi: East African Literature Bureau, 1970).

[52] Kwame Bediako, *Theology and Identity: The Impact of Culture on Hritian Thought in the Second Century and Modern Africa* (Oxford: Regnum, 1990).

The process was constructive, invigorating, and revealing. What it obscured was that many of the ideas, beliefs, institutions, beliefs, assumptions, and practices associated with "African traditional religion" also occur outside Africa. They are to be found in locations and among peoples as far from Africa, and from each other as the Pacific Islands, the Arctic, the mountains and forests of South America, among the First Nations of North America, the aboriginal tribal peoples living within India outside Indic culture, and the ancient ethnic minorities of China and Southeast Asia. The fact is that much of what in Africa is called "African traditional religion" is not uniquely African. Using Mbiti's terminology, we may recognize a range of systems of belief and practice that one may call African religions, which assume a similar view of the spiritual world (what Mbiti calls "philosophy"). But those worldviews, and that "philosophy," and very similar religious systems may be found in the other continents. It is highly desirable that those who study African religions look beyond Africa for a full understanding of their field.

For African Christian theologians, there is a further reason to do so. The peoples who share these worldviews with traditional Africa for the most part also share with Africans the experience of widespread appropriation of the Christian faith. Taken together, these peoples constitute a large proportion of World Christianity. As African theologians and pastoral practitioners wrestle with the issues that arise from the interaction of the Christian gospel with African culture, their insights may have much relevance outside Africa.

Kwame Bediako would probably have acknowledged himself a member of what James L. Cox[53] has denominated the "Aberdeen School," for he regularly used the term "primal religions" to indicate both the religions of traditional Africa and for religious systems anywhere, ancient or modern, that reflect similar worldviews. The word "primal" expresses two of their crucial aspects. Primal religions are earlier than and anterior to the so-called world religions; they are also about the basic elements of religion, that is, the relationship of human beings with the transcendent world.[54]

One of Bediako's last major projects, directed by himself and his wife, Professor Gillian Mary Bediako, supported by the Nagel Foundation and still in progress at the time of his passing, was a study with the title "The Primal Religions as the Substructure of Christianity." It was addressed to the shared experiences of Christian communities from Africa, Asia, Latin

---

[53] See James L. Cox, *From Primitive to Indigenous: The Academic Study of Indigenous Religions* (Aldershot, UK: Ashgate, 2007).

[54] Cf. Andrew F. Walls, "Primal Religious Traditions in Today's World," in *The Missionary Movement in Christian History* (Maryknoll, NY: Orbis Books, 1996), 119–39.

America, and the Pacific who share a background in the primal religions and who together belong to the bedrock of contemporary World Christianity. The project brought together Christian scholars from west, east, and southern Africa, from the forest and mountain peoples of the Americas, from the Pacific Islands, and from minority cultures in Asia. It expressed Bediako's conviction that dialogue between Christians of Africa, Asia, Latin America. and the Pacific is as urgent as the much more easily attained dialogue between African and Western Christians. The main report of the project is still to appear.[55]

For guidance as to the nature of primal worldviews, and the basic elements of religion to which they relate, we need look no further than the Old Testament. The history of Israel as described there reflects the experience of many Christian communities across the world today. The Old Testament presents a story of conflict within primal religion,[56] the conflict between Yahweh, the God of heaven, and his competitors. Sometimes those competitors were alien gods, as when Elijah provoked a confrontation with Melkart, the Tyrian Baal, on Mount Carmel. But time and again the record points to the competitors being the gods of the land, the territorial spirits, the *baʾalim,* lesser beings who divert the attention of Yahweh's worshippers from him and to whom farmers are tempted to look for fertility.

This is a story often repeated in Africa and elsewhere. In many forms of primal religion the God of heaven is recognized and has a vernacular name. In some, the God of heaven is the object of direct worship; in others, while God is recognized as supreme, it is the gods of the land that are the focus of religious activity; in others again the focus is on the ancestors, the spirits of the clan, or group or nation. The Old Testament prophets denounce those who, while acknowledging Yahweh as God, give their priority to the gods of the land that their predecessors served.

The Old Testament story is a repeated call to conversion; a call for Israel to turn from the false to the real, to the God of heaven and earth, who as the story goes on is revealed as the God and Father of the Lord Jesus Christ. And African Christianity is both the African chapter of Christian history and the Christian chapter of the history of African religion.

---

[55] A number of essays from the project have appeared in the *Journal of African Christian Thought.*

[56] Some key issues in this regard are discussed by Gillian M. Bediako, *Primal Religion and the Bible: William Robertson Smith and His Heritage* (*Journal for the Study of the Old Testament* Supplement Series 246) (Sheffield, UK: Sheffield Academic Press, 1997).

10

Kwame Bediako and Christian Scholarship in Africa

Manasseh Kwame Dakwa Bediako, late rector of the Akrofi-Christaller Institute for Theology, Mission, and Culture, in Akropong, Ghana, was born on July 7, 1945. He died, following a serious illness, on June 10, 2008. Over many years he pointed others to Africa's proper place in contemporary worldwide Christian discourse. He charted new directions for African Christian theology. He labored so that generations of scholars, confident equally of their Christian and their African identity, might be formed in Africa, and to that end he created a new type of institution where devotion to scholarship and understanding of the cultures of Africa would be pursued in a setting of Christian worship, discipleship, and mission.

These were huge undertakings, and he was called from them at the height of his powers, when still full of visions and plans for their implementation, and the institution that was meant to model and facilitate all those visions still in its youth. It would be premature, therefore, to pronounce his legacy so soon after he has gone from us. All who knew him or his work are still achingly conscious of the gaps caused by his departure, the business unfinished, the books half written, the plants that have budded and blossomed but are yet to bear their intended fruit. His achievements, great as they are, point to a future not yet realized. He was both a visionary and a skillful entrepreneur, but he was also an inspirer and encourager of others, holding out a vision for the whole church in Africa and beyond, sending out a call to those who would heed it to dedicate themselves to scholarship as a costly form of Christian service. His life, his vision, and his objectives can be set out, but we do not yet know how far others will take up what he has laid down. It is as though we are present at the reading of a will; decades must pass before it will be manifest how others, in Africa and elsewhere, made use of what Kwame Bediako bequeathed to them.

Early Life

Kwame—he always used his traditional Akan "birth-day" name, indicating his birth on a Saturday—was the son of a police inspector and the grandson of a Presbyterian catechist and evangelist. Though his parents came from the central region of what was then the British colony of the Gold Coast, he grew up in the capital, Accra, at the Police Training Depot. His first schooling was thus not in his beloved mother tongue, Twi, but in the Accra language, Ga, in which he was also fluent. An outstanding pupil, he was able to gain secondary education at Mfantsipim School, Cape Coast, founded in the nineteenth century by the British Methodist mission. Missionary emphasis on education and an exceptionally enlightened period of educational policy under an exceptionally enlightened governor had given the Gold Coast some of the best schools in colonial Africa, and Mfantsipim was one of the best of these. Kwame received an excellent education of the English type.

The period of his secondary education coincided with the transformation of the Gold Coast into Ghana, the first of the new African nations, led by Kwame Nkrumah, with his emphatic rejection of Western rule in Africa and high sense of Africa's past glories and future destiny. Kwame Bediako left Mfantsipim as its head prefect and in 1965 entered the University of Ghana, set up after World War II with the aim of being an Oxbridge in Africa. There he developed as an eloquent orator and debater, a person who could make a mark in politics; he also attained the academic excellence in French that won him a scholarship for graduate studies in France and the promise of an academic career. By this time he was a confirmed atheist under French existentialist influence, apparently deaf to the pleas of Christian classmates.

In France he gained master's and doctoral degrees at the University of Bordeaux, not surprisingly choosing African francophone literature as his area of research. During his time in France he underwent a radical Christian conversion—so radical that at one stage he thought of abandoning his studies in favor of active evangelism. Happily, he was persuaded otherwise; the time was coming when he would recognize scholarship as itself a missionary vocation.

His new life brought him new associates—above all, a fellow student of French, from England, who joined him in a mission to migrant Arab children. In 1973 Kwame and Gillian Mary were married, forming a wonderfully happy partnership that was rich both intellectually and spiritually. The following year came the Lausanne Conference on World Evangelization, enlarging Kwame's world vision and deepening his acquaintance with other Christians from the non-Western world—or as he liked to call it, the Two-Thirds World. His studies now moved from literature to theology, and their base from France to London, where he took first-class honors in his theological degree. Then it was back to Ghana, to teach for two years at the Christian Service College (the name of the institution precisely describing its purpose) in Kumasi. Here the family links were rebuilt with the Presbyterian Church, where his grandfather had given signal service, and he was accepted for ordination in that church.

Vocation to Theology

Kwame's Evangelical convictions and credentials were manifest, but he was wrestling with issues that were not at the front of most Evangelical minds, or on the agenda of most Evangelical institutions at that time. Could Africans become fully Christian only by embracing the mind-set of Western Christians and rejecting all the things that made them distinctively African? Ordinary African Christians daily faced acute theological issues that were never addressed in the sort of theology that apparently served the needs of Western Christians well enough.

It was not that this theology was necessarily wrong; it simply could not deal with issues that went to the heart of relationships with family, kin, or society, nor deal with some of the most troubling anxieties of those who saw the world in terms different from those thought normal in the West. Africans were responding to the gospel, and in unprecedented numbers, but the received theology did not fit the world as they saw the world. Great areas of life were thus often left untouched by Christ, often leaving sincere Christians with deep uncertainties. Much Evangelical thinking was not engaging with the issues of culture, or was doing so simplistically or superficially.

It was such concerns that brought the Bediakos back to academic study and Kwame to a second doctorate in the Department of Religious Studies at the University of Aberdeen, Scotland. At the same time Gillian took first-class honors in the Master of Arts in religious studies; she later went on to complete an Aberdeen PhD in the area of primal religions.

Kwame's studies pursued two lines of investigation. One lay among the then quite small body of African academic theologians. Why did the starting point of their thinking so often lie in the pre-Christian religion of their peoples, so rarely in the sort of topic thought interesting or important by Western theologians? Why did the efforts of pioneers such as Bolaji Idowu and John Mbiti cause such disturbance both in the Evangelical stables in which they were nourished and among African intellectuals such as Okot p'Bitek, who had rejected Christianity?

Kwame pursued such questions in parallel with another question: how had the early church faced such issues? How had theologians in the Greco-Roman world dealt with questions that arose from Hellenistic culture, how had they viewed their pre-Christian intellectual, literary, and religious heritage, and their cultural ancestors? How far was it possible to be both Greek and Christian? His doctoral thesis, approved in 1983 and described by the external examiner as the best thesis he had ever read,[1] explored how second-century theologians faced the issues posed for Christians by the Greco-Roman past, and how twentieth-century African theologians dealt with the African past. The similarity of the issues was striking; consciousness of identity was at the heart of both processes. The second-century question was the possibility of being both Christian and Greek; the twentieth-century question was the possibility of being both Christian and African. We are made by our past; it is our past that creates our identity and shows us who we are. We cannot abandon or suppress our past or substitute something else instead, nor can our past be left as it is, untouched by Christ. Our past, like our present, has to be converted, turned toward Christ. The second-century quest was the conversion, not the suppression or replacement, of Hellenistic culture, and in that case conversion had led to cultural renewal. Today's quest is the conversion of African culture, and perhaps thereby its renewal. And second-century theologians discovered that God had been active in that past; with the same conviction African Christians could recognize that God always goes before his missionaries.

Over the years that followed, Bediako was to develop these ideas in his teaching and writing. The activity of the divine Word, the signs that God had not left himself without witness in the African past, the multitudes of Africans coming to Christ in the here and now, all pointed to a special place for Africa in Christian history; but this special place lay within, and not separate from, the history of the church as a whole. All Christians share the same ancestors, and those ancestors belong to every tribe, kindred, and nation.

---

[1] The thesis was later published as Kwame Bediako, *Theology and Identity: The Impact of Culture upon Christian Thought in the Second Century and in Modern Africa* (Oxford: Regnum Books, 1992).

The Department of Religious Studies at Aberdeen at that time contained the embryo of the Centre for the Study of Christianity in the Non-Western World, better known in its later manifestation at the University of Edinburgh (where it is now called the Centre for the Study of World Christianity). In a lively mix of graduate students from many parts of the world, Africa was particularly well represented. For the most part their research topics fell into two categories that in many cases overlapped. Many members of the department were working in the area of the primal religions of traditional, usually preliterate, societies; others were engaged with the history, life, and thought of Christians in some part of Africa, Asia, or the Pacific. Increasingly, Kwame Bediako was drawn to the study of the primal religions and their relation to Christianity. These religions were primal in the sense of bring anterior to the so-called world religions. Throughout Christian history they have proved the most fertile soil for the Christian message, so that they form the background, the substructure as one might say, of the faith of a high percentage of the world's Christians, and influence their worldview. And the Bible, the Old Testament in particular, shows us a good deal about primal worldviews in action, instantly recognizable in Africa and many other parts of the world. Thus they are primal in a second sense, of being basic, elemental, reflecting fundamental elements of human response to the divine. Studies of writers of the conversion period in Europe, Bediako discovered—Gregory of Tours, for instance, or Bede, or Boniface—reveal how Western Christianity emerged in the interaction between the biblical tradition and the primal worldview of the peoples of Northern and Western Europe. Western Christian history was also a story about the conversion of the past.

Networking and Pastorate

Kwame was meanwhile engaging in an activity that marked much of his life: building networks sustained by caring friendships. He established a link for mutual support and stimulus between African Christian researchers in Britain. It was the germ of the Africa Theological Fellowship, which later linked scholars across the African continent. Contact continued with like minded people in the Lausanne movement, such as Vinay Samuel from India and Tito Paredes from Peru, embodied eventually in the International Fellowship of Evangelical Mission Theologians (INFEMIT), an international body in which leadership came from the "Two-Thirds World" and which gave rise to the Oxford Centre for Mission Studies.

Following the completion of his second doctorate, Kwame taught for a year as a temporary lecturer during a vacancy in the Aberdeen department. It was the first of a series of engagements that made him for some time part of the Centre for the Study of Christianity in the Non-Western World. That center moved from Aberdeen soon after Kwame finished his temporary lectureship, finding a new home in the Faculty of Divinity of the University of Edinburgh, and for many years Kwame was a visiting lecturer there. But his immediate call was to Ghana and to the pastorate of the Ridge Church in Accra. In colonial times Ridge Church had been the church of the expatriate officials; by this time it had a burgeoning and very diverse congregation, where Anglicans, Methodists, and Presbyterians in rotation provided the resident pastor. The three years (1984–87) that Kwame spent there were formative for him in what they revealed of the concerns, aspirations, and anxieties of African Christians, and in later years he was never less of a pastor for being a scholar and academic. Indeed, even before he left Aberdeen he had a clear vision of what his ongoing work was to be, and pastoral concerns were at its heart.

The Akrofi-Christaller Centre

With such formidable academic credentials as Bediako now had, a teaching post in the West could well have beckoned; in later years there were many such invitations, all firmly declined. In Ghana he could readily have returned to the university world; equally, he could have become a key figure in training for the ministry. But he had heard a call to theological scholarship of a sort that neither universities nor seminaries were yet able to mount. The assumptions underlying their programs frequently depended on Western intellectual models. But vast numbers of African Christians were continually facing situations that demanded theological decisions for which Western intellectual models provided no help. Fresh informed biblical and theological thinking, along with sensitive understanding of society, was needed to help in situations where the identity and obligations of Christians intersected with their identity and obligations as members of a family or a community or a state. In such cases textbook theology rarely provided answers.

Church tradition where Christianity had been received from Western sources in a period of Western dominance too often led either to blanket rejection of all things evidently African or to a division of life into parallel streams of "Christian" and "African" activities that never met. The end product could be a sort of religious schizophrenia, a fractured identity.

The key theological issues of the day, as in the early Christian centuries, demanded integral identity, being simultaneously thoroughly African and thoroughly Christian, confidently Christian, assured that the divine Word was taking African flesh and pitching his tent there. Theological reflection of this sort would require a new type of institution. Bediako had begun to visualize such an institution before he left Aberdeen. When he left Ridge Church in 1987, he found, with the full approval of his church and the support of friends in and beyond Ghana, an opportunity to put the vision into practice. The outcome was the Akrofi-Christaller Centre for Mission Research and Applied Theology, later called the Akrofi-Christaller Institute of Theology, Mission, and Culture. Its establishment and development lay at the heart of Bediako's work for the rest of his life.

Any consideration of the life of Kwame Bediako must take account of the institute and the principles on which it was based. Crucial to its purpose was the commitment to Christian scholarship in Africa. Bediako believed that Africa was now, as a result of its experience as a major theater of Christian mission, a major theological laboratory, with theological work to do that would not and could not be done elsewhere. Furthermore, the shift in the center of gravity of Christianity from the global West to the global South that was such a feature of the twentieth century made the quality of African theological activity a matter of universal, not just continental, Christian concern. Africa needed scholars, and needed them not only for its own sake but also for the sake of the world church.

The Centre (as it was first named) came into being as a research institution. It was not long before it became a center of postgraduate study. Initially this was by means of an arrangement with the University of Natal (now the University of KwaZulu Natal) in South Africa. Under this arrangement students for the Master of Theology in African Christianity degree spent their first semester in South Africa and the second in Ghana, with Kwame and Gillian Bediako teaching in both places. Later, on the initiative of the Ghana government, the Akrofi-Christaller Institute became an independent postgraduate institution within the Ghana university system. It has seen a steady stream of success at the master's level, but the Master of Theology program was from the first designed to prepare those with conventional theological training for specialist study and research in the fields of theology, mission, and culture in Africa, and the institute now has a significant group of doctorates to its credit. The aim of the center, however, was never to produce PhDs (there are many recipients of such who do nothing for scholarship) but to produce mature, disciplined, dedicated scholars who recognize the pursuit of learning as a calling from God and follow it sacrificially. The institute set itself against shortcuts and soft options. Courses of study were often longer and more demanding than those at other institutions.

The institute also recognized that the duties of scholarship go beyond the boundaries of the academic world and certainly extend to informing the life and work of the whole church. The program for the institute in any year has typically included activities for ministers, catechists, Bible translators, and Scripture-use specialists. There have been workshops on gospel and culture for Christian workers from all over the country, consultations on the local history of such major issues as slavery, and regular meetings of those engaged in writing Bible commentaries in the languages of Ghana.

The institute's aim was to promote scholarship rooted in Christian mission. The word "mission" occurs in both the old and the new forms of its title. It marks the deliberate rejection of Western attempts at detached or uncommitted scholarship; Bediako saw the Christian scholar as holding responsibility in the church, and the church as needing the measured scholarly quest for truth, the scholarly activities of investigation, and testing. At the same time, Bediako advocated—and practiced—public engagement of theology with other disciplines. He was elected a fellow of the Ghana Academy of Arts and Sciences and was active in its affairs; he lectured for the academy on the religious significance of one of the pioneers of Ghana's independence, J. B. Danquah.

The institute was intended to function as a Christian community; not only teachers and students but also office and domestic and catering and garden staff attended, participated in, and led daily worship. In many institutions scholarship had become an individual, even a competitive, activity, with career enhancement the driving motive. Tapping into an earlier tradition of Western learning, Bediako looked to the worshiping community, living in a situation of mission, as the proper matrix of scholarship.

The focus of the scholarship of the institute was on Africa—its religious, cultural, social, and linguistic realities, and the history, life, and thought of its Christians. The preparatory courses in the master's degree program explored the principles underlying the interaction of gospel and culture, the worldviews of primal societies, theology in Africa, the Bible in Africa, and Christian history in Africa from the early centuries and in different parts of the continent. The institute's students have come from all over Africa, with a sprinkling from Western and Asian countries. The small resident faculty is supported by scholars from other parts of Africa. But the focus on Africa was always against a wider background. A course on world Christian history took account of two millennia and six continents, and that on primal worldviews considered the primal worldviews of the peoples of Europe and their early interaction with the gospel. Bediako was essentially a world Christian. In particular, he was an advocate of what he called South–South dialogue. Bilateral arrangements between Africa and a Western partner were relatively easy to arrange, but potentially mutually beneficial links between Africa and Asian or Latin American partners were much harder to sustain. One of his last major undertakings was a collaborative study of primal religions as the substructure of Christianity, involving scholars from different parts of Africa, Asia, the Americas, and the Pacific.

The location chosen for the institute was itself significant. Akropong is a relatively small town, but it is the capital of the Akan state of Akuapem, where traditional patterns of rulership and the attendant rituals remain intact, and there is great pride in a long and colorful history. The building that is the institute's nucleus retains many features of its nineteenth-century Basel Mission origin and of its long association with the training of teachers and ministers of an earlier time. Within a short walk are the palace, scene of traditional activities such as the great Odwira festival of national purification; the vast old church; and the place of assembly, where the first missionary was received by the king of that day. The church, some compounds in the town, and the institute's own building commemorate names well known in the records of Akan church history. The whole town bears the marks of continuous interaction between the Christian gospel and Akan society from the 1830s to the Internet age. It is a reminder of how richly stored Africa is with the materials for religious research. The linking of the names of Johann Gottlieb Christaller and Clement Anderson Akrofi in the institute's title is also significant—the one a German missionary translator who devoted himself to the Akan language and traditional lore, the other a Ghanaian reviser of the Twi Bible and author of a grammar of that language. The vernacular principle in Christianity, the significance of theological expression in the mother tongue, and the capacity of African languages to illuminate biblical concepts were themes that Bediako regularly visited.

The Legacy

Kwame Bediako was the outstanding African theologian of his generation. A distinguished academic himself, he knew that academics were not the only theologians, and he drew attention to the informal or, as he would say, implicit theology to be found among people of little formal education. He delighted in the vernacular songs of Madam Afua Kuma,[2] traditional

---

[2] An English version of some of the songs is available in Afua Kuma, *Jesus of the*

midwife and Pentecostal poet, who sang the praises of Christ in the exalted language of praise songs to traditional rulers. He called them "a liberating force for African academic theology and for the academic theologian."[3] He did perhaps more than anyone else to persuade mainstream Western theologians and mainstream Western theological institutions that African theology was not an exotic minority specialization but an essential component in a developing global Christian discourse.

His all too few writings will continue their influence, as will his institute's *Journal of African Christian Thought*, to which he so often contributed. There are other books that he never completed, rich material lying in those electrifying lecture courses and biblical expositions. But much of his finest work has been written in the lives and thinking of his students, colleagues, and friends, in the concept of the institution he founded, and in the networks he helped to establish, enhance, and maintain. It is a rich legacy, much of it prudently invested for future use.

Deep Forest: Prayers and Praises of Afua Kuma, trans. Jon Kirby (Accra, Ghana: Asempa Press, 1981).

[3] Kwame Bediako, *Christianity in Africa: The Renewal of a Non-Western Religion* (Edinburgh: Edinburgh University Press and Maryknoll, NY: Orbis Books, 1995), 59.

Part Three

THE MISSIONARY MOVEMENT
AND THE WEST

11

Missions and the English Novel

At the beginning of the twentieth century, over 80 percent of those who professed and called themselves Christians lived in Europe or North America. At the end of the century, something approaching 60 percent of professed Christians lived in Africa, Asia Pacific, or Latin America. Christianity began the twentieth century as the religion of the West and as an essentially Western religion; it began the twenty-first century as a progressively Non-Western religion, where the center of thought and action looks increasingly to belong to Africa, Asia, and parts of Latin America, with Africa assuming the place in its counsels once occupied by Europe.

This extraordinary change in the demographic and cultural composition of the Christian church is one marker of the significance of the missionary movement. This is not to suggest that Christian missions are the sole reason for the change; there are many reasons for it, indigenous to each of the continents. But it is difficult to imagine that the change could have occurred without the missionary movement. Missions were not the bomb, but they were the detonator, and as a result Africa and Asia and Latin America have become the important theaters of Christian activity, the representative Christianity of the twenty-first century.

If this is the case, then the movement that produced Christian missions must be one of the most important developments within Western Christianity. Beginning in Catholic Europe in the early sixteenth century, fading there in the eighteenth and early nineteenth centuries but developing in Protestant Europe at the same time, reaching its climax alike in Catholic and Protestant Europe and Protestant North America in the late nineteenth and early twentieth century, the missionary movement makes the Reformation itself look like a little local difficulty. And yet, it has never been a major theme of church historians; it has typically been left to the less-regarded company of mission historians. Perhaps that is inevitable; the missionary movement was rarely at the center of the life of the Western church: it was for most of its history the sphere of enthusiasts within the church. Sometimes its popular image in Britain was high, sometimes it was a figure of fun or a byword for folly; but even when its reputation was highest—I suspect this was in the 1840s—it did not draw many participants; and in the period when it drew most participants (in Britain, this was the period from the 1880s to the First World War) its reputation was already beginning to decline. It is instructive to see how few references to the movement occur, for instance, in the two large volumes of Owen Chadwick's magisterial work on the Victorian Church: the excommunication of Bishop Colenso and the funeral of David Livingstone are the high points. This is not a criticism of that great book, either; the book is about the church from the perspective of Westminster, the cathedral closes, and the university senior common rooms; and these were rarely the powerhouses of the missionary movement. They were busy with other things.

In other words, one of the most significant developments in Western Christianity, in terms of its impact on the future of Christianity, left a comparatively slight impression on the sources from which we usually study Western Christianity.

This observation may lead us to consider what impact missions made upon other sources, such as literature. And to begin with, we may note that the missionary movement created a substantial literature of its own, and several new literary genres. Perhaps more importantly, it created a readership for this literature.

The missionary magazine is worth a study in itself, well worth comparing both in circulation and in influence with the weighty journals of opinion such as the *Edinburgh* and the *Quarterly Reviews*. The big quarterlies found their way into country house libraries; they were addressed to and read by the classes with a voice in decision making in the era before the First Parliamentary Reform Act. The missionary magazines—the *Missionary Register* (the most ambitious), the *Scottish Missionary Register*, the Baptist *Periodical Accounts*, the various publications of the Church Missionary Society (CMS), the *Wesleyan Missionary Notices*—reached a far wider audience. The devout among the middle classes read them, but so did multitudes of godly artisans and shopkeepers, and these were the people from whom the early generations of missionaries were principally drawn. They reached beyond these circles; groups sprang up specifically to hear "missionary intelligence," read aloud. Thomas Chalmers's downtown parish in Glasgow had a regular weekly meeting for this purpose. The form of organization developed by many missionary societies from the early nineteenth century, pioneered by the British and Foreign Bible Society, favored this development. Local auxiliaries were formed. Local bigwigs or clergy were usually the titular officers of these auxiliaries, but the key to their working was the local collector, who went around to the neighbors to collect, often a penny a week. These people became stakeholders, interested, eager to hear what was happening far away in response to their prayers and gifts. Chalmers dilated upon the significance of the Aberdeen Female Servants' Society for the Distribution of the Scriptures among the Poor; here, people at the very bottom of the employment market, female domestic servants, were raised to the dignity of donors, if it were only in halfpennies, and developed an interest in the work toward which their halfpennies were directed.

In the 1850s, Henry Venn, secretary of the CMS, could write that the fact that the little West African state of Abeokuta had repulsed the armies of the King of Dahomey had given satisfaction to everyone from Her Majesty's ministers to the humble collector of a penny a week. Her Majesty's ministers had state papers to guide them about Abeokuta, but for the rest of the population, it is questionable how many had heard of Abeokuta, or could distinguish the King of Dahomey from the Queen of Sheba. One would hazard a guess that a high proportion of those who were aware of both had gained that awareness first from the pages of a missionary magazine. Careful followers of "missionary intelligence" would have been well briefed as to why the continued independence of Abeokuta was a matter of Christian concern, and aware of the massive involvement of the King of Dahomey in the Atlantic slave trade. It is worth noticing that the point at which the CMS began to get English recruits for the mission field was the point at which it ceased to be a fraternity of Evangelical clergy, corresponding amongst themselves, and took over the Bible Society's model: a mass membership organization with local auxiliaries maintained by voluntary collectors of small but regular sums, sustained by mass-circulation illustrated magazines.

Another literary genre issuing from the missionary movement might be called "missiography": those accounts of missionary work with sustained description of the context, so that, depending on the gifts and interests of the author, a book might combine discussion of missionary activity with essays on matters of public policy, geographical, scientific, or ethnographic record, or a narrative of travel and adventure. There were widely selling examples of this genre, such as Robert Moffat's *Missionary Labours in South Africa* and John Williams' *Missionary Journeys in the South Seas*, and a famous bestseller, David Livingstone's *Missionary Travels and Researches in South Africa*, which partook of all the elements mentioned. Such books had a multiple readership—not only enthusiasts for missions, but the scientifically minded, and a category of reader with a limited appetite for devotional or theological literature who needed something that was allowable to read on Sundays. The latter years of the nineteenth century saw a huge expansion of missionary literature as missions began to appoint editorial secretaries, some of them prolific writers themselves, such as Eugene Stock of CMS and Richard Lovett of the London Missionary Society. One aspect of this not sufficiently explored is the immense literature generated for children's reading.

Also needing study is the development of an antimissionary literature. This is most noticeable in the late nineteenth and early twentieth centuries; we have already noticed that the period, which seems to be the high point of the missionary movement, is also the point where it comes most heavily under fire. Mary Kingsley probably would not wish to be classed as an anti-missionary writer; but she represents the voice of the trader, the commercial men, whom missionaries regularly blamed for spreading bad influences and setting bad examples. Kingsley argues that it is a misconceived mission education that causes moral breakdown in African coastal areas. Another line of argument derived from the writings of the Harrow schoolmaster Reginald Bosworth Smith, and supported by many agents of colonial governments, extolled the advantages of Islam over Christianity as a source of civilization in Africa, and as a religion more suited to African capacities than was Christianity. Sir Hiram Maxim, inventor of the gun that bears his name, pretended to write as Viceroy Li Hung Chang to show the futility of missions in China. So much literature was produced during the colonial period to show how missions worked against British interests that the mission societies found it necessary to publish independent testimony to the value of missions. Thus, in the 1890s, thousands of copies were circulated of such testimonies by the celebrated lady traveler Mrs. Isabella Bird Bishop. By the 1920s, Charles Bradlaugh's daughter Hypatia Bradlaugh Bonner was attacking the missionaries from the standpoint of rational atheism.

These bodies of literature, however, lie beyond our immediate concern. Let us turn to the inky-handed professionals who wrote just for the story's sake. The value of these as a source is precisely the incidental nature of their testimony; since in most cases they are not essential to the story, any references to missions or related matters may reflect something of the mental context in which the author sees them or attitudes prevalent when the author wrote.

I confess at once my limitations. Not being a literary specialist, I am at the mercy of what, and how little, I have read, and that is a tiny fragment of what is available. It will be noted that I dwell mostly on what F. R. Leavis called the Great Tradition, and finish comfortably before the present day. It is more than likely that I will omit any number of examples that could illuminate the subject better than those I have chosen.

There is another limitation, made reluctantly. If the "English novel" means "the novel in English," then it should embrace American as well as British novels. The problem is that in the great American novels, to an extent that (as far as my knowledge goes) is not reflected in the British novel, missionaries are sometimes central, rather than incidental, to the story. Part of this arises from American experience that had no historical equivalent in Britain: the relationship of Anglo-America with Native America and with Afro-America. And at least two major American novelists write very specifically on overseas missions as the central theme of a novel. Herman Melville's early animadversions on the mischief done by missions in *Typee* might be passed over, were *Typee* to be accepted for what it seemed in its own day to be, that is, a traveler's tale combined with an ethnographic essay; but it is now clear that *Typee* is in more senses than one an artful book, which prepares us for *Moby Dick* and the noble savage Queequeg, the Polynesian harpooner on the American whaler; the pagan who guilelessly reveals the corruption and hypocrisy of Christians. Melville's argument with God, the dark subtext of his greatest book, had already begun in *Typee*. *Omoo*, which follows it, takes the argument further, and even includes a mock missionary sermon. As for Michener, both Hilde Levonius and Alan Tippett have demonstrated the systematic misuse of historical evidence in *Hawaii*, a tract for the swinging sixties. Passing to American novelists of a lesser rank, there is Pearl S. Buck, who had a place on my mother's bookshelves. Daughter of missionaries, and for a time wife of a missionary, she broke away not only from the missionary calling but from mainstream Christianity; but her books, as with *The Good Earth*, the best known, are shot through with a love of China of a sort that would be readily recognized by many missionaries.

I retreat, therefore, to a British Parnassus, where the missionary movement is generally treated at oblique angles—at least until well into the twentieth century. Even the novelist of the Great Tradition with the widest personal acquaintance with the non-Western world keeps missions at arm's length. Joseph Conrad writes one of the great novels of Africa, *Heart of Darkness*, and one of the great novels of Southeast Asia, *Lord Jim*. Both center on moral and cultural dilemmas without any complications introduced by missionaries; and he writes one of the great novels of Latin America, *Nostromo*, with only background reference to effective Catholics and ineffectual Protestants. It seems to be the cinema that makes the missionary theme popular; or is it that, by the 1930s, novels about human weakness on the mission field were popular? Somerset Maugham's *Rain*, a story about a missionary's fall, published in 1923, became a film in 1932; *The Keys of the Kingdom*, about a conflict of a missionary with the church, followed; and how many people of a certain age draw their images of missionaries from Bogart and Hepburn in *The African Queen,* again based on a novel by a British author, C. S. Forester? There was even a sort of British Pearl Buck: Robert Keable was a missionary of the Universities' Mission to Central Africa, who wrote a book about the mission's work with the eloquent title *Darkness and Light* and composed *Songs for the Narrow Way*. One of his earlier books carries a preface by the then Archbishop of Canterbury. But in 1920, when, as a missionary priest in Leribe, in what is now Lesotho, he resigned his orders and started a new life as the author of novels of passion. His last book is a revisionist life of Jesus, provoked by the Conference on Faith and Order held at Lausanne in 1927. So long had he been away from orthodox Christians, he says in the preface, that he had not realized there were still four hundred people left to reach such reactionary conclusions. Keable's Jesus, not surprisingly, is a proponent of sexual freedom.

In parentheses, we may mention George Bernard Shaw's one foray into the mission field: one of his plays for Puritans, *Captain Brassbound's Conversion*, is set on a Scottish mission station in North Africa, where the only (and highly ambiguous) convert is a dissolute European.

And so to what those of the Great Tradition let slip about missions while talking of something else, we have, of course, to treat their evidence circumspectly to allow for their interests, knowledge, and methods. It is no use, for instance, taking Dickens as a historical source for the period of which he writes; he has neither the requisite attitude nor the requisite information; he wears his prejudices proudly on his sleeve. The miscellaneous religious influences in his formation make him an interesting witness to the Christian framework of Victorian thought and life, but do little to describe particular religious people or institutions. But they do reveal assumptions and attitudes, and his oblique references to missionary themes are cases in point.

His friend Wilkie Collins, creator of the detective story, was an atheist. His sympathetic characters are decent worldlings, while obvious piety is infallibly an indication of a villain. He has little direct to say about the missionary movement, but the spring of *The Moonstone* lies in India. India is represented as alien in thought and life and violent. "Caste is precious, life is cheap," says the Indian traveler, Mr. Murthwaite, who had passed in India as a "Hindoo-Boodhist" and spoke the language (whatever that might have been). In the end, the moonstone returns to Somnath, from where it had been stolen by a British officer, and is restored with high ceremony in the temple. And the novel's closing words evoke the idea of the cycle of Samsara: "The years pass and respect each other, so that the same events revolve in the cycles of time. What will be the next adventures of the moonstone? Who can tell."

Of Thackeray, one expects more because he has pretensions: he wrote not only historical novels but historical essays. But he does not always get things right. At the beginning of *The Newcomes*, he gives a marvelous picture. The mansion of Mrs. Sophia Alethea Newcome is a resort of the most favored among the religious world.

> The most eloquent expounders, the most gifted missionaries, the most interesting converts from foreign islands were to be found at her sumptuous table; in Egypt itself there were not more savoury fleshpots than those at Clapham.

The business of the life of Sophia Alethea is

> To attend to the interests of the enslaved Negro; to awaken the benighted Hottentot to a sense of the truth; to convert Jews, Turks, Infidels and Papists; to arouse the indifferent and often blasphemous mariner; to head all the public charities of her sect and do a thousand secret kindnesses that no one knew of, to answer myriads of letters, pension endless ministers; imperious but doing her duty, severe but charitable, and untiring in generosity as in labour.

One can recognize here the portrait of Clapham Evangelicalism; and one recognizes also that of her less resilient husband, who grew weary of the prayer meetings, yawned over the sufferings of the Negros, and wished the converted Jews at Jericho. But then Thackeray introduces a note that spoils it all. The household turns out to be a hotbed of sectarianism. The head gardener was a Scots Calvinist who had dated the end of the world two or three years hence (a curious occupation for a Scots Calvinist of the early nineteenth century); the housekeeper, a follower of Joanna Southcott; the guinea fowl are apparently Quakers; and on Sunday the whole household marches out in couples to sit at the feet of their diverse favorite ministers. But such did not really happen at the real Clapham. There the saints marched to the parish church and heard the rector, the Reverend John Venn, call them to their missionary task in the world. So Thackeray, too, we must use with caution.

With Jane Austen we are on surer ground; she speaks only of what she knows, and she has a marvelous ear so that we have first-rate authority for the topics addressed in general, especially female conversation, in the small gentry and clerical circles in the earliest period of British Protestant missions. Charlotte Bronte, like Jane Austen, was brought up in a parsonage, but a generation later, and she shows us how the status of the missionary movement had changed in a generation. George Eliot had a sensitive approach to some of the marginal religious movements of her time: the worlds of Silas Marner and Dinah Morris. But in reading her we must remember the tears that streamed down her face as she translated Strauss's *Life of Jesus* and realized that for her the days of faith were over. So when, *in Felix Holt the Radical*, we encounter the dissenting minister skimming the pages of a missionary report (which must certainly have been from the London Missionary Society) and emitting a slight "hmm," which seems expressive of criticism rather than of approbation, we may be sure that the deprecating "hmm" is George Eliot's own and guess what she thought about missions.

Trollope is something of an oddity: good on atmosphere, unobservant of detail; would Mrs. Proudie have remained in her Evangelical sepulcher after her husband—and he a bishop—had placed over it an inscription so repugnant as RIP?

We must therefore use our witnesses of the Great Tradition each according to his or her own canons. And we are fortunate in having in the earliest of them, Jane Austen, an explicit reference that offers us the social context of the missionary movement at the end of the first decade of the nineteenth century. Mary Crawford, in *Mansfield Park*, belongs to the smart set in London. A sojourn in the country has awakened affection in her for the earnest Edmund Bertram, who is both a clergyman and son of a baronet. Mary wishes he would be less of the first and more of the second. Events bring them to a rupture, and at their farewell interview, Mary tries to laugh off Edmund's earnestness.

> A pretty good lecture, upon my word! Was it part of your last sermon? At this rate, you will soon have converted everyone in both parishes, and when I hear of you next it may be as a celebrated preacher in some great society of Methodists or as a missionary into foreign parts.

Now Edmund was a beneficed English clergyman, and when these words were written, not a single beneficed English clergyman had become, in the strict sense of the word, a missionary into foreign parts. Edmund, born a country gentleman, is behaving like a fanatic. Enthusiasm can go no further—except as a ranting Methodist or as a missionary. Mary Crawford's world is that of Sydney Smith, who in that same year, 1808, was writing in the *Edinburgh Review*, "Why are we to send out little detachments of maniacs to spread over the five regions of the world the most unjust and contemptible notions of the gospel? The wise and rational part of the Christian ministry find they have enough to do at home . . . but if a tinker is a devout man, he infallibly sets off for the East."

Missionaries did not, in 1808, come from "the wise and rational part" of the Christian ministry, but from the tinkers, or more precisely, the cobblers: he is writing about William Carey and his Baptists.

When Jane Austen and Sydney Smith were writing, the Anglican CMS had been in existence for nine years; it had not been able to recruit a single English clergyman or any laymen who had the education or social status required for ordination. Every one of their missionaries to this point had been German.

George Eliot also has a reference to the low educational and social position of the first generation of missionaries. Felix Holt's father was a traveling salesman who invented quack medicines. His widow tearfully remarks of him, "My husband's tongue would have been a fortune to anybody; and there was many a one said it was as good as a dose of physic to hear him talk." She admits that his eloquence got him into trouble, but remarks that he always said, if the worst came to the worst, he could go and preach to the Blacks. Of course, had he really decided to do that, he would have had to get past the committee of the London Missionary Society; nevertheless, the passage reflects a popular perception that anyone with the gift of gab can preach to the Blacks.

To move the single generation from Jane Austen to Charlotte Bronte is to see how far the middle-class world had shifted in relation to the missionary movement. *Jane Eyre* was published in 1847, not the period of the missionary movement's loudest impact, but within the period of its greatest public acceptance. And in *Jane Eyre*, the movement is represented, not by a tinker or a snake oil salesman, but by Jane's cousin and suitor, St. John Rivers. Rivers is a highly educated beneficed clergyman, with at least modest independent means. He is determined to sacrifice all to follow a missionary vocation, in which he invites Jane to join him. His sisters deplore the decision, sure that it will bring his early death; the local grandee calls it a waste; the grandee's daughter dotes on Rivers but cannot share his vision. After much heart searching, Jane, too, refuses him—not for fear of the missionary life, though she clearly has no feeling of calling to it, but because her kinsman's martyr constitution has no place for the passionate personal self-offering that she craves. He wants not a wife so much as an assistant, a deacon. But she never doubts the nobility of his aim, and there is no hint of derision about what he believes he must do; and when the book closes, ten years later, its last words are for Rivers, wearing himself out in India, like a giant hewing down the forests of creed and caste, about to sink into the early grave that his sisters predicted. And Jane, thinking of him, sheds human tears and feels divine joy. The missionary life is not for her; but it is a noble calling worthy of a heroic gentleman, not the sphere of the fanatical tinker.

If we were to follow the internal indications of date, we may assume *Jane Eyre* to be set in about the same period as *Mansfield Park*; but Charlotte Bronte is not writing a historical novel. There are plenty of indications of the 1840s within the book, and we may take the attitudes expressed as reflecting those of Charlotte Bronte's own time, a time when people of Rivers's background were serving in India; even if the average missionary of the CMS (the natural home of someone of Rivers's outlook) was still a Wuerttemburg farmer or someone pushed through the society's Islington College because he had no hope of a university education. The picture of Rivers surely owes something to the young Cambridge scholar Henry Martyn who did, like Rivers, study Hindustani before going to India, whose offer of marriage was rejected by a young woman who did not feel able to take on the missionary life, and who did wear himself out in India and found an early grave in Iran. By this time, Sargent's memoir of Martyn had appeared, as had Samuel Wilberforce's edition of Martyn's journal. One suspects that one or both had found their way to Haworth parsonage.[1]

In the less-intense atmosphere of *Shirley*, Charlotte Bronte introduces an institution that one strongly suspects was a bane of her life in Haworth parsonage: the missionary basket. This was

> in size, a good-sized family clothes basket for conveying from house to house a monster collection of pincushions, needle books, card racks, work bags and articles of infant wear, made by the Christian ladies of a parish and sold perforce to the heathenish gentlemen thereof at prices unblushingly exorbitant. The proceeds are applied to the conversion of the Jews or to the regeneration of the interesting coloured population of the globe. Each lady has

---

[1] I am grateful to Professor Brian Stanley for pointing out that the connection between Martyn and Rivers was proposed by Valentine Cunningham in Fiona Bowie, ed., *Women and Missions: Past and Present* (London: Bloomsbury, 1994).

it for a month and foists it on to the male public. Some with a good trading spirit enjoy forcing up the price of useless articles, others would rather see the Prince of Darkness at the door than the phantom basket.

In other words, in Charlotte Bronte's country society, the fund-raising for missions is taken for granted as a social duty of middle-class ladies. Another reflection of missions occurs in a passage in her last and greatest novel, *Villette*, where a child of six points to a picture of thousands of wild men gathered in a desolate place around a man in black, "a good, *good* Englishman, who is preaching to them under a palm tree." What is more, the book has been given to her by a not very pious schoolboy.

Dickens reflects the passage of missions from the Evangelical margins to general acceptance. In his early work *The Pickwick Papers* it is the backstreet preacher Stiggins who promotes the sending of handkerchiefs, embellished with moral sentiments, to the West Indies; in *Bleak House* (1852) Dickens satirizes middle-class philanthropists' schemes for economic development in Africa; in *Little Dorrit*, written in 1855, a bishop, no less, advances the idea of a mission to Africa at a dinner given by a financier. By this time even bishops who were not of Evangelical persuasion were proposing new missions: Samuel Wilberforce, Bishop of Oxford, was arguing that earlier missions had proceeded in the wrong order, sending missionaries to build the church with a view to adding bishops later, whereas the bishop should be present from the beginning. This principle was adopted in the following decade by the Universities' Mission to Central Africa. By 1861, Trollope, in *Framley Parsonage,* is depicting an ambitious politician with a scheme for civilizing "the Australian archipelago." It is taken for granted that Christianity is to be part of the scheme of civilization; but the politician, in a public lecture, forgets to mention this until interrupted from the floor by the bishop's wife, and he hastily adds "and Christianity, of course." A separate charity is set up to administer the new missions. The whole arrangement suggests, and was probably suggested by, the scheme of James Brooke, the White Rajah of Serawak, which led to the setting up of the Diocese of Labuan.

We are now at the threshold of the high imperial era, and suddenly the trail becomes harder to follow. If we leave the Great Tradition of the novelists so far as to consort with W. S. Gilbert, we may meet the bishop of the remote island of Rum-ti-Foo. This Bab ballad is a skit on the Melanesian Mission—High Church Anglican, public school educated missionaries, a mission for gentlemen, as Bishop Selwyn of New Zealand demanded. The Bishop of Rum-ti-Foo leaves his flock untended to visit the Lambeth Conference and returns to find it sadly corrupted—naturally, by White traders.

> *Some sailors whom he did not know*
> *Had landed there not long ago,*
> *And taught them "Bother!" also "Blow!"*
> *(Of wickedness, the germs.)*
> *No need to use a casuist's pen*
> *To prove that they were merchantmen;*
> *No sailor of the Royal N*
> *Would use such dreadful terms . . .*

In addition to these vices learned from civilization, the islanders have reverted to their preregenerate ways. All ends happily, however, when the bishop adopts the customary rite as a liturgical dance, and caps this daring piece of enculturation by marrying the youngest of his flock.

Though a skit, not to be taken seriously, it is a sign of the times, an indication of the increasing embattlement of the missionary movement in the last decade of the century, when there were more missionaries than there had ever been before. The era of its most manifest presence was also the period that marked the beginning of the sustained critique of missions within the British intellectual establishment. It is not simply that missionaries can be treated as figures of fun; the subtext, as in countless other critiques, is that the missionary task is impossible. As Kipling said,

> *And when the goal is nearest, the end for which they sought,*
> *Watch sloth and heathen folly bring all your work to naught.*

Kipling is in some respects the lay theologian of this period, but he was not a Christian theologian, and certainly not a missionary theologian:

> *There are nine and sixty ways of constructing tribal lays*
> *And every single one of them is right.*

This era produced the imperial novel, tingling tales of high adventure from pens such as those of Rider Haggard and John Buchan. Missionaries are not usually very noticeable in these imperial novels. Haggard knew South Africa—he had indeed been Theophilus Shepstone's secretary, and in retirement he had strong ideas about Church of England matters. But we do not meet missionaries on the way to King Solomon's mines. (Charlotte M. Yonge declined to include the book with that title in her Young People's Library, because of the deceptions performed on the natives, and especially the bad language used by a prominent character.) Buchan's *Prester John* introduces us to the Reverend John Laputa, an outstandingly well-educated African clergyman whose sermon preached on the liner from England deeply impresses the passengers; but Laputa, while undoubtedly of great ability, turns out to be a savage at heart, the Christian persona only a cloak. The book sends a message: do not trust the apparently converted product of the missionaries. And Kipling brings Kim to his Catholic school, not through missionaries, but through the agency of army chaplains.

One theme associated with missions runs through the Great Tradition: the engagement with slavery and its outcome in the Caribbean and Africa. We know that Jane Austen, who was not an Evangelical, and whose devotional tastes lay with old-fashioned eighteenth-century High Church divines, nevertheless read works from the Clapham circle, and she read Claudius Buchanan on India, and writers on slavery such as Thomas Gisborne. The slave trade makes an appearance in her novels on two occasions; and what is remarkable is that it is almost the only social and economic question that does so, certainly the only one mentioned by women, who were not supposed to speak on political topics. And yet, in *Mansfield Park* (written at about the time the British Parliament had passed the act abolishing the trade), the landowner Sir Thomas Bertram returns after attending to the cumbered affairs of his estate in Antigua. It is his shy niece Fanny who timidly asks him a question about the slave trade. Fanny is the member of the family most likely to have read serious works from Clapham and to have done so with moral sensibility. Similarly, in *Emma*, Jane Fairfax talks about the sale of human flesh; Mrs. Elton assumes that this is "a fling against the slave trade" and assures her that her grand brother-in-law is "rather a friend to the Abolition." But Jane was thinking of agencies for governesses, "very different as to the guilt of those who carry it on," and in so saying, makes it clear that the slave trade is a matter of guilt. Both passages are indications of the great success of the Clapham Evangelicals in raising consciousness about the slave trade to the extent that, of all political issues, it alone could be talked of by young ladies in country houses and rectories.

In Thackeray's picture, in *The Newcomes*, of an actual Clapham household, there is a Black footman. His pious mistress encourages his addresses to her stepson's nurse, having the idea of sending the couple to Africa as missionaries. If Thackeray feels repugnance at the proposed interracial marriage, he at least recognizes that the Clapham lady felt no such repugnance; and when she orders the footman to flog her recalcitrant stepson, the author points to the irony that she feels unaffected pity for the lashes under which her footman's brethren suffered.

For Dickens, the campaign against slavery inhibits charity at home. The borough of Eatanswill, scene of a remarkable election in which Mr. Pickwick becomes unintentionally involved, sent an equal number of petitions against slavery and against factory reform. Sam Weller's critique of the Reverend Stiggin's handkerchiefs is that "blacks don't need handkerchiefs." But Dickens's most sustained piece of mockery relates to the Niger Expedition of 1841. The Evangelical Sir Thomas Fowell Buxton, lately the leader in Parliament of the campaign to emancipate the slaves, had designed the expedition to help to strangle the slave trade forever, to open Africa to Christianity and to economic development, redeeming Africa by the Bible and the plow, and calling out its own economic and human resources, thus bringing Africa into economic parity with Europe. State-of-the-art vessels and hand-picked crews and the best of contemporary technology, together with a crowd of scientific experts, went on the Niger Expedition; yet in three months it had turned back from the Niger; virtually all the European members of the expedition had been ill—forty-one of them had died.

Dickens reviewed the published account of the journal of the expedition for a magazine, and he makes at least two references to it in the novels. One is in *Our Mutual Friend*, where African kings are referred to as cheap and nasty—the evidence being that they wear European clothing in what, to Europeans, are unbecoming combinations. The other is in *Bleak House*, which presents Mrs. Jellyby, who is full of philanthropic concern for cultivating coffee on the left bank of the Niger, while shamefully neglecting her own family.

But Dickens was rather behind the times here. The Niger Expedition was over by October 1841, its sponsor, Buxton, died, brokenhearted, in 1845. Dickens was still scoffing over the expedition in 1853, when *Bleak House* was published; but by that time the Yoruba Mission was well established and cotton, if not coffee, was to be found growing, by missionary intervention, if not on the left bank of the Niger, not all that far away from it.

Behind the scoffing lies the conviction that all African projects are useless. "Blacks" do not need handkerchiefs, with or without moral sentiments; African kings wear jackets that do not belong with the trousers.

I do not think that the one major novelist known to be an outright supporter of missions, the devout tractarian Charlotte M. Yonge, actually wrote a novel, as distinct from a biography, based on a missionary life; but I have not read all her 161 books, and I doubt that I ever shall. But the general conclusion that appears from our survey must be that while the missionary movement made a substantial impact on British society, it was far from being a great national project arousing major enthusiasm. Missions were never a mainstream British concern in the nineteenth century, which is often called the Great Century of Missions. Missions began as the preserve of Evangelical extremists; it passed before mid-century to recognition and respect, but not to universal commitment. After that period, the mention of missions is often followed by a knowing wink: because "everyone" knows that what they are attempting is impossible. As the colonial period lie develops, the jokes get broader, and the critique of missions sharper.

At the heart of all this lies the ambiguous relationship between Christianity and Western civilization. The critics wrote off the missionary project, some from the belief that Christianity was incommunicable cross-culturally. Some thought that Christianity was passé in any case, but more held the belief that Western culture, necessarily associated with the Christian faith, was incommunicable. The central critique of missions in the late nineteenth and early twentieth centuries rested on racist premises.

12

World Parish to World Church

John and Charles Wesley on
Home and Overseas Mission

"I Look upon All the World as My Parish"

One of the most famous of John Wesley's sayings, uttered quite early in his itinerant career, was "I look upon all the world as my parish." This was not an announcement of a program for world evangelization, but a justification for preaching in other people's parishes, and a declaration of intent to go on doing so. Nonetheless it has a place in the development of a characteristically Methodist doctrine of mission. It signals a breach in the concept of Christendom, to which the parish was integral; and the Christendom concept was foundational to the Western experience of Christianity. It contains a hint of the transition from the church as an essentially Western institution that characterized Wesley's day to the world church in every continent that characterizes our own.

So there is reason to explore how the idea of a world parish led to the reality of the world church, and how the sphere of Methodist activity shifted from English parishes to distant parts of the globe. This essay is confined to the earliest part of the process, the words and actions of John Wesley, and the hymnody of his brother Charles. Other studies must consider the transitional figure of the mission expansionist Thomas Coke,[1] Wesley's troubleshooter in America and the Caribbean, and some significant Methodists of the generation that followed John's death who formed the Wesleyan

---

[1] Meanwhile, see John Vickers, *Thomas Coke, Apostle of Methodism* (London: Epworth Press, 1969).

Methodist Missionary Society and in the process built the Wesleyan Methodist Church.[2] The Wesleys saw Methodism as a mission; their successors turned the mission into a church with a mission society.

Western Christendom and the Idea of Parish

Europe had become Christian in a process lasting several centuries in which the peoples of the north and west came to accept Christianity as the basis of custom. Christendom, which is only another word for Christianity, became a geographical expression, "the Christian part of the world." The presence of an Islamic world to the east and south as Europe's only near neighbor reinforced the association of Christianity with territory.

This geographically expressed Christianity of Europe was organized in territorial units, of which the basic unit was the parish. The parson (the "person") of the parish notionally had the "cure of souls" of everyone resident within it. All were baptized in infancy, all, notionally, were taught the Christian faith and shared in the Christian worship of the community. The concept implied a single church, a concept unchallenged by the Protestant Reformation, which envisaged the purification of the whole church within each nation. And although by Wesley's day some degree of religious plurality was a political reality, the basis of church thinking remained that of the parish minister with the cure of souls for all within his parish. The idea was carried over into parts of the New World, including Georgia, where Wesley's unhappy missionary service took place.

The letter[3] which contains the celebrated phrase about the World Parish is a reply to one from a former Oxford pupil, James Hervey, who now held the cure of souls in the rural parish of Weston Favell. In this letter Hervey remonstrates with Wesley for his irregular behavior toward the parish system, and urges him either to return to college teaching in Oxford, or else get a parish of his own. Wesley summarizes:

---

  [2] Among recent studies, see Andrew Walls, "Wesleyan Missiological Theories: The Case of Richard Watson" in *The Global Impact of the Wesleyan Traditions and Their Related Movements*, Charles Yrigoyen, 27–47 (Lanham, MD: Scarecrow Press, 2002); Andrew F. Walls, "Methodists, Missions and Pacific Christianity," in *Weaving the Unfinished Mats: Wesley's Legacy—Conflict, Confusion and Challenge in the South Pacific*, ed. Peter Lineham, 9–32 (North Auckland: Wesley Historical Society of New Zealand, 2007).

  [3] The letter appears in Journal, June 11, 1739. Nehemiah, ed., *The Journal of the Rev. John Wesley*, standard edition, 2:216–18.

[Y]ou think I ought to sit still; because otherwise I should invade another's office if I … intermeddled with souls that did not belong to me. You accordingly ask, "How is it that I assemble Christians, who are none of my charge, to sing psalms, and pray, and hear the Scriptures expounded.[4]

It is noteworthy that Wesley uses the word "Christians" here where one might have expected simply "people." The point is that those being assembled were baptized members of a community explicitly identifying itself as Christian. As such their spiritual welfare was the responsibility of the clergyman of the parish. Wesley's practices invaded the parish clergyman's sphere both by public preaching (in the church if permitted, out of it if necessary) and by establishing meetings for those "who have the form of godliness and desire the power thereof." This produced a longer-term evangelistic and pastoral instrument, independent of the parish structures.

The concept of Christendom was built on the idea of a community that had a "form of godliness," even if all knew that this was rarely attained in practice. To set up a body consisting of those parishioners "desiring the power of godliness" was to introduce a more radical expression of Christianity than the church structures provided for, now that the Reformation had abolished the monasteries. Wesley's hymnbook was later to speak of "real" Christianity, and "inward" over against "formal" religion.[5]

The distinction between "real" or "inward" Christianity and the formal and nominal expressions required or assumed by Christendom is the hallmark of the Pietist and Evangelical movements that transformed Protestant Christianity in the eighteenth and nineteenth centuries. Wesley's expression of it was perhaps the more subversive of the parish structures by *not* establishing a gathered congregation on the independent or Baptist model. By drawing together societies of "Methodists" committed to radical Christian discipleship inside the parish but independent of its structures and oversight he was setting up an organization for mission not so much *of* the church as *to* the church, outside its lines of authority.[6]

---

[4] Ibid., 217.

[5] John Wesley, *A Collection of Hymns for the Use of the People called Methodists*, first appeared in 1780, and was reissued with successive supplements several times during the nineteenth century. In the preface (dated October 20, 1779), Wesley claims the hymns are "carefully arranged under proper heads, according to the experience of real Christians." These "proper heads" include "Describing Formal Religion" and "Describing Inward Religion."

[6] Wesley could cite these lines of authority when it suited his purpose. For instance, when, shortly before the letter recorded, Beau Nash of Bath had challenged him for his authority, Wesley's reply was, "By the authority of Jesus Christ, conveyed to me by the

James Hervey, Wesley's correspondent, was himself a radical who asserted the difference between formal and inward religion. A moderate Calvinist doctrinally, he was one of the small group of parish clergy early touched by the Evangelical revival. He, too, was seeking conversions, but essentially as a mission *of* the church, within, and by means of, the parish system. Charged with the cure of souls within one tiny segment of Christendom, he saw Wesley's mission project as interfering in the exercise of that responsibility.[7] Both men were aware that there were multitudes of parishes where no one exercised responsibility effectively, and a growing number where no one could do so. For Hervey, this was irrelevant to the issue: one's duty lay with one's parish. Wesley had a less circumscribed guiding principle:

> If you ask on what principle, then, I acted, it was this: A desire to be a Christian; and a conviction that, whatever I judge conducive thereto, that I am bound to do; wherever I judge I can best answer this end, thither it is my duty to go. On this principle I set out for America, on this I visited the Moravian Church, and on the same am I ready now (God being my helper) to go to Abyssinia or China, or whithersoever it shall please God, by this conviction, to call me.[8]

The letter continues with the scriptural duty to "instruct the ignorant, reform the wicked, confirm the virtuous," duties only possible for one in Wesley's position by entering some other clergyman's parish. And so,

> I look upon all the world as my parish: thus far I mean that in whatever part of it I am, I judge it meet, right and my bounden duty to declare unto all who are willing to hear the glad tidings of salvation.[9]

The argument and the context make it plain that, however ready Wesley may have been in principle to go to Abyssinia or to China, he did not expect to go to either; he expected to preach the glad tidings of salvation in English parishes to baptized people in a society that claimed to be Christian. The Evangelical revival challenged a Christian civil society that was not Christian enough, positing "real Christianity" over against the formal or nominal.

(now) Archbishop of Canterbury, when he laid hands on me and said "Take the authority to preach the Gospel." Journal June 5, 1739, in Curnock, *The Journal of the Rev. John Wesley*, 2:212.

[7] Hervey (1714–58), a Holy Club member at Oxford, even formed religious societies similar to the Methodist form; but he kept them under his own eye as parish minister.

[8] Curnock, *The Journal of the Rev. John Wesley*, 2:218.

[9] Ibid.

As one of Charles Wesley's hymns puts it, the Christian world is guilty of damning unbelief. Baptized people need the glad tidings of salvation leading to conversion, just as the Chinese do.

In this view of the preacher's task, there is no place for a special category of "cross-cultural" or even "overseas" mission. Wesley makes a revealing remark after reading Jonathan Edwards's publication of the journal of David Brainerd, missionary of the Scottish Society for Promoting Christian Knowledge to the Native Americans of Massachusetts. Wesley admired Brainerd and made a version of the journal for his *Christian Library*; but he notes in him the human tendency to overplay the significance of one's own work. Mighty as the movement was where so many of the Indians turned to Christ through Brainerd's preaching, the movement of the Spirit in Northampton under Edwards and in Cambuslang and Kilsyth in Scotland (Wesley modestly goes no further south for his examples) were still more remarkable.[10] But surely, we people of today protest, Northampton and Cambuslang were communities with a long Christian tradition; Brainerd was preaching to people different in language and culture who hitherto had been outside the Christian faith. This feature does not appear to have struck Wesley as important; for him revivals of religion are comparable, irrespective of their historical, cultural, or ethnic features.

This helps to explain the apparently haphazard early development of Methodist overseas missions, Wesley's damping down of Coke's enthusiasm for new overseas enterprises, and in particular the long delay in establishing a mission society for Methodists. The 1790s saw the formation of mission societies for most major British Protestant groups; not until 1814 was the Missionary Society for the Leeds District founded, and not until 1818 did the Connexion-wide Wesleyan Methodist Missionary Society come into being. Yet there were Methodist missions in four continents before 1818. In 1792 William Carey, usually credited with originating missionary societies in Britain, had seen "pleasing accounts" of their success.[11] Nor

---

[10] Journal December 4, 1749, in Curnock, *The Journal of the Rev. John Wesley*, 5:449. See also Andrew F. Walls, "Missions and Historical Memory: Jonathan Edwards and David Brainerd," in *Jonathan Edwards at Home and Abroad*, ed. David W. Kling and Douglas A. Sweeney (eds.), 248–65 (Columbia: University of South Carolina Press, 2003); see Chapter 13 below.

[11] William Carey, *An Enquiry into the Obligations of Christians to Use Means for the Conversion of the Heathens* (Leicester: UK, 1792), 37 refers to Wesley's ministers "now labouring amongst the Caribbs and Negroes" in the West Indies. Methodism in Antigua had begun through the conversion when visiting England in 1757 of the planter Nathaniel Gilbert and several of his slaves. There were Black Methodists, formerly serving in British regiments in the American Revolutionary War, in Nova Scotia. In 1792 they brought a

did Methodism suffer, like the Church of Scotland, where organization of missions was still later, from disputes about the principle of missions. No need was felt for a mission society because missions overseas were not seen as in essence different from other Methodist work. Appointing a missionary was in principle like appointing any other preacher, to be settled by establishing priorities.

The Fullness of the Gentiles' "Call": The Eschatological Framework

Wesley sets out the theological basis of his approach in Sermon 63, headed *The General Spread of the Gospel*.[12] The text is Isaiah 11:9, "The earth shall be full of the knowledge of God as the waters cover the sea." The "general spread of the gospel"—worldwide mission—is set in the framework of the fulfillment of God's purposes for humanity. Wesley's eschatology is standard for the period, rooted in the prophecies that speak of the Messiah having the heathen as his inheritance, interpreted in the light of Paul's argument in Romans 9–11 that God's economy involves the call of Israel, its hardening in part, and the admission of the Gentiles to the privileges once unique to Israel. Then, when that process has reached a climax ("the fullness of the Gentiles") there follows the recognition by all Israel of its Messiah. The great themes of this eschatology, intertwining the Old Testament, Romans, and the book of Revelation, are set out by Charles Wesley in the great hymn "Head of Thy Church Whose Spirit Fills":[13]

> *Come Lord, the glorious Spirit cries,*
> *And saints beneath the altar groan;*
> *Come Lord, the Bride on earth replies,*
> *And perfect all our hearts in one.*

Methodist society to Sierra Leone. Coke sent a (disastrous) agricultural mission, intended for Futa Jallon, to Sierra Leone in 1796, and a regular missionary was appointed to Sierra Leone by the Connexion in 1811. The mission party headed by Coke reached Sri Lanka, and Samuel Leigh Australia, in 1814. Thus there was established Methodist work in every continent before the foundation of the Wesleyan Methodist Missionary Society in 1818.

[12] I have used the text in *Sermons on Several Occasions by the Rev. John Wesley* (London: Wesleyan Conference Office, 1866), 2:261–71.

[13] For convenience I cite the hymns according to their numbers in the 1876 version of *Hymns for the People Called Methodists, with a New Supplement.* "Head of Thy Church Whose Spirit Fills" is no. 749.

The Spirit and the Bride—that is the church—here call for the completion
of divine love (all loves excelling), the finishing of God's new creation, the
fulfillment of salvation in the holiness without which none shall see God.
The hymn resumes:

> *Pour out the promised gift on all,*
> *Answer the universal "Come."*
> *The fullness of the Gentiles call,*
> *And take thine ancient people home.*

This is the order of Romans: the fullness of the Gentiles, the completion
of the preaching of the gospel to the nations, followed by the salvation of
Israel.

> *To thee let all the nations flow. . . .*

(a glance here at Isaiah 2:2ff, where the Gentiles crowd up the temple mount
to learn the ways of God, beating their swords into plowshares)

> *Sinners obey the gospel word*
> *Let all their bleeding Savior know*
> *Filled with the glory of the Lord.*
> *Oh for thy truth and mercy's sake*
> *The purchase of thy passion claim;*
> *Thine heritage, the nations, take*
> *And cause the world to know thy name.*

The climax thus comes with a reference to the second psalm where the
King, to whom God has just said "Thou art my Son," receives the nations as
his inheritance—the fullness of the Gentiles.

It is a theme that comes again and again in Charles Wesley's hymns of
the kingdom:

> *Saviour whom our hearts adore*[14]
> *To bless our earth again*
> *Now assume thy royal power*
> *And o'er the nations reign.*

---

[14] *Hymns* no. 730.

The subsequent verses enlarge on this call to Christ "the world's desire and hope" to set up the last great empire in our ruined world, sodden with the blood of murdered millions. By claiming the heathen tribes Christ begins the endless reign where no one learns war anymore.

But this is not a vision of another world; it is a natural extension of what has already begun as a result of Methodist preaching, as another hymn indicates:

> *With joy we now approve*[15]
> *The truth of Jesus' love.*
>
> *God the universal God*
> *He the door hath opened wide.*
> *Faith on heathens hath bestowed,*
> *Washed them in his bleeding side.*

The "heathens" that Charles Wesley is thinking of do not live in Africa or the Pacific. They are the baptized heathens of London and Kingswood and Bristol, who have been

> *Purchased and redeemed of old,*
> *Added to the chosen race,*
> *Now received into the fold*
> *Heathens sing their Saviour's praise.*

It is English heathens who have been incorporated into Israel, a contribution toward the fullness of the Gentiles that will precede the salvation of all Israel. A better-known hymn, "Head of thy Church Triumphant,"[16] is still clearer:

> *Thou hast employed thy servants*

(that is, the Methodist preachers)

> *And blessed their weak endeavours*
> *And lo! in thee we myriads see*
> *Of justified believers.*

Thanksgiving for this evangelistic success leads into prayer for the completion of the process:

---

[15] *Hymns* no. 735, v. 2.
[16] *Hymns* no. 853.

But show thy power and myriads more
Endue with heavenly graces

(that is, bring them not just to forgiveness of sin but to scriptural holiness)

But fill the earth with glory
And, known by every nation,
God of all grace
Receive the praise of all thy new creation.

Or again, in the hymn "Ye Neighbors and Friends of Jesus Draw Near"[17]:

To us and to them

(that is, the blind, lame, dumb, deaf, leprous and poor)

Is published the word
Then let us proclaim
Our life giving Lord
Who now is reviving
His work in our days
And mightily striving
To save us by grace.

The mighty work taking place in the writer's days is in the English parishes through Methodist preaching. This leads naturally to prayer for the completion of the process, its extension to all nations:

O Jesus ride on till all are subdued,
Thy mercy make known and sprinkle thy blood
Display thy salvation and teach the new song
To every nation and people and tongue.

In other words, the eschatological vision of the conversion of the nations is organically linked with the present calling of Methodists to preach the gospel in England. Present ministry, with its divine endorsement shown by repentance, faith, and changed lives, is part of a single continuous process whereby Jesus "rides on" toward the time when all things everywhere are put under his feet.

---

[17] *Hymns* no. 40.

The General Spread of the Gospel

This is spelled out in matter of fact prose by John Wesley in the sermon on *The General Spread of the Gospel*, already mentioned. It addresses the problem why five-sixths of the earth was then pagan or Muslim, and why so little of the remaining sixth was truly Christian. The newly discovered peoples of the Pacific, though Wesley could not bring himself to believe that they were actually cannibals, were undoubtedly indiscriminately violent, a standing refutation of contemporary theories of the benevolent effects of natural religion. If Muslims, outnumbering Christians, were without true religion and mercy, their Christian neighbors—Georgian, Circassian, Mengrelian—were proverbial for ignorance and irreligion, and the Christians of Abyssinia little better. Europe might offer more knowledge and more scriptural and rational ways of worship, but two-thirds of it was subject to the corruptions of Rome, and the majority of Protestants led far from Christian lives. How can we reconcile this prevailing darkness with the power and love of God?

It is an Arminian problem; high Calvinists may settle it by the mystery of election. Wesley finds in the prophecies the assurance that the darkness will be replaced by the knowledge of God, and, as foretold in that text so beloved by his brother, the Messiah will claim the nations as his inheritance (Psalm 2:8). John, like Charles Wesley, expects this event of the last times to come about by extension from God's present activity in the revival of religion in the Methodist movement. It is possible to conceive how God will work, he argues, by considering how he has already worked, and specifically how he has worked over the last fifty years or so: "In the same manner as God has converted so many to himself without destroying their liberty, he can undoubtedly convert whole nations, or the whole world."[18] Wesley urges his hearers to think how from the little circle in Oxford (Oxford, notice, not Aldersgate Street) the leaven has worked throughout England, and then spread to Scotland and Ireland, and a few years later into New York and Pennsylvania and beyond, even to Newfoundland and Nova Scotia. Traditionally, Wesley argues, the pattern has been for large-scale movements of the preaching of justification to last for some weeks or months and then subside, after which progress is by gentle degrees. But the Methodist movement has already lasted for fifty years, and it is reasonable to expect its further continuance. The most likely direction for it to spread now would be to Holland and then to the Protestants of France, Germany, and Switzer-

---

[18] *Sermons*, 2:261.

land, and then to Denmark, Sweden, and Russia. It could then spread to the Catholics in those areas where Catholics and Protestants live on close terms, which would enable true religion to spread to the Catholic countries: Italy, Spain, Portugal. (Wesley says nothing to indicate that awakening among European Catholics would make them Protestants.) He expects the renewal movement to proceed from the bottom upward, affecting rulers last, and the learned last of all.

Such a movement would bring about a return to the model of the church of the Acts of the Apostles, with shared property and the abolition of poverty—but without an Ananias and Sapphira. It would remove the main stumbling block to the conversion of Muslims, which lies in the evil lives of Christians. Muslims will thus turn to the true Messiah, and similar considerations will bring in the heathen peoples, beginning with those closest to the European settlements in India.

That leaves only those peoples who do not have regular contacts with Christians. But God can find ways of reaching the Pacific Islanders and the "recesses" of Africa and the Americas. When that happens, it will surely be time for the Jews to return, and all Israel will be saved, and all the promises to the church will have been fulfilled.

Wesley's vision is of the fulfillment of prophecy by contagion; the effect of scriptural holiness that proceeds from the gospel of forgiveness spreading from community to community. Considerations of culture differences and power relationships are left aside.

The sermon explains why Africa and some other parts of the world moved in and out of consideration for the stationing of Methodist preachers during Wesley's lifetime. On Wesley's principles the stationing of a preacher must relate to the prospects of doing most good at the particular moment.[19] Wesley is sure that the turn of Africa will come, as providence opens the way; but Africa never reached the main agenda during his lifetime. Fittingly, the slave trade, the topic of his last letter, was to place Sierra Leone firmly on the agenda soon after his death.[20]

---

[19] Inevitably Charles Wesley has a hymn, though unpublished, on this economy of preachers. Meditating on how Philip is guided to the Ethiopian eunuch (Acts 8) he says,

Not by voice angelic taught
Yet, Lord, we plainly know
Whether, and to whom we ought
At thy command to go.

S. T. Kimbrough and Oliver A. Beckerlegge, eds., *The Unpublished Poetry of Charles Wesley* (Nashville, TN: Kingswood Books, 1990), 2:322.

[20] Wesley's last known letter was written to William Wilberforce in 1791 to

Some parts of Wesley's analysis of the way Methodism might contribute to the general spread of the gospel have proved sound. Crucial developments have sometimes flowed from Methodists doing Methodist things—praying, preaching, meeting in class or society, singing, talking to neighbors or workmates. Portable Methodist structures, dependent on the gifts and graces of laymen and women and independent of heavy ecclesiastical investment have sometimes been crucial to new churches.

But for the most part, events relating to the general spread of the gospel have taken a path quite different from Wesley's expectations. He might be amazed (but surely delighted) to find teeming churches and vigorous Christian life in the "recesses" of Africa; he might be puzzled and dismayed at the decline from Christendom in the English parishes where his best years were spent. Perhaps the general spread of the gospel that he foresaw has happened and is still in progress, with the missionary movement (now entering a new, non-Western phase) the product of the Evangelical movement he knew. And surely both brothers were right to see that movement stretching into a future in which the Messiah will receive all the nations as his inheritance.

---

encourage him in the parliamentary campaign against the slave trade. See John Telford, ed., *Letters of the Rev John Wesley* (London: Epworth Press, 1931), 8:265. The next year, 1792, the Sierra Leone Colony was founded, with many Methodists of African birth or descent settling there from Nova Scotia.

13

Missions and Historical Memory

Jonathan Edwards and David Brainerd

The Missionary Movement
and Western Christianity

The missionary movement was a result of the shock impact upon Europe of the worlds beyond the West; in the religious sphere it was the most important outcome of that impact, not least because it occurred at the high point of the Europeanization of Christianity. Over the centuries in which Christianity was being honed to the conditions of Europe, and taking a distinctively Western form, the once buoyant and expansive forms of Christianity that had been characteristic of much of Asia and parts of Africa were going into eclipse. The form of Christianity that Europeans knew, and seemed to them normative, was territorial in expression. Conceptually, Christendom consisted of contiguous territory ruled according to the Law of Christ by Christian princes subject to the King of kings, with no public place for idolatry or blasphemy or heresy.

When Europe emerged in the late fifteenth century from its long insulation into a much wider world, the first instinct of Western Christians was to seek to incorporate the lands they now came upon into Christendom. For this purpose the already established model of crusade was adapted. In the Spanish Americas and some other places conversion followed conquest, and the boundaries of Christendom were thereby enlarged. A few places—the Congo kingdom of Soyo, for instance—entered Christendom voluntarily. But in most of the new world now open to the West, especially in the great Asian land mass, conversion was at best a distant dream, and conquest an impossibility.

This reality produced differing reactions among European Christians. Economic and political considerations now tied the Western powers—first Spain and Portugal, then the powers of Northern Europe—to ongoing involvement in the non-Western world; but the concept of the maintenance and extension of Christendom, originally integral to the enterprise, gradually receded from view. The public policy of the states of Christendom no longer actively pursued it as a goal desirable in itself. Europeans settled or working in the non-Western world could ring-fence their own Christian profession, and get on with the business of war or settlement or simply making money, without much concern about the religious systems of the host societies.

It was radical Christians, what one might call totalitarian Christians, those for whom the religious imperatives overcame the economic and political, who found this state of disengagement unacceptable. And it was among the radical Christians that the missionary movements, first Catholic and then Protestant, arose. The missionary principle differed from the crusading principle in that it was based on demonstration and persuasion rather than coercion. It did not in itself extend Christendom (though for a long time, many, perhaps most, missionaries hoped that it eventually would do so). It operated outside the sphere of Christian law and beyond the concept of a Christian civil society.

Relations with the non-Western world, and the colonial relationship in particular, helped to undermine the Christendom principle in Europe.[1] At the same time, largely through the agency of the missionary movement, new Christian communities developed in the non-Western world, communities that did not embody the territorial Christendom principle. The missionary movement was rarely a primary concern of the official Western church, and usually involved the energies of only a minority among those in Europe who professed and called themselves Christians, but it did much to change the demographic and cultural composition of the Christian church. What began as an attempt to extend Christendom ended by superseding Christendom. The extent of the revolution effected through the missionary movement was not visible until the second half of the twentieth century. Since European minds were shaped by the experience of centuries of Christendom, Western missionaries held to Christendom concepts even when the logic of their activities and of the situation pointed in other directions. For a long time after the beginnings of the movement the only instruments, intellectual or logistical, that missionaries and their sponsors had were instruments that had been forged in Christendom. The very concept of a

---

[1] This is argued in Andrew F. Walls, *The Cross-Cultural Process in Christian History* (Maryknoll, NY: Orbis Books, 2002), 27–48.

missionary had to be built from European patterns of Christian ministry; and those patterns were conditioned by territorial concepts, such as the parish. (It was fortunate that there were additional structures available in Western Christianity—Catholic orders and societies, Protestant voluntary societies, Methodist itinerancy—that had arisen where parochial and other territorial models had manifestly failed). The message that the missionary was expected to proclaim, the duties that he (inevitably "he"; since the foundation on which the missionary concept was raised was that of the male territorial ministry within Christendom) was expected to carry out, were in all essentials those thoroughly tested by experience in Europe. The responses to be expected to the missionary's message and the result of his activities were similarly shaped by the experience of Christendom. Radical Christians, who sought reformation and renewal and were dissatisfied with the normal standards of attainment in Christendom, had particularly clear expectations about the forms of response, both positive and negative, that would follow faithful proclamation of the Christian message. Missionaries began by doing what they had always done, usually in the way they had always done it, expecting the patterns of response that had emerged in the experience of Christendom. They entered upon the great learning experience of Western Christianity when, as representative Western Christians, they discovered the limitations of the confident encyclopedia of knowledge, theology, and practice that had been built up over the centuries of Christian interaction with European cultures, and sought to expand or transcend it. In the process they found themselves cultural and theological brokers between two worlds.

The Historical Memory of the
Missionary Movement

The missionary movement had its own historical memory and a highly developed sense of pedigree. As it was a product largely of peripheral forces within Western Christianity, few of the central, norm-setting figures of church history figure prominently in it. Its main dynamic always came from radical Christians, and among radical Protestants, the Reformation and the Evangelical revival always held a high symbolic place in the memory. But attempts to detect a serious concern for mission in the non-Western world in Luther or Calvin have never looked convincing, and it might be argued that John Wesley (despite meanings imported into his famous phrase "The world is my parish") did as much to restrain Methodists from activity outside the Western world as to promote world mission.

Jonathan Edwards was in this respect rather unusual, a central, norm-setting figure whose place in the historical memory of the missionary movement is secure. He can, like John Wesley, be held to have been personally a participant in missions, even if largely by default, through his Stockbridge exile. More significantly, he was an important theological influence on early Protestant missionaries from the English-speaking world. A stream of thinking passed from Edwards through Hopkins and watered the soils in which the early American missionary recruits grew and flourished. Edwards's theological principles on the freedom of the will and the religious affections also helped to liberate English (and perhaps Scottish) Calvinism and to make a dynamic theology of mission possible for Calvinists.[2] The greater number of the English-speaking missionaries whose service began in the last decade of the eighteenth century and the first three decades of the nineteenth had their background in that liberated Calvinism.

A good representative of Edwards's indirect influence is David Bogue,[3] a Scot who influenced a whole generation of missionaries. The Missionary Society, as the body later known as the London Missionary Society was originally called, initially demanded no theological education of its would-be missionaries. The assumption was that most candidates would come from the shop or the forge, rather than from the usual sources of supply of the ministry, and that the manual skills of such people would fully compensate for any inadequacy in the dead languages that underlay conventional theological education.[4] There were enough unmitigated disasters among missionaries recruited on this principle to persuade the Missionary Society otherwise, and from 1800 until his death in 1825 the society entrusted the theological education of missionaries to Bogue. Candidates continued to come from the shop or the forge, but they were put through a demanding course of study. Bogue did not lecture; he wrote an outline of a topic, leaving several inches of space under each heading, and gave a reading list. Students were expected to copy the outline, fill in the intervening spaces, and enter into oral dialogue with Bogue on the results. The readings were from books in his own library, and Edwards is prominent in the lists. That the system was judged effective by

---

[2] See J. van den Berg, *Constrained by Jesus' Love. An Enquiry into the Motives of the Missionary Awakening in Great Britain in the Period between 1698 and 1815* (Kampen, the Netherlands: Kok, 1956); Sidney H. Rooy, *The Theology of Mission in the Puritan Tradition* (Grand Rapids: Eerdmans, 1965).

[3] On Bogue (1750–1825), see James Bennett, *Memoirs of the Life of the Rev David Bogue D.D.* (London: F. Westley and A. H. Davis, 1827); John Morison, *Fathers and Founders of the London Missionary Society* (London: Fisher, 1844).

[4] See Andrew F. Walls, *The Missionary Movement in Christian History* (Maryknoll, NY: Orbis Books, 1996), 160–72.

those who went through it is shown by the fact that a group of his students conspired to publish the outlines (without the intervening spaces) after his death, and by the appearance of an American edition immediately thereafter.[5] When a college was established in the 1840s in Raratonga for the training of Polynesian evangelists for service in the Pacific, the resident missionary, Aaron Buzacott, took the students through Bogue's lectures, and eventually translated them into the vernacular and printed them.[6] Under such circumstances a somewhat diluted version of Edwards's teachings was spreading in the South Pacific long after his death.

But great as his direct and indirect influence undoubtedly was, Edwards the theologian, with one well-known exception, does not figure greatly in the historical memory of the missionary movement. Individual missionaries, as Stuart Piggin has shown,[7] read him avidly, but not all missionaries were avid theological readers. And the mentor that a generation of London Missionary Society missionaries remembered was not Edwards, but Bogue.

The exception, the one element in the Edwardsian theological inheritance that entered into the collective missionary memory, is, of course, the *Humble Attempt to Promote Explicit Agreement and Visible Union of God's People in Extraordinary Prayer*.[8] More than forty years after its composition, this tract helped to inspire the Baptist circle to which William Carey belonged, and was thus instrumental in the founding of the Baptist Missionary Society,[9] despite the fact that the book's eschatological scheme was by then demonstrably flawed. One of the circle, John Sutcliff, produced a cheap new edition,[10] and Carey himself cited the work in his *Enquiry into the Obligations of Christians to Use Means for the Conversion of the Heathens*.[11]

---

[5] Joseph Samuel C. F. Frey, *Theological Lectures by the Rev. David Bogue* (New York: L. Colby, 1849).

[6] J. P. Sutherland, *Mission Life in Islands of the Pacific, being an account of the life and labours of the Rev. Aaron Buzacott* (London: Snow, 1866).

[7] See Stuart Piggin, "The Expanding Knowledge of God: Jonathan Edwards's Influence on Missionary Thinking and Promotion," in *Jonathan Edwards at Home and Abroad: Historical Memories, Cultural Movements, Global Horizons*, ed. David W. Kling and Douglas A. Sweeney (Columbia: University of South Carolina Press, 2003).

[8] Jonathan Edwards, *Humble Attempt to Promote Explicit Agreement and Visible Union of God's People in Extraordinary Prayer* (Boston: D. Henchman, 1747).

[9] See, for example, Arthur Fawcett, *The Cambuslang Revival* (London: Banner of Truth Trust, 1971).

[10] On Sutcliff, see Ernest A. Payne, *The First Generation, Early Leaders of the Baptist Missionary Society in England and India* (London: Carey Press, 1937), 38–45.

[11] William Carey, *Enquiry into the Obligations of Christians to Use Means for the Conversion of the Heathens* (Leicester, UK: Ann Ireland, 1792).

The story, involving as it does contact and interaction between Congregationalists in New England, Presbyterians in Scotland, and Baptists in the English Midlands, illustrates the informal networks that linked practitioners of Evangelical religion across barriers of geography and confession.[12] It also offers a study in the application of ideas. The *Humble Attempt* is not a book about missions; it is a book about prayer. It became a book about missions because the group of people who were reading it already had the germ of the idea of an overseas missionary enterprise. Edwards's expansive ideas of the sovereignty of Christ and the postmillennial eschatology that these latter-day Puritans inherited served to enrich, inform, and confirm an enterprise already conceived.

The Life of Brainerd and the Missionary Movement

Despite legend, the work of Carey does not mark the beginning of the Protestant missionary movement, only the significant entrance of British Christians into it. The movement had begun almost a century earlier in Germany and Central Europe.[13] But in one sense it had begun earlier still. The missionary movement as it developed was essentially maritime in its thinking; Christendom and the non-Christian world were divided by oceans. But in North America, Protestant Christians for the first time lived side by side with non-Christian people. As happened elsewhere, the initial desire to bring these peoples into the Christian fold, while never abandoned, receded before temporal considerations. Theological principle—the Redeemer's throne set up in America where Satan had once ruled—sat uneasily with the practical realities of daily relations between Western Christians and Native Americans. The latter were not a distant people to be evangelized by specially devised means; they were the neighbors, and neighbors with whom relations were, to say the least, ambivalent. It is from this borderland of Christendom, a mission field without the maritime element that came to be an essential ingredient in Western thought about missions, that Edwards's greatest impact on the historical memory of the missionary movement was made.

---

[12] See, for example, Susan O'Brien, "Eighteenth Century Publishing Networks in the First Years of Transatlantic Evangelicalism," in *Evangelicalism: Comparative Studies of Popular Protestantism in North America, the British Isles and Beyond, 1700–1990*, ed. Mark A. Noll, David W. Bebbington, and George A. Rawlyk, 38–57 (New York: Oxford University Press, 1994).

[13] See Walls, *Cross-Cultural Movement*, 194–214.

Incomparably the fullest and most direct influence of Edwards on the later missionary movement lay in his making available the journal of David Brainerd, missionary to the Native Americans of the Society in Scotland for Promoting Christian Knowledge.[14] Many hundreds of missionaries and prospective missionaries read the book in some shape or form, and many were stirred by it. By the early nineteenth century Brainerd had become the Protestant icon of the missionary, its ideal type, as a result of the published journal. Every new missionary—typically, a man in his twenties—was taught thereby to see this young man as the pattern for what his own life ought to be.

Brainerd's status as the icon of the Protestant missionary was perhaps attained by only one other figure, the English clergyman Henry Martyn, who ironically was not in the technical sense a missionary but a chaplain of the East India Company.[15] Martyn was himself deeply influenced by Edwards's presentation of Brainerd's journal. And Martyn's story had much in common with Brainerd's—young, cultured, articulate, consumptive, depressive men, marriage unfulfilled for the gospel's sake, burning themselves out in the work. The portraits elided; Martyn was Brainerd for a new generation.[16]

---

[14] Jonathan Edwards, *An Account of the Life of the Reverend Mr. David Brainerd, Minister of the Gospel, Missionary to the Indians, by Jonathan Edwards, A. M.* (Boston, 1749). References in this essay are to Jonathan Edwards, *The Life of David Brainerd*, ed. Norman Pettit, *The Works of Jonathan Edwards*, vol. 7 (New Haven, CT: Yale University Press, 1985) [hereafter Edwards, *Works*]. Edwards indicates the work is "chiefly taken from [Brainerd's] own diary and other private writings, written for his own use." William Bradford had already published parts of the diary in two parts as *Mirabilia Dei inter Indicos* and *Divine Grace Displayed or the Continuance and Progress of a Remarkable Work of Grace among Some of the Indians* (both Edinburgh, 1746). Edwards omitted the parts already printed (what he calls "the public journal"), though many later editions conflate the texts. For the publishing history of both *Journal* and Life of Brainerd, see Edwards, *Works*, 7:71–85.

[15] The influence of Martyn on different generations of missionaries is reflected in his biographies, each going through several editions. See John Sargent, *Memoir of the Rev. Henry Martyn* (London: Seeley, 1816); Samuel Wilberforce, ed., *Journal and Letters of the Rev. Henry Martyn* (London: R. B. Seeley and W. Burnside, 1837; New York: Dodd, 1867); George Smith, *Henry Martyn: Saint and Scholar, First Modern Missionary to the Mohammedans, 1781–1812* (London: Religious Tract Society, 1892); Constance E. Padwick, *Henry Martyn, Confessor of the Faith* (London: SCM, 1922; revised edition, IVF, 1953).

[16] The Congregational divine R. F. Horton, addressing student volunteers on "The Spiritual Preparation of the Missionary," says "so far as I know the history of missionaries, whether I read the life of Henry Martyn who learned the secret from David Brainerd, or the life of Mackay who learned the secret from Henry Martyn . . . their success and that power and their Christlikeness in service are all accurately measured by their powers and Christlikeness in prayer" (*Students and the Missionary Problem: Addresses Delivered at the International Student Missionary Conference* [London: Student Volunteer Missionary

Martyn felt Brainerd coming alive from the page, so that he entered into a sort of conversation with him. He confides, "I feel my heart knit to that dear man, and really rejoice to think of meeting him in heaven."[17] On another occasion he says, "That dear saint of God David Brainerd is truly a man after my own heart. Although I cannot go half way with his spirituality and devotion, I cordially unite with him in such holy breathings as I have attained unto."[18]

When his ship put into Cape Town en route for India, and he made the acquaintance of James Read of the London Missionary Society, his mind again went to the book: "I was so charmed with his company that I fancied myself in company with David Brainerd."[19] For Martyn, born more than thirty years after Brainerd's death, Brainerd had become a contemporary.

And at the end of the nineteenth century, the high peak of the missionary movement, Brainerd's life was still being set before missionary recruits. Eugene Stock, the historian of the (Anglican) Church Missionary Society (CMS), writing in the 1890s after referring to the great Native American movement to the church at Crossweeksung in response to Brainerd's preaching, goes on: "But Brainerd did less in his lifetime than his biography, by President Edwards, did after he was gone. In its pages is presented the picture of a man of God such as is rarely seen. No book has, directly or indirectly, borne richer fruit."[20]

The spiritual fathers of late Victorian times who pointed new missionaries toward Brainerd recognized that we know Brainerd only because of Edwards. When Sereno Edwards Dwight produced an enlarged edition of the Brainerd journals in 1822, he described Brainerd as the person "who would probably be selected by all denominations of Christians as the holiest missionary, if not the holiest man of modern times," and he suggested that the time was near when Brainerd would be better known all over the world than Alexander, Julius Caesar, or Napoleon.[21] Nevertheless he did not include the book in his collected works of Jonathan Edwards, his reason

---

Union, 1900], 181). At the same conference a High Church Anglican, Leonard Dawson, remarked of Martyn's life, "Although there is a certain melancholy tone about that life, yet personally, I found in it my first inspiration as a missionary" (ibid., 533).

[17] Wilberforce, *Journal and Letters of the Rev. Henry Martyn*, 80.

[18] Ibid., 200.

[19] Ibid., 133.

[20] Eugene Stock, *The History of the Church Missionary Society* (London: Church Missionary Society, 1899), 1:27. Stock links Brainerd with Martyn, as well as with a more recent missionary hero, James Hannington.

[21] Sereno Edwards Dwight, *Memoirs of the Rev. David Brainerd, Missionary to the Indians . . . by Rev. Jonathan Edwards. . . . Including His Journal Now for the First Time Incorporated with the Rest of His Diary in a Regular Chronological Sequence* (New Haven, CT: S. Converse, 1822), 9.

being that so little of the work was by Edwards himself.[22] The fact remains that the book owed its origin and its shape to Edwards, and it probably had a more profound effect on a wider range of people than did many of the master's weightier treatises.

But there was a dash of gall mixed into this spiritual elixir, and every reader could taste it. It is impossible to disguise the depressive strain in Brainerd's journals, and Edwards does not attempt to do so. He reproduces sections where the writer is "filled with sorrow and confusion,"[23] "distressed by a sense of spiritual pollution,"[24] and so confused by inward anguish that he lost the track of his sermon.[25]

Edwards actually warns the reader against this "melancholy," which he did not regard as a necessary ingredient of proper self-examination. He reflected that it might have been contained had Brainerd gone with a companion; after all, the Lord sent his disciples in pairs. He also identified a physical element and thought Brainerd willfully reckless in putting his life into danger.[26] Martyn, with depressive tendencies himself, takes up the hint. He concludes it was improper for Brainerd to attempt what he did at a time when he should have been in medical care—was Brainerd perhaps overanxious to obtain his own good opinion?[27] The editor of an early short version advises the reader to discount the melancholy as "purely animal,"[28] that is, arising from Brainerd's distressing physical condition. Others found its origin in the theological and pastoral inadequacies of Calvinism. "How much of his sorrow and pain had been prevented" cries Wesley, "if he had understood the doctrine of Christian perfection!"[29] For the spiritual mentors of the Student Volunteers, deeply influenced by the doctrines and experiences of the Keswick Convention, Brainerd's melancholy was a theological puzzle. "I know nothing more resembling Pentecost than the scenes following [Brainerd's] preaching at Crossweeksung," says A. J. Gordon of Boston,[30] but he goes on to ask how someone who manifestly displayed the

---

[22] Ibid.

[23] Edwards, *Works*, 7:272. 24.

[24] Ibid., 7:278.

[25] Ibid., 7:284.

[26] Ibid., 7:95.

[27] Wilberforce, *Journals and Letters of Martyn*, 204.

[28] *An Account of the Life of the Rev. David Brainerd* (Newark, NJ: J. A. Crane, 1811), preface.

[29] John Wesley, *Letters of the Rev. John Wesley, A. M.*, ed. John Telford, 5:95 (London: Epworth Press, 1931).

[30] A. J. Gordon, *The Holy Spirit in Missions* (London: Hodder and Stoughton, 1893), 207.

indwelling of the Holy Spirit did not know the exultant spiritual liberty that was part of the Keswick message and a regular ingredient of much contemporary Evangelical teaching.

Brainerd—Missionary or Minister?

For a period at the beginning of the nineteenth century, Edwards's presentation of Brainerd occupied another place in the historical memory of the missionary movement. Not only did the *Life of Brainerd* provide the icon of the missionary as regards motivation and inner life; it was also one of the very few accessible accounts in English of the day-to-day work of a missionary in contact with people of another language and culture, and one of the very few works that reflected on what a preacher so circumstanced should say and how he should communicate it.

When the group of Anglican clergymen who formed the CMS in 1799 set up their first library, "Brainerd's Life" was the first of the titles they selected. There were only thirteen titles in all, and five of these were current periodicals. Apart from Edwards's presentation of Brainerd's journals, the committee could find only a few continental works in translation describing the work of Moravian missions and that of the Danish Lutheran Hans Egede in Greenland[31] to provide firsthand accounts of modern Protestant endeavors to present the gospel across a cultural divide.

It is something of a shock to realize that this is not how Edwards viewed Brainerd's work. The founders of the CMS who compiled this library had the maritime consciousness characteristic of the developing missionary movement; for them, missions lay overseas. Edwards was looking out at the New England that he knew, with its diverse layers of population.

The chapter that Edwards appended to *Life of Brainerd*,[32] in which he assesses the significance of Brainerd, is instructive. The first and longest section focuses not on the Indians' conversion, but on Brainerd's own. It analyzes the marks of authenticity in his experience that were missing from the testimonies of many who claimed the same experience of conversion to God. The second section distinguishes between the genuine and the spurious in religious affections as displayed in times of revival, rebutting the idea that Brainerd's work at Crossweeksung was of the same kind as some recent revivals among White settlers. Edwards's point, however, is not that

---

[31] Charles Hole, *The Early History of the Church Missionary Society for Africa and the East to the End of of 1814* (London: Church Missionary Society, 1896), 48.

[32] Edwards, *Works*, 7:500–541. 33.

the Crossweeksung movement took place in a Native American community, but that (unlike some contemporary movements among the settlers where the response was spectacular, but transient) it effected a lasting transformation. The third section argues that Brainerd's life displays the sharp difference between experimental religion and mere emotional imaginations. The fourth seeks to demonstrate that Brainerd's ministry proves the efficacy of the doctrines of grace, in opposition to Arminian objections. The fifth displays Brainerd as an exemplar for candidates for the ministry, and the sixth as an exemplar for religious practice, notably with regard to fasting. Only with the seventh reflection, a short one, do we reach what one might call the specifically missionary dimension of Brainerd's career: how it encourages God's people to prayer and endeavors for the advancement and enlargement of the kingdom of Christ in the world, and in particular for the conversion of the Indians "on this continent!" Edwards pauses to consider how Crossweeksung might be the forerunner of something much more glorious and extensive of that kind. But the visionary pause is brief; he quickly passes to practical matters like sending missionaries in pairs (we have already seen that he believed this might have kept Brainerd's depressive tendencies in check) and to a consideration of the special providences attending Brainerd's last illness and death.[33]

For people building up a library for an infant mission agency, the life of Brainerd was a rare example of Christian preaching among people of another language and culture, or, as they would have said, other manners and customs. For Edwards, who made that life known to the world, it was primarily a demonstration of the true character, authentic experience, and proper doctrine of a Christian minister. An almost contemporary throwaway remark by John Wesley suggests a similar conclusion. Wesley believed that "even so good a man" as Brainerd overestimated his own work. "The work among the Indians, great as it was, was not to be compared to that at Cambuslang, Kilsyth, or Northampton."[34] For Wesley, who made the first of the hosts of popular abridgements of the memoir, it was valuable not because it would call people to the mission field, but because it would teach them devotion and acceptance of harsh conditions in their service in England.[35] For Wesley and Edwards alike, what we would call the cross-cultural aspect of Brainerd's work was coincidental. For them, Crossweeksung is of one kind with Cambuslang and Northampton. A generation

---

[33] Ibid., 7:531–34.
[34] John Wesley, *Journal of the Rev. John Wesley, A. M.*, ed. Nehemiah Curnock (London: Charles H. Kelly, n.d.), 3:449.
[35] Wesley, *Letters*, 5:282.

later, in the historical memory of a missionary movement that saw its task as the establishment of the Church of Christ among non-Western and hitherto non-Christian peoples, Brainerd, as presented by Edwards, was reconceived as the missionary par excellence.

Evangelical Preaching, Christendom, and the Missionary Movement

The missionary movement, with its requirement to live on terms set by the life of a society other than one's own, marked a breach with the centuries-old idea of Christendom. This posited a civil society in nominal allegiance to Christ, and a pastoral duty of the church to bring that civil society into true harmony with its Christian profession. There is very little sense of such a breach in Edwards, very little to indicate that he saw any particular significance in the missionary office that was not already present in the ministerial.

Edwards and Brainerd—and for that matter Wesley—are transitional figures in the history of the missionary movement. They operated before the movement emerged in the English-speaking world as a distinct element in Protestant consciousness. They thought in terms of Christendom and the traditional responsibility of the Christian ministry within it. But they thought as Evangelicals, that is, as radical, "totalitarian" Christians.

Evangelical consciousness saw all humanity as one in sin, misery, and loss, one in redemption and holiness in Christ. There was thus a single message for the money-making merchant in Massachusetts and those whom merchant and minister alike might describe as "rude savages." Brainerd refers to "white heathens" being affected during the movement among the native peoples at Crossweeksung.[36] Heathenism was not a religion but a state of mind, and it had nothing to do with race.

Evangelical religion was a product of Christendom. It assumed a civil society that nominally accepted Christian symbols and Christian norms, but that fell drastically short of those norms in reality. Evangelicalism was thus about "real Christianity" over against the formal and the nominal profession of it, about the inward religion of the heart turned toward God. Evangelicalism was by its nature protest religion, a protest movement against a society that claimed to be Christian but denied that claim in its practice. Classical Evangelicalism required nominal Christianity in order to define itself, and assumed the presence of a Christian (even if defectively Christian) civil society.

---

[36] Cf. Edwards, *Works*, 7:309. He found one group of Whites "behaved more indecently" during his preaching" than any Indians I ever addressed" (ibid., 7:318).

The Native Americans that Brainerd and Edwards knew lived on the margins of Christendom. These damaged, dislocated, partially demoralized, and frequently alcoholic communities had lost the integrity of traditional life. Their whole existence was a marginal one, on the fringes of White society. Brainerd calls them "poor pagans," but his own journals reveal that they were not *mere* pagans. A whole spectrum of attitudes toward Christianity can be discerned in what he says about them. Brainerd's interpreter, Moses Tinda, though at first "a stranger to experimental religion" was nevertheless very desirous that his people should "renounce heathenish notions and practices and conform to the customs of the Christian world."[37] These are very much the principles on which Christendom operated. Among those converted in the movement at Crossweeksung were people whom Brainerd describes as "secure and self-righteous," which suggests that they were at least regular church attenders. Among these was a man who claimed to have been a Christian for ten years.[38]

Brainerd was clearly not working in entirely virgin territory but among people where gradual and uneven accommodation to White society had produced at least a degree of Christian profession and absorption of Christian ideas and practice. The native community was also well aware that there were "white heathens" who paid little or no heed to the religious norms of White society. Brainerd was working in a frontier district of Christendom, and that district responded to the radical, totalitarian Evangelical preaching of Brainerd in a way similar to that in which contemporary White society in other parts of Protestant Christendom responded to similar preaching. Crossweeksung saw the mourning for sin and the testimonies to personal experience of the love of Christ that characterized revivals in the nominally Christian areas of old Christendom, according to the recognized Evangelical paradigm of conversion. Brainerd the missionary is thus seen by Edwards as the model of a young minister, working under conditions of exceptional hardship.

Not surprisingly, the early Protestant missionary movement, which was for a long time principally Evangelical in character, initially brought to the non-Western world the same message and the same methods that it brought to the nominally Christian world that produced Evangelical radicalism. And it expected the responses (and Evangelicals had plenty of experience within Christendom of hostile or indifferent response) to be along the same lines.

This had an important and often overlooked outcome. It meant that the early missionary movement was not racist, however "culturist" it might be. Evangelical conviction about the solidarity of humanity in sin and in grace

---

[37] Dwight, *Memoirs of the Rev. David Brainerd*, 218.
[38] Ibid., 210.

meant that even those viewed as "rude savages" or "poor pagans" were open to the highest operations of divine grace, just as "white heathens," not to mention "secure, self-righteous" churchgoers, were open to the same condemnation as the "savage heathens."

Brainerd was as "culturist" as his contemporaries in general. He had little sympathy for Native American ways of life and was puzzled that the unregenerate actually preferred these ways as superior to the unremitting busy-ness of White society. Even the regenerate were not eager to start cultivation and the more laborious lifestyle that would accompany it. When one group refused to abandon a noisy dance despite the presence close by of a very sick man, Brainerd attributed the decision to the callous inhumanity of the heathen heart. But justice immediately forced him to add, "Although they seem somewhat kind in their way"[39]—even if it was a different way.

No doubt Brainerd took for granted that regeneration would dispose converted Native Americans to adopt "civilized" ways. He was engaged in moving his converted people to conditions where this would be easier when he was overtaken by his last illness. But he was in no danger of identifying regeneration and civilization.

Pastoral experience within Christendom suggested that there was a recognizable pattern of authentic response to the gospel, a paradigm of genuine religious experience. It also recognized certain common deformations of that experience, and some blind alleys that prevented its attainment. Neither Edwards nor Brainerd had any reason to doubt that the paradigm was universal, and Crossweeksung appeared to prove the point.

If the Native American community there was already reflecting a fair degree of acculturation, the high degree of conformity to the paradigm established among Whites is not altogether surprising. A substantial section of the Native American community may have had sufficient knowledge of and nominal adherence to Christianity to be shatteringly convicted of their deficiencies and delightedly responsive to the hope of "an interest in Christ."

Brainerd does reflect a degree of puzzlement about how the paradigm worked within his Delaware society in at least one instance. We have already seen that his interpreter, Moses Tinda Tautamy (or Tattamy), was, even before he met Brainerd, strongly in favor of "civilized" ways and wanted his people to renounce idolatry. Presumably this was at least part of the reason that Brainerd offered him the post, and that Tinda accepted it. Nevertheless, Brainerd believed him to be without experimental knowledge of the

---

[39] Brainerd had particular difficulty with a group influenced by Quakers, who seemed to him to be trusting in sobriety and sincerity for salvation (Edwards, *Works*, 7:346).

gospel. Already distressed to find that the language had no words for the staple terms of Evangelical preaching—salvation, grace, justification—and disposed like some later missionaries to blame the language for this, Brainerd was thus further frustrated by an interpreter who showed no fervency. All this changed a short time before the striking events at Crossweeksung. The interpreter, who had already shown signs of genuine concern for his soul, fell seriously ill. Brainerd recognized the signs of conviction of sin, and the evidence of the changed life that followed his recovery. Tinda's style of interpretation also changed; he conveyed Brainerd's fervor as he became fervent himself. He became so committed to spreading the gospel that he hardly knew when to stop. Brainerd found that when he himself had left a place, Tinda would stay behind to explain or reinforce what the missionary had said. The Crossweeksung movement with its flood of conversions, baptisms, and communions followed Tinda's transformation.

And yet Brainerd was never entirely satisfied about Tinda's personal experience. It was clear that he had known awakening, conviction of sin had been evident, his conduct was exemplary, his fervor unbounded, and no one could have been more devoted to the work of the gospel. It was through his effectiveness that the missionary had become effective. But Brainerd felt unhappy that Tinda could not give distinct views of Christ, nor a clear account of his soul's acceptance "which," concludes Brainerd sadly, "makes his experience the more doubtful."[40]

It is fair to assume that Tinda played a critical role in the movement that led to the ingathering at Crossweeksung. Yet his own experience conformed only in part to the paradigm of conversion that had emerged from Evangelical preaching in Protestant Christendom.

The Later Missionary Movement and the Paradigm of Conversion

Such mismatches with expectations increased as missionaries crossed the seas and proclaimed their message in settings where there was no trace of the Christian civil society that was characteristic of Christendom.

---

[40] See Dwight, *Memoirs of the Rev. David Brainerd*, 210–11, 213. Edwards preserves few of the references to Moses Tinda Tautamy in his version, though he refers to the interpreter's awakening (Edwards, *Works*, 7:277) and to his being "amazingly assisted and I doubt not but the Spirit of God was upon him, (though I had no reason to think he had any true and saving grace, but was only under conviction of his lost state)" (ibid., 7:279). On Tinda, see also ibid., 7:254 and note.

The Evangelical paradigm of conversion was shaped by the distinction between real and nominal Christianity. Missionaries, converted people themselves and true to their Evangelical heritage, declared a single gospel for all humanity without distinction of race or religious profession. They continued to recognize conversion as a requirement for all. But attitudes to indigenous culture softened as acquaintance deepened. A key factor in deepening acquaintance was language. Brainerd did his best, but he never mastered the Delaware vernacular: hence the crucial position of his interpreter.[41] Beyond the boundaries of Christendom the only way of proceeding was by agonizingly, and for a long time inexpertly, struggling with someone else's language. At first language seemed, as it had to Brainerd, to be simply a barrier to be overcome in order to communicate the gospel. Gradually language was seen to be the outer gate to an inner world in which the gospel must take root if meaningful conversion was to take place. Sometimes that conversion did not follow the paradigm, yet appeared to missionaries to be the work of God. Beyond Christendom people might respond to the gospel without responding to the missionaries' experience of the gospel. And this was sometimes particularly evident where the communication took place through indigenous people—through the likes of Moses Tinda, in fact.

In the Pacific, for instance, Calvinistic Evangelical missionaries of the London Missionary Society who had learned Edwardsian theology through study under Bogue saw mass movements to the faith in Tahiti and Raratonga. In the latter case, indigenous preachers had been particularly important in bringing the movement about. Kings and chiefs sought baptism, multitudes threw their cult objects into bonfires, whole villages crowded into church and school and demanded to be taught the Christian way. What was happening appeared to match the New Testament phrase "turned from idols to serve the living and true God."[42] No missionary could fail to rejoice at such events, yet elements of the paradigm of conversion were missing. Sometimes there was little sign of conviction of sin, despite an obvious break with idolatry; and frequently what Brainerd called "views of Christ" were vague, even though there might be signs of conviction of sin. What was undeniable in Pacific Christianity was the renunciation of traditional cult and the assertion of public allegiance to Jehovah.

In Tahiti the perplexed missionaries waited six years after the first professions of faith—when the names of those who declared their faith were written down—before baptizing anyone. During that time they studied all

---

[41] Brainerd refers to the frustrations of having only a pagan interpreter in a place (Juniata Island) where the traditional religion was intact (ibid., 7:326).

[42] 1 Thessalonians 1:9.

the theological authorities available to them, and they concluded that none of the theological works they could find envisaged the circumstances of Tahiti. They worked out a position for themselves, distinguishing between church members, who had renounced idolatry and declared their allegiance to Jehovah, and communicants, who showed the marks of regeneration.[43]

Protestant missionaries were beginning to discover what their Catholic predecessors had found two centuries earlier, that a theology, however comprehensive, which had been shaped by the experience of Christendom, was not extensive enough or flexible enough to cover the unprecedented situations that arose from the preaching of Christ in the worlds beyond the West. That David Brainerd himself perhaps had some inkling of this is suggested by one curious incident.

Brainerd had no doubt that Satan ruled in the howling wilderness, with complete sway over the Native Americans in their natural state. He speaks of their religious practices as foolish, puerile, and depraved, and of their notions of the divine as confused and indistinct. One day he encountered that religion in its full satanic horror: a shaman advancing toward him, in colored mask with hideous mien, dancing with calabash rattle in hand. "Of all the sights I ever saw, none appeared so frightful, so near akin to what is imagined of 'infernal powers.'"[44]

Involuntarily, he shrank away, even though it was broad daylight and he knew the identity of the person behind the mask. But sitting down with the same shaman, he found in him a reforming prophet who believed he had been called by God and claimed that he had come to know God. His task was to summon his people to repentance. Those people were sinking into alcoholic demoralization because they were forsaking God and the old ways under White influence. Brainerd went through with him some of the themes of Christian teaching; "Now that I like" or "So God has taught me," was the shaman's response on several occasions. Their main item of difference was not over the work of redemption but over the existence of the devil. This, the shaman said, was not to be found in traditional cosmology; he evidently had less difficulty over the work of Christ. "Some of his sentiments seemed very just," Brainerd notes, and he adds, "There was something in his temper and disposition which looked more like true religion than anything I have ever discovered among other heathens."[45]

---

[43] William Ellis, *Polynesian Researches during a Residence of Nearly Eight Years in the Society and Sandwich Islands* (London: Fisher and Jackson, 1831), vol. 2, ch. 2. On Raratonga, see Richard Lovett, *The History of the London Missionary Society 1794–1895*, 1:262ff.

[44] Edwards, *Works*, 7:329–45.

[45] Ibid., 7:330.

One senses a strange fellow-feeling between the reforming shaman and Evangelical missionary, both seeking to turn a people to God, both converted men after their respective fashions, both assured of their divine calling, both outsiders ("precise Zealots," as Brainerd puts it) in their own communities.

Brainerd had lived long enough among the Native Americans to qualify some easy assumptions about the nature and results of the devil's role in the wilderness. He knew that the Native Americans had suffered robbery, dispossession, and exploitation at the hands of his own kinfolk, though his vivid apprehension of the transitoriness of earthly life and the transcendence of the eternal may have blinded him to the depth of the consequent trauma. He could see that the experience of mistreatment by Whites was a serious obstacle to conversion, and he sought to explain the matter in Evangelical terms—such deeds were the work of nominal, not real Christians. After his initial frustrations at having no words for the standard themes of Evangelical preaching, and despite his not acquiring competence in the vernacular himself, he began to break down such abstractions as grace and justification into translatable language, a first step beyond Christendom, a first movement toward living intellectually and theologically on terms set by others.

Here again we see Brainerd's and Edwards's transitional status in the Protestant missionary movement. They stand within the bounds of Christendom and work as agents in Christendom's revival. Brainerd stretches these bounds to the limit as his preaching embraces the most marginal people in Christendom. The movement as it developed was to go much farther. Its historical memory acknowledged its debt to Edwards. The debt to Edwards the theologian, indeed, was scarcely remembered, for it was an inheritance shared with Evangelical theology as a whole, and largely mediated to the mission field through others. What the historical memory retained was the impression of the life, work, and death of young David Brainerd, as Edwards had presented him from his journals. Brainerd was not remembered in the movement as Edwards remembered him, the model of a Christian minister whose ministerial charge happened to be among Native Americans; he was reinterpreted for the new century, a model missionary pioneer of the maritime age of missions.

The resetting of the image is not illegitimate. Brainerd is a transitional figure linking the revival in Christendom with the evangelization of the non-Western world and showing early traces of the way the missionary movement became the learning experience of Western Christianity.

14

Distinguished Visitors

Tiyo Soga and Behari Lal Singh in Europe and at Home

The Rev. Tiyo Soga[1] from South Africa and the Rev. Behari Lal Singh[2] from India were contemporaries, though Singh was somewhat the elder and lived to a greater age. Both were in Europe at around the same time, Soga for a substantial period, Singh primarily as a visitor, though he seems to have kept up his links with Scotland, and to have had family members living there in the later part of the nineteenth century.[3] Both were well educated in Western terms, both fluent, not to say eloquent, in English; both became ministers of Scottish churches, and were recognized as missionaries of those churches. Soga first came to Britain in 1846 as a youth of seventeen, while one of the South African Frontier Wars was in progress. He was then a student at the Lovedale Institution in South Africa.[4] He stayed in Scotland for two

---

[1] On Soga, see J. A. Chalmers, *Tiyo Soga: A Page of Mission History* (Edinburgh: Elliot, 1877); Donovan Williams, *Ufumdisi: A Biography of Tiyo Soga, 1829–1871* (Lovedale, South Africa: Lovedale Press, 1978); M. Gideon Khabela, *The Struggle of the Gods: A Study in Christianity and African Culture* (Lovedale, South Africa: Lovedale Press, 1996). Chalmers was a Scottish missionary colleague of Soga.

[2] I have traced no biography of Behari Lal Singh, despite the obvious interest of his life and career, beyond the entry in William Ewing, ed., *Annals of the Free Church of Scotland* (Edinburgh: T & T Clark, 1914). But see his pamphlet *Leading Incidents Connected with a Missionary Tour in the Gangetic Districts of Bengal* (Calcutta: Baptist Mission Press, 1853).

[3] See a note dated June 4, 2008, in the family history website Ancestry Rootsweb: archiver.rootsweb.ancestry.com/th/read/INDIA/2008-06/1212616839.

[4] The Lovedale Institution was quite new at the time: it had been set up at the Lovedale mission station (established in 1821 by the Glasgow Missionary Society) with a view

years and then returned, now baptized, to his homeland in independent Kaffraria—that is, the area occupied by Xhosa people beyond the limits of the British colony at the Cape—as a mission school teacher. Another two years later, war broke out again, and he took the opportunity to come back to Scotland where he spent the next seven years in the study of arts and divinity and acquired a Scottish wife. He was licensed as a preacher of the United Presbyterian Church of Scotland and ordained as their missionary. No Black South African had hitherto been ordained as a minister of any church; with Soga, Protestant missions in South Africa began to follow the pattern of indigenous ministry already established in West Africa.

By the time of his return the Frontier Wars had changed the shape of Soga's homeland. Emgwali, the mission station that was to be his home for most of the rest of his life, was now within British Kaffraria, a territory ruled from Cape Colony, though retaining traditional chiefly rule at the local level. In colonial terms, Soga was an anomaly in a way he would not have been in West Africa. No other Black African in the Cape or British Kaffraria had such an educational background or such professional status. He could not be readily ignored or patronized by any White man.

Over the years that he had spent in Scotland, his own Xhosa people had been ravaged, not only by the Frontier Wars, among the nastiest in the long record of the little wars of empire, but by the traumatic event of the cattle killing of 1856–57. This had followed an outbreak of bovine tuberculosis, which had been introduced by an imported herd of cattle, and was widely attributed to witchcraft. Cattle were at the heart of Xhosa traditional life; thousands of them were slaughtered in response to an indigenous prophet movement that owed much of its inspiration to biblical sources and Christian preaching. The outcome for Xhosaland was starvation and penury; it also brought an end to effective Xhosa resistance to White expansion.[5] The remainder of Soga's life, curtailed as it was in duration and activity by tuberculosis, was spent in seeking the Christian evangelization of his people and their social and economic amelioration, in the shadow of these devastating experiences. Essentially, he encouraged them to take the path that he himself had taken: Christianity, education, development of skills. This was the path, he argued, to economic betterment, enabling Xhosa people to acquire money, and by that means, acquire land. Any other path would

to the education of a ministry for South Africa. At this stage it was biracial, with White students (including the children of missionaries) as well as Black.
    [5] On the background to the Cattle Killing and its effects, see J. B. Peires, *The Dead Will Arise: Nongqawuse and the Great Xhosa Cattle Killing of 1856–57* (Bloomington: Indiana University Press. 1989).

leave them the clients and servants of the Whites and helplessly dependent on them.

Behari Lal Singh's origins lay in the Punjab, but his father, seeing the way the wind was blowing in India, wanted his sons to have an English education, with government posts to follow. This not being easy to achieve in the Punjab at that time, he moved to Calcutta and entered his sons at the General Assembly's institution there. This was the English language school that, with local assistance from the Hindu reformer Ram Mohun Roy, had been opened by Alexander Duff, the first missionary of the Church of Scotland, with the object of reaching high-caste Hindu youth with Christian influences.

At the General Assembly's institution, Singh received a thoroughly Scottish education, inspired by the arts curriculum of Duff's own University of St. Andrews, shot through with the rational Enlightenment Calvinism that formed Duff's own worldview.[6] Singh, by his own account, at this period of his life was reading the Bible as he would read any other class book; what led him to Christianity was the personal impact, first of Duff and his missionary colleagues, and then of David MacLeod, a Christian East India Company official; a man, said Singh, of utter integrity who, while spending little on himself, laid out his substantial salary in sponsoring the education of such boys as Behari Lal Singh. From the Scots College in Calcutta, Singh went to the government medical college, and thereafter to the job under government that his father had desired for him. But by this time, after much reading of the Bible, both he and his brother had decided to become Christians. Their father did not oppose the step; he, too, had been reading the Bible, and his only objection to Christianity was that its ethical standards were too high for realization. The brothers thus embraced the Christian faith without the family trauma and ostracism suffered by many whose conversion had followed study at the Scots colleges.[7] Behari Lal Singh resigned his government post and offered for missionary service with the Free Church of Scotland.[8] He taught in the church's college in Calcutta, and

---

[6] This is well explored by Ian Maxwell, *Alexander Duff and the Theological and Philosophical Background to the General Assembly's Mission in Calcutta to 1840* (PhD thesis, University of Edinburgh, 1995).

[7] This account of Singh's early life reflects what he says of it in his address to the "Second Missionary Soiree" at the Liverpool Conference on Missions (see below). Secretaries to the Conference, eds., *Conference on Missions Held in 1860 at Liverpool: Including the Papers Read, the Deliberations, and the Conclusions Reached; with a Comprehensive Index Shewing the Various Matters Brought under Review* (London: Nisbet, 1860), 80–85 [hereafter *Conference*].

[8] In 1843 (the year of Singh's baptism) the Disruption brought about a major divi-

then was successively a missionary to the Jews, senior minister in Calcutta, and a missionary to Muslims. In 1868 the Free Church seconded him to the English Presbyterian Mission to open work in an unevangelized area of Bengal. The appointment lasted until his death in 1878.

In 1860, Singh, by then an established figure in the church with seventeen years of service, was in Britain and attended the Conference on Missions held in Liverpool that year.

The Liverpool Conference (or Conference) has had less attention than it deserves,[9] for it is arguably the first international conference on missions in any meaningful sense, and a true ancestor of the World Missionary Conference of Edinburgh 1910. Singh's interventions at the conference reveal him as a perceptive observer of the European Other.

The Conference brought together 126 delegates, representative of most branches of British Protestant missionary activity, the most notable absentees being the Society for the Propagation of the Gospel and the Society for Promoting Christian Knowledge, the old official societies of the Church of England. (Evangelical Anglicans, those of the Church Missionary Society [CMS] in particular, were plentifully represented.) But while most of the participants were British, an international dimension was given to the conference by several representatives of the Basel Mission and several CMS missionaries of continental origin, by one American missionary—and by Behari Lal Singh. To Singh, therefore, it fell to be the voice of the peoples to whom missions were addressed, and in particular the voice of the Christian churches overseas that had arisen from the work of missions. That voice was raised frequently, clearly, and uncompromisingly. The Conference record shows that he often intervened in the debates; he was also a featured speaker at one of the few public meetings (and it may be noted in passing that this is one of the very few places where the Conference record indicates laughter on the part of the audience).

In a response to the Conference's opening paper, he argued that the value of native agency had not yet been understood. Translation work in particular had suffered from an assumption that only expatriate missionaries could be competent translators; translations were needed of greater

---

sion within the Church of Scotland, those withdrawing from the church forming the Free Church of Scotland. Duff and the other Church of Scotland missionaries in India identified with the new body and established a new mission.

  [9] A recent study is Andrew F. Walls, "The 1860 Liverpool Conference on Missions," in *Communities of Faith in Africa and the African Diaspora: In Honor of Dr. Tite Tienou with Additional Essays on World Christianity*, ed. Caseley B. Essamiah and David K. Ngaruiya, 347–60 (Eugene, OR: Pickwick Publications, 2014).

purity and precision than had yet been attained, and this required indigenous translators.[10] Twisting the knife, he added that the same was true of
preaching. A further trenchant contribution from Singh came following
criticism of the Scottish missions for overconcentration on education. Singh
replied that the standards of the Scottish institutions were in fact too low;
they provided a mere smattering of Greek and Hebrew, whereas much more
was needed if Christians were to keep up in debate with learned Hindus
and Muslims. He himself had found it necessary to study with a rabbi and a
classical scholar for that purpose. And not nearly enough Arabic was taught
in mission institutions.[11] Another target of Singh's was Protestant denomi-
nationalism, which he saw as irrelevant in India. Indian Christians did not
ask whether a particular situation represented a better form of theology or
church government than that of another mission, but whether it offered
greater opportunities for usefulness.[12] Singh is even ready to enter unafraid
the sensitive financial topic of the salaries of indigenous mission agents.[13]
One way and another, Behari Lal Singh was as effective as the voice of the
indigenous church as anyone in those circumstances could have been. He
always speaks as a missionary, from within the missionary project, but from
an independent perspective, constantly bringing into view not only the
indigenous contribution to the project, but the potential further contribution, the indigenous resources as yet untapped.

That the voice of the indigenous church at the Conference should be
Indian was fully in line with the ethos of the meeting. India represented
the most considerable investment of the contemporary missionary movement, and for many of the delegates it clearly held the highest interest. It was
the field that the majority of the missionaries, ex-missionaries, and mission
executives who formed the backbone of the Conference knew best; and
the largest group of delegates outside that category were current or former
members of the Indian civil or military establishments. The chairman of the
Conference was an Indian Army general; the secretary had been civil admin-
istrator of Banaras.[14] Further, the Conference met at a time when memories
of the climactic events of 1857–58 were still fresh; the mutiny, the shock
of the atrocities on both sides, the administrative revolution that brought
the winding up of the East India Company and its replacement by direct

---

[10] *Conference,* 26–27.

[11] Ibid., 216–18.

[12] Ibid., 292.

[13] Ibid., 217–18.

[14] See the introduction to the Conference volume (ibid., 1–3) and the list of
members that follows.

British rule over much of India. Evangelical grievances about lukewarm government attitudes to missions remained; the arch-Evangelical Earl of Shaftesbury, who presided over the closing meeting of the Conference, had not long before presided over another meeting, called to discuss the future relations of the British government to religion in India, and had declared there that it was the government's business and duty "boldly and unreservedly to proclaim that it is a Christian government. . . . that it will pursue a Christian course, that it desires that its people should be brought within the knowledge, and if possible within the compass of India Christianity."[15]

Like most contemporary Indian Christians, Behari Lal Singh was an unblushing supporter of British rule in India, believing that, despite its faults, it was the best guarantee of social and educational advance; and he also believed that the spread of Christianity in India would strengthen that rule.[16] Britain as the Other was already manifest in India; whether in India or in Liverpool, Singh could view it as a critical friend.

But Soga's homeland, "Kaffraria," had also undergone traumatic experiences over the same period: recurrent warfare, leading to the inexorable spread of British rule and the extension of the Cape Colony, the apocalyptic excitement that led to the great cattle killing of 1856–57, and the mass starvation that followed. In South Africa, as in India, the power of the European Other had for a short time been threatened, and had then reasserted itself in more complete form, so that it was now beyond immediate challenge. And in South Africa, the Other was present and visible in ways that the vastness and complexity of India sometimes hid. Cape Colony had its own little Europe functioning within its borders, setting up towns, cities, and communities on the European model, sharing the living space with the indigenous and the traditional, but controlling the environment. In South Africa, even more than in India, it might be possible to reject or ignore the Other for a while; but there was no escaping it completely. The options were absorption, subjection, or negotiation.

Behari Lal Singh and Tiyo Soga were, in their different ways, negotiators. They had met the Other at close quarters in Europe, knew it well in its strengths and its weaknesses; they had appropriated what they saw as its strengths, without losing their original identity. Singh could lament the failure of the Scottish colleges to reach the academic standards that

---

[15] *Christianity in India. Proceedings of a public Meeting Held at Exeter Hall . . . to Consider the Future Relations of the British Government to Religion in India* (London: Reed and Parden, [1868]), 5–6. Another speaker at the meeting had declared Britain to be the only conqueror of India not to make its religion known.

[16] See his remarks at the Missionary Soiree, *Conference*, 181.

the missionary task in India required, and could offer to a large assembly of missionaries a compelling critique of aspects of mission practice, doing so as a colleague, not as an outsider. Soga's long acquaintance with Scottish life enabled him to deal confidently with Cape society and to be discriminating in his views of traditional Xhosa society. In the colony he met plenty of crude racism: when he disembarked at Port Elizabeth on his return from Scotland with a White woman on his arm, the couple had been greeted with shouts of "Shame on Scotland!"[17] There was a colonial manifestation of Little Europe, King William's Town, not far from his usual place of residence. There Soga was open to harassment and insult from petty officials who could not bear the sight of a Black man who was, as they put it, a "fine gentleman." (A fruitless complaint by him to the Town Council of King William's Town about such an incident got into the local newspaper.[18])

But Soga had met the Other on its own ground, and concluded that his people would gain by appropriating, as he had done, what was good in the life of Europe, while avoiding the bad and rejecting the dangerous. In this respect, one of his most interesting writings in English (what he published is mostly in Xhosa) is an address he gave to the Cape Town branch of the Young Men's Christian Association (YMCA) in 1866,[19] while he was recuperating in the city after serious illness. We should remember that the audience he was addressing would have been principally, if not entirely, White. The topic was "Some of the Current Popular Opinions and Tendencies of the Times"; the text offers a sustained critique of the "unblushing infidelity" of contemporary European society, as he had met it in Britain.

Soga finds this infidelity in academic circles, instancing the philosophical reconstructions offered by Principal Tulloch[20] of the University of St. Andrews. When applied to theology, Soga argues, these would dismantle the doctrines of the Reformation from whence derived the Evangelical teaching with which he clearly identifies. He is equally scathing about Isaac Taylor[21] and the quest for a new exegetical method that would enable a new

---

[17] Donovan Williams, ed., *The Journal and Selected Writings of the Reverend Tiyo Soga* (Cape Town, South Africa: Balkema for Rhodes University, 1983), 3 [hereafter *Journal and Writings*).

[18] Ibid., 182.

[19] The lecture was reported in full in *The Cape Argus* for June 7, 1866. It is reprinted in ibid., 183–94.

[20] John Tulloch (1823–86), though an influential philosophical and theological liberal, was essentially an establishment figure, a chaplain to Queen Victoria, and later (1876) Moderator of the General Assembly of the Church of Scotland.

[21] Isaac Taylor (1787–1865) was a lay theologian who wrote especially about corrupting factors in Christian history that had produced fanaticism or other unhealthy

way of understanding the Bible—though the new method and the new understanding was still indefinable. What were Christian preachers like himself to say to Africans while this method was being constructed? Were they to suspend their work until the method was ready? He knew what the response among his own people would be. They would say, "Old or new, it is all the same to us, you may now take it all away! We have been suspecting that this thing you said was God's word was only a fabrication of the white man, and this uncertainty is a proof of it!"[22] The idea of inevitable human progress was similarly defective[23]; it took no account of, and gave no consideration to, such areas as Kaffraria.

From the academic and theological, Soga then turns to popular opinion in Britain and to the widespread demands to relax the observance of Sunday. In this connection it is worth reflecting how in the history of African Christianity, the observance of Sunday has been a marker of Christian progress, rather as the degree to which the Ramadan fast has been observed has marked the progress of Islam. Soga sees the degree to which British people were in his day challenging the centrality of Sunday worship as a sign of drift from Christianity itself. He gives as an example the bibulous captain of a ship he traveled on who had clearly found the worship services that the missionaries had provided for the passengers to be a nuisance. But Soga's reflections on Sunday observance led into a much wider critique of British society as he had seen it.

He had witnessed crowded city life, and observed how huge populations were virtually imprisoned for long hours, week after week in factories, warehouses, and shops. Some aspects of the boasted Western civilization, he concludes, resemble the great car of Juggernaut in the callous sacrifice of human life they bring about:

> I would ask my African-born friends[24] here present to go to London, to Edinburgh, to Glasgow, and other great cities of trade. Let them visit the great manufacturing estates—let them watch breakfast,

---

manifestations. It is noteworthy that Soga chooses quite mainstream intellectual figures to demonstrate his perception of a drift from Christian moorings—not, for instance, the translation (by George Eliot) into English of *The Life of Jesus* by D. F. Strauss that had appeared in 1846.

[22] *Journal and Writings,* 189.

[23] It is interesting to find Soga referring in this connection to the American Baptist theologian Horace Bushnell, though with mixed reactions: applauding his portrayal of Christ but fearful when he "diverges from the road"—presumably on eschatology and soteriology.

[24] In the context of the lecture, "African-born" will refer primarily to White men born in South Africa.

dinner and closing hours when their thousands of labourers are relieved of their toil; let them see the pale, sickly, careworn factory girls who have no hope of life but in that imprisonment, and they will thank God for having been born in the free air of the desert.[25]

Soga has been led to this account of industrial Britain by his reflections on Sunday observance. Those in Britain arguing for a dilution of that observance often cited the recreational needs of busy workers. Reflecting on what he had seen of the lives of industrial workers, Soga heartily agreed that they needed to escape from the crippling routine of the factory. They also needed the space that Sunday afforded in order to worship and attend to their souls. These two things should not be incompatible: the solution lay in the hands of the employers, who should be prepared to give their workers adequate time for recreation:

> The guilt in the whole of this question, I humbly submit, lies neither at the door of a rigid orthodoxy nor at the door of the Decalogue; it lies at the door of the commercial world! Nothing, it appears, must stand in the way of its interests. Its laws are as unchangeable as those of the Medes and Persians!
>
> Is it too much to ask the commercial world, by a compact agreed upon for the interests of suffering humanity, either to allow a more frequent and regular recurrence of holidays, or to shorten the hours of labour, or to give one day in the week free? Such propositions of course, are deemed absurd and ruinous![26]

Soga thus finds British society to be defective in its observance of the humane, not to say the Christian ethical standards it professed, and be in real danger of slipping away from its Christian moorings both in doctrine and in practice. His message to the young White South African-born Christians of the YMCA, representatives of that little Europe now at home in Africa, is that they should be bold and articulate in defence of Christian truth and Christian standards.[27]

We can learn much of his message to Xhosa people from his articles in the Xhosa and English language magazine *Indaba*,[28] a periodical addressed to the literate African community influenced by church teachings. In one of

---

[25] *Journal and Writings*, 190.

[26] Ibid.

[27] *Journal and Writings*, 193–94.

[28] New English translations of seven articles that he originally wrote in Xhosa for this magazine are included in *Journal and Writings*.

them he urges them to discriminate when viewing the things that the Whites have brought. Jackets, trousers, hats and shoes are both more comfortable and more efficient than karosses made of animal hide; the now common use of metal ploughs and spades instead of wooden ones has improved our agriculture. But some of the other things that White men insist on peddling, notably their liquor, should be sedulously avoided.[29]

Such discriminating conduct is one of his constant themes. Soga seeks for Xhosaland a selective and controlled relationship with the European Other. This will include a discriminating attachment to the African past as well as a discriminating acceptance of things coming from the West. In a letter to his mission he quotes with approval words he heard in a prayer offered at the opening of a new church: "No good ever came of people who did not give the old its due."[30] His articles in *Indaba* reflect his continuing interest in Xhosa history and tradition.[31] One necessary element in giving the old its due was respect for chiefs, who gave cohesion to Xhosa traditional society. Chiefs, not without reason, often feared that the spread of Christianity would take people away from them and their authority: Soga was anxious to prevent this happening in practice. In his account of the occasion when the prayer just quoted was offered, he tells how the chief, who was not a Christian, was present, and was addressed by the Christians with tender attachment, even when they were appealing to him to abolish the most offensive of traditional customs. He appeals to Scottish history: the attachment of the Highland clans to their chiefs, he argues, had been an important factor in maintaining Scottish patriotism to the present day.

An article in *Indaba* on "Christians and Chiefs"[32] treats both the issue of the respect Christians owe to traditional rulers and the obverse, the attitudes they should take to White people. In this sphere, civility, but not servility, should mark the relationship. Discrimination was necessary here too. White people had their chiefs, and, like traditional rulers, these should be greeted with respect. What was not acceptable was to treat all Whites, regardless of their status, as if they were chiefs; indiscriminate use of the address "Sir" to White people was "very annoying."

---

[29] *Indaba* 1, no. 11 (1863): 166–70; English version in *Journal and Writings,* 167–69.

[30] *Missionary Record of the United Presbyterian Church* (n.s.) 4 no. 66 (1871): 553–55; reprinted in *Journal and Writings,* 132–49 (the quotation is from page 144).

[31] This is especially evident in his articles in each of the first three issues of the paper (translations in *Journal and Writings,* 151–63).

[32] *Indaba* 2, no. 6 (1864): 353–54; translated in *Journal and Writings,* 171–75.

Soga turns to another aspect of community relations in an article in *Indaba* entitled "Mission People and Red People."[33] The latter term designates traditional Xhosa, those outside the sphere of church and school, those who had retained the red ochre body paint that those who took the path of church and school normally eschewed.[34] Soga speaks of the two groups as "the two sections of our people." There were inevitably differences between them, but it was important that Christians should not generate unnecessary divisions, and that fellowship and cooperation should be maintained where possible. It was particularly important, for instance, that Christians maintain the duties of hospitality; it was scandalous if Christians left "red" people stranded on a journey, without a meal or a place to sleep.

Soga's attitude to the European Other, whether in its Scottish or its South African expressions, is one of selective appropriation. It does not involve total rejection of the Xhosa past, but the selective incorporation of the Other into it. This is strikingly to be seen in the vision of the future of Africa expressed in a long letter to a Cape newspaper in 1865.[35] The letter is a reply to an article in the paper that had predicted the doom of the African—or specifically the "Kaffir"—race that had so manifestly rejected civilization. Soga proposes an alternative view, rooted in the history of Africa, the teachings of Scripture, and Christian missionary activity. He begins with a gentle indication of the inadequacy of the term "Kaffir" for ethnographic purposes[36] and then moves into a historical demonstration of African durability:

> Africa was of God given to the race of Ham. I find the Negro from the days of the Assyrians downwards, keeping his "individuality" and "distinctiveness" amid the wreck of empires, and the revolution

---

[33] *Indaba* 2, no. 10 (1864): 424–26; translated in *Journal and Writings,* 175–77.

[34] The prophet–poet–preacher Ntsikana, whom Soga calls "the first notable Caffre convert" (*Journal and Writings,* 86), though he did not embrace mission Christianity, nor receive baptism through the missions, nevertheless washed off the red ochre in an act of obedience to the presence that he believed controlled him. Soga used Ntsikana's hymns, with their rich traditional imagery, and they clearly influenced his own hymn-writing.

[35] *King William's Town Gazette and Kaffrarian Banner,* May 11, 1865; reprinted in *Journal and Writings,* 178–82. Soga's preliminary thinking on the matter appears in his journal for April 25, 1865 (*Journal and Writings,* 38–40). On the whole issue, see Williams, *Ufumdisi,* chap. 7.

[36] Soga accepts the term—which he spells "Kafir"—for himself and told his mixed-race children to accept it proudly (*Journal and Writings,* 6). But in his letter to the newspaper he is showing how simplistic and imprecise is the language about African peoples employed by the author of the article. Soga indicates the ethnic kinship of the inhabitants of Kaffraria with peoples all the way into Central Africa.

of ages. I find him keeping his place among the nations, and keeping his home and country. I find him opposed by nation after nation, and driven from his home. I find him enslaved—exposed to the vices and the brandy of the white man. . . . I find him exposed to all these disasters, and yet living—multiplying and never extinct.[37]

Now, indeed, with "the prevalence of Christian and philanthropic opinions on the rights of man," Africans uprooted by slavery were returning to Africa, and, as the Republic of Liberia demonstrated, taking Christianity and civilization with them. All historical evidence opposes the extinction theory.[38]

Nor is that theory compatible with the promises of Scripture, which make clear that "Ethiopia shall soon stretch her hands to God." As for civilization, this is a gradual process, the product of generations, indeed centuries: no people has ever moved suddenly and completely to embrace it. And in South Africa, only the missionaries, with their very limited financial resources, have even attempted the hard work of education. "Would that the Government of Great Britain, the Father of its many people, would come forward with aids worthy of the Greatness."[39] Hitherto Africa had received mixed blessings from its contacts with the West. Far from being doomed, all that Africa now needed to preserve and renew and uplift its life was "the Gospel by itself and Christian civilization by itself."[40]

A South African historian has identified in Soga the dawn of Black Consciousness in South Africa.[41] The views expressed, however, fit very well the Christian pan-Africanism being expressed in this period in West Africa, and notably in Sierra Leone, which in the 1860s could claim a higher degree of literacy, and a higher proportion of children at school than many European nations. Soga, like the Sierra Leonean J. A. B. Horton, can look forward to a Christian Africa, which will play its own part within the comity of nations.[42]

---

37 Ibid., 180.
38 Ibid., 180–81.
39 Ibid., 181–82.
40 Ibid., 182.
41 Donovan Williams, in a note in ibid., 178.
42 See James Africanus Beale Horton, *West African Countries and Peoples, British and Native . . . and a Vindication of the African Race* (London, 1868, reprinted with introduction by George Shepperson, Edinburgh: Edinburgh University Press, 1969). Horton is discussed by Robert W July, *The Origins of Modern African Thought* (London: Faber and Faber, 1968). Cf. Andrew Walls, "Meditations among the Tombs: Changing Patterns of Identity in Freetown, Sierra Leone," in *Rethinking African History*, ed. Charles Jedrej, Kenneth King, and Jack Thompson, 489–504 (Edinburgh: Centre of African Studies, University of Edinburgh, 1997).

Soga, it will be noted, identifies *two* needs of Africa, not one: "the Gospel by itself and Christian civilization by itself." He does not identify the gospel with Christian civilization, even though he desires the latter to spread among the Xhosa. The sad fact of Xhosa experience had been that gospel and civilization had alike been introduced to them with additives of European origin.

Soga and Singh begin their thinking with their appropriation of the Christian faith. The fact that Christianity is associated with the European Other is incidental: as we have seen, Soga believed that Britain was, or might well be, slipping away from that faith; and Singh could offer robust criticism of European Christian practice. Both recognize Christianity as the source of (but not as identifiable with) other desirable developments, intellectual, cultural, and technical, that Soga includes under the head of civilization, and Singh thinks of in terms of social and educational advance. In neither case does embrace of this involve wholesale rejection of the past of their nation; they do not obliterate that past, but refine it.

We no longer have a word in English to express what they and the Evangelical usage of their day meant by civilization, with its historical, cultural, literary, technological, and religious dimensions. These dimensions meant that "civilization" was seen as improving agriculture, enhancing living standards, encouraging intellectual and aesthetic activity, reducing violence, protecting family life, and diffusing Christian influences. Singh and Soga had appropriated that discourse and lived in that world of ideas, not as strangers or visitors, but as proprietors. Perhaps the nearest word in contemporary discourse is "development"; but that is a miserably attenuated and sanitized concept compared with theirs, which, like their Christian faith, remained undiminished by the less than satisfactory aspects of the Other that they encountered in Europe, in India, and in Africa.

15

Western Christians in China

A Chapter in a Long History

Christianity is of its nature multicultural. The church during the period of the New Testament writings maintained two distinct cultural models simultaneously. One, the older, retained the Jewish law, with its regulations on food avoidances, ablutions, festivals, and ritual circumcision of male infants; the other required none of these things but revised normal Hellenistic social and family life by introducing moral institutions inspired by the figure and teaching of Christ. The New Testament writings insist that both these contrasting lifestyles were necessary to the proper functioning of the Christian body; they were representations of the life of Christ in different segments of social reality. As a result, Christianity has always been global in principle; early Christianity spread eastward, westward, and southward, and in its first six centuries its main centers lay in Asia and Africa as well as in Europe. Its career has not been progressive, a steady growth from a permanent center, but serial, from centers that change over time; it has often withered and sometimes died in areas that once formed its centers of apparent strength while finding fresh growth in areas previously little touched by its influence. Christianity has no permanent geographical or cultural center or form of expression; at different times it has been associated with different areas of the world and different cultures and languages. Indeed, its history, and on occasion its very survival, has been determined by cross-cultural diffusion. Had it not crossed the cultural frontier from the Judaic to the Hellenistic world, it could hardly have survived the destruction of the Jewish state after AD 70. Had it not made the transition from the Greco-Roman world to those the Romans called barbarians, it might not have survived its eclipse by Islam in the Middle East and North Africa. Within the twentieth century the recession from the Christian faith

217

that took place in Europe and North America occurred at the same time as a great accession to it in Africa and some parts of Asia. As a result, the majority of Christians today are Africans, Asians, and Latin Americans, and that proportion is increasing year by year. It seems clear that the future of Christianity will increasingly be determined by developments in Asia and Africa, and that its shape will increasingly be influenced by its interaction with the cultures of Asia and Africa.

Christianity first came to China in the seventh century of the Common Era, about the same period as it came to many of the peoples then inhabiting England; indeed the second T'ang emperor was studying the writings brought to him by Arab missionaries at almost the same time as the king of Northumbria was considering whether to abandon the traditional cult of his people in favor of Christianity. The imperial decree of 638 CE permitting Christianity to spread in the empire seems to imply that the emperor found Christianity broadly in line with Confucian principles. The decree declares that both the expression of the Dao and the form of the Sage are environmentally conditioned. Which Christian writings led the emperor (and the decree declares that the documents were studied "in the private apartments") to this conclusion? The evidence suggests that the documents submitted to him included a life of Christ and a text of the Sermon on the Mount. The latter could indeed be seen to present Christ as Sage, and might well convince the emperor that Christian teaching would not undermine traditional teaching on society and the family. But how were Christians to declare that Christ was more than Sage, how show the transcendent significance of the divine Son? It seems that they adopted categories from Buddhist discourse, bestowing on Christ such titles as the World Honored One. Later representatives of the Christian faith in China were to find the same difficulty in translating that faith into Chinese terms. The classical tradition afforded a splendid framework for Christian moral teaching, but provided no vocabulary to convey the full identity of the Christ who stood at the heart of that faith. But a new idea can only be conveyed in terms of ideas already present. It was Buddhism, to the official mind a foreign religion and often seen as sectarian with explosive social connotations, that supplied the Christians with vocabulary and analogies.[1]

Western missionaries, both Catholic and Protestant, were to encounter this situation. The missionary movement is a single story from the sixteenth to the twentieth century, with a Catholic phase based in Southern Europe. This was followed by a Protestant phase beginning in Germany and Central

---

[1] An account, with a convenient translation of the imperial decree, is given by John Foster, *The Church of the T'ang Dynasty* (London: SPCK, 1939).

Europe, gaining new impetus from British and other northern European (and later American) participation, followed by a phase in which Catholics and Protestants from all over the West participated. Looked at from one point of view the missionary movement is part of the Great European Migration that began around 1500 CE and continued until the middle of the twentieth century, bringing millions of people out of Europe into the lands beyond Europe, and setting up the world order that may now be in the process of implosion. But the missionary movement was always a semidetached component of the migration. Though the Western powers sometimes sought to co-opt it, and often made use of its work, they as often found it a nuisance or even an obstruction. The initiatives for the movement, and the resources that maintained it, came from radical movements within Christianity with aims and priorities quite independent of those of the state; while it is arguable that the roots of European secularization lie in colonialism.

China had a distinctive role in the history of the missionary movement. The Catholic story was interrupted by the Rites Controversy and the response of the Emperor Kang Xi,[2] leaving Catholic Christianity in China to operate underground until missionary enterprise began again in the 1840s. At this point the Protestant mission enterprise, a tiny presence until that time, rapidly expanded.[3] The sudden opening of China to missionary activity after 1842 put immense strain on mission resources; it took place before the great wave of missionary enthusiasm in the last two decades of the nineteenth century. There was general recognition that the evangelization of China was a necessary new commitment and that it would be a particularly demanding task; mission agencies accordingly tended to allocate the best equipped of their candidates to the China field, as they had hitherto allocated them to India. With the acceleration of the missionary movement late in the nineteenth century, missionary involvement in China grew exponentially. The institutional infrastructure grew as nowhere else: Christian colleges, universities, hospitals, even fully equipped Christian medical schools, appeared across China.[4] As this process reached its height, so did China's turmoil; the first half of the twentieth century saw the collapse of the empire, the rise of the republic, the civil wars, the Japanese wars, World War II, civil war again. Over this period, Chinese public attitudes to the

[2] See Andrew C. Ross, *A Vision Betrayed: The Jesuits in Japan and China 1542–1742* (Edinburgh: Edinburgh University Press and Maryknoll, NY: Orbis Books, 1994).

[3] On the whole modern story of Christianity in China, see Daniel H. Bays, ed., *Christianity in China from the Eighteenth Century to the Present* (Palo Alto, CA: Stanford University Press, 1996).

[4] See, e.g., Daniel H. Bays and Ellen Widmer, eds., *China's Christian Colleges: Cross-Cultural Connections 1900–1950* (Palo Alto, CA: Stanford University Press, 2009).

West and to missions as the most ubiquitously visible face of the West went through every gradation from the hysterical antiforeignism of the Boxers to apparent readiness to welcome the missions as mediators in the process of modernization.

When the World Missionary Conference met in Edinburgh in 1910 and reviewed the state of the Christian gospel across the world, its report on China was broadly optimistic; the heavy missionary investment in China seemed amply justified. A generation or so later, missions, still catching their breath after the dislocation of World War II, were facing the effective closure of all their operations in China and the withdrawal of all missionary personnel. Many were searching their hearts as to what it all meant, and some were writing books about it with such titles as *Christian Missions and the Judgment of God.*[5]

We can now see that the missionary movement from the West was a transitional episode in Christian history; a bridge between a period when Western Christianity was the representative, the normative Christianity, and a period when the center of gravity of Christianity has moved toward Africa, Asia, and Latin America. In considering this bridge period in relation to China, I propose to look at several missionaries who between them span the period from the beginning of the nineteenth century to the middle of the twentieth—the whole lifespan, in effect, of Protestant missions in China, considering what each was trying to do, and how far that relates to the issue of the authenticity and the rootedness of Chinese Christianity. In counterpoint to these are placed the stories of certain Chinese with whom they were associated.

All my representative missionaries were Europeans (though China was the American mission field par excellence) and all but one were British. It was stated earlier that the missionary movement, Catholic and Protestant alike, was especially the province of radical Christians, those desiring an exceptional degree of Christian commitment. The form of radicalism most characteristic of European Protestantism during the early phases of the missionary movement was to be found in the circles called Pietist on the continent and Evangelical in Britain. Pietist and Evangelical had much in common. Their distinguishing feature was less a specific set of doctrines than a distinction between "real" Christianity and the "formal" or "nominal" Christianity characteristic of "Christendom," Christian civil society as it existed in Western Europe. They saw the Christian profession of mainstream society—what the Anglican Evangelical politician

---

[5] David M. Paton [a former China missionary], *Christian Missions and the Judgment of God* (London: SCM Press, 1953).

William Wilberforce called "the prevailing religious system of professed Christians in the upper and middle classes of this country"—as deeply defective. "Real" Christianity involved personal experience as well as intellectual belief and behavioral conformity. In practice that experience often included a period of personal crisis with a deep sense of sinfulness followed by a liberating realization of forgiveness as a result of Christ's atonement and a heightened desire to live a life pleasing to God. Such a progress marked the typical "Evangelical conversion," and Evangelical faith was tied into social criticism of a nominally Christian civil society. Evangelicals produced a high proportion of the early missionaries and a good proportion of all missionaries, and many, especially in the early period, took the paradigm of "Evangelical conversion" as the sign of authentic Christian experience. As missionaries, they were not simply seeking adhesion to Christianity; they were seeking Evangelical conversion, that would reflect something like the experience of conversion they themselves had known. They therefore stressed human sinfulness, Christ's atonement through the cross, the need for Christians to live holy lives. Sometimes, as occurred in some Pacific island societies, a mass response to Christianity would follow missionary proclamation, with every sign of sincerity but without evident conviction of sin, and missionaries were forced to revise the paradigm. But in China there was no early mass response (save in the Taiping movement, to be considered later) and no evident reason to seek a new paradigm; especially as from time to time the Evangelical message did find resonance in nineteenth-century Chinese society. This is illustrated in the experience of Robert Morrison and Liang Fa.

Robert Morrison and the Linguistic Hurdle

Robert Morrison,[6] the first, and for a long time the only Protestant missionary to China, was born in a Scottish family in the north of England in 1782. Like many British missionaries of his generation, he came from the class of skilled craft workers; his father made wooden frames used to give shape to boots, and Morrison became his father's apprentice. He started work early in life, with little opportunity for formal education, but following his Evangelical conversion in teenage years he devoted himself to intense study. Such activity was a common accompaniment of Evangelical

---

[6] On Morrison, see Christopher Hancock, *Robert Morrison and the Birth of Chinese Protestantism* (London: Clark-Bloomsbury, 2008); *Memoirs of the Life and Labours of Robert Morrison DD... by His Widow* (London: Longman, 1839), 2 volumes, is still useful.

religion in this period; the first mark of an Evangelical was the scrupulous use of time, the abandonment of trifling pursuits. Some words of Morrison's widow reflect this:

> The cordial reception of Christianity is as favorable to general improvement as it is essential to spiritual character. It elevates at the same time as it purifies the mind. The whole field of investigation which it opens inspires the love of knowledge.

Contemporaries saw Evangelical religion as stimulating the intellect and giving a thirst for knowledge. Thus missionary candidates, though often coming from a sector of society that had not received much formal education, often underwent a strenuous search for learning in order to fit themselves for missionary service. Candidates' papers of the early missionary societies regularly lament among the sins of youth, the frittering away of time, and the neglect of the duty to improve one's talents. The young Robert Morrison certainly did not fritter away time. He schooled himself to read while walking, so as not to waste time on the way to work. Then he realized he could save still more time if he took his bed to the workshop. He learned shorthand to enable himself to take notes rapidly. He went to classes in Latin for an hour a day, starting work an hour earlier to compensate. It is hardly surprising that all his life he suffered from headaches. In later years he expressed two regrets: that he had not had access to more books in his early years, and that missionaries in general did not have all the books they needed in order to be fully efficient.

When about twenty years of age Morrison offered for the Presbyterian ministry, and early in 1807, while still studying for the ministry, he approached the London Missionary Society with a view to service in South Africa. He was accepted and assigned to China, with a commission from the society's directors to translate the Scriptures into Chinese.

The commission displays the extraordinary ambition and confidence of the early missionary movement. A more experienced mission leadership might well have concluded that such an assignment was out of the question; for how could it possibly be carried out? China allowed no foreigners on her soil other than licensed traders, and these were restricted to the "factories" or trading posts in certain ports. British trading interests in China were a monopoly of the East India Company (or Company), which in India had developed a fear of missions bordering on paranoia, and was more likely to be obstructive than helpful in China. And the Qing government impeded foreigners learning the language; no one was permitted to teach it, nor might Chinese books be exported or sold to foreigners. As to learning Chinese in Britain, there were no facilities whatever. As far as anyone knew, the one British person who knew the language served the East India Company in China.

Nevertheless, Morrison was appointed to China, and set himself to learn Chinese. The British Museum, he found, had two Chinese manuscripts, a harmony of the four gospels and a translation of the Acts and Pauline epistles, both the work of Jesuit missionaries and belonging to the seventeenth century. He set to work to copy them, character by character—without, of course, having any idea of the sounds they represented. He then found that the Royal Society, the nation's chief scientific body, held a Chinese–Latin manuscript dictionary, six hundred pages long, again of Jesuit origin, and set about copying this also. All this time he was undertaking other studies: attending a London hospital to get some knowledge of medicine and Greenwich Observatory in view of the well-known Chinese interest in astronomy.

Then came an extraordinary opportunity to learn more: the arrival in Britain of a young Chinese visitor, Yong Sam Tak. The two young men were introduced, but do not seem to have taken to each other. With the ideas each had of the barbarous state of the other's nation, it could hardly be otherwise. Morrison later said that he learned little Chinese through this early encounter; but he did get experience of culture clash and an insight into the lurking dangers in conflicting codes of etiquette. In after years they met again, in China, and Morrison then found Yong Sam Tak a helpful friend in need.

For Morrison, though with much difficulty, did get to China. The East India Company, which controlled British access to China, refused to transport a missionary. So Morrison took a ship for New York, and someone in the mission network there knew Secretary of State Madison, and by this means Morrison got to the port then known as Canton, and now as Guangzhou, and took up residence in the American trade factory.

The American traders were no more pleased than the British to have a missionary in their midst. Morrison's way was strewn with pitfalls. Seeking identification with Chinese people, he adopted Chinese dress, grew his nails long and his hair in a queue—and was denounced as a spy. He shaved his hair, pared his nails and donned the black coat of a Presbyterian minister—and was denounced as a missionary. The only form of dress that would attract no suspicion was the white suit and straw hat of a licensed foreign trader. How galling for this earnest missionary to appear to deny the position of a preacher of the gospel that in fact he gloried in. The word went around in the port that he was very wealthy, since he did no trading. He tried to justify his place in the factory by offering to act as their chaplain; but everyone was too busy to come to services. Morrison soon realized that he was outstaying his welcome in the American factory, and he moved into a disused building.

His situation now was dire. He had no status in the country; he belonged to no one. He had come to China desiring to preach the gospel, but if he attempted to do so, he would certainly be ejected. Or, he wondered, was this simply the voice of cowardice? He was by temperament depressive, and he agonized over his vocation as a missionary. But his mental strife always led him back to the duty to learn Chinese in order to translate the Scriptures. He plodded on. He was able to acquire Chinese books, though their sale to foreigners was forbidden, and he had to hide them when anyone came. After a couple of years he had a library of 1,220 volumes on law, history, religion, language, and medicine. All this cost money, more money than the Missionary Society had reckoned on. Morrison offered to cut down on living expenses to compensate.

He got some help with the spoken language; a Chinese Roman Catholic convert proved especially valuable, and Yong Sam Tak resumed the acquaintance they had begun in England and put him in touch with other assistants in speaking and writing. Gradually, as he combined his various sources, he was able to piece together a knowledge of Chinese. He learned of the two main spoken forms of the language, Mandarin and Cantonese, and their differences. He learned something of the regional dialects of South China. He learned that city speech was different from country speech. And he applied what he learned to his central task of translating the Scriptures, using the transcription of the old Jesuit partial version—quite a good translation, he decided—that he had made in the days when he had had no idea what the characters meant or how they sounded. Day after day he labored, staying in his room to avoid attracting attention, while using every opportunity to converse with Chinese people, and always lamenting his inability to do more. All that early discipline of maximizing study time and note taking now paid dividends. His knowledge of the language clearly surpassed that of Europeans who had lived in China much longer—so much so that the East India Company that had refused him passage, countenance, or protection now offered him the post of Company translator. After some hesitation, he accepted.

By this strange route the missionary became part of the Western commercial presence—a semidetached part still, for he had little in common with most of the Company traders and officials; "a distant civility" is how he describes his relations with them. The advantages of the appointment were immense, the chief being that he now had a legal status for residence in China. He got opportunities for travel that would have come in no other way; accompanying an ambassador from the British government to Beijing, for instance, and the chance of a long, carefully recorded journey by river boat. He also had a comfortable salary, which relieved the mission of his support; a burdened mission secretary noted that Morrison, with his book buying, cost more than was usually allowed for an unmarried missionary. And the salary allowed him to marry the daughter of a visiting Irish family. The letters of the time reflect the early happiness of the union. Then comes the birth of a child, and soon afterward, its death, and then the reader is conscious of something wrong, until it becomes plain from the bleak, understated writing that Mary Morrison is sinking into postnatal depression and mental breakdown.

Such was the personal background against which much of Morrison's translating was done. Plodding on through the domestic shadows he produced a grammar of Chinese. And then his version of the New Testament was published, and the alliance of mission and trade briefly disintegrated. Though the Company knew quite well what he had been working on when not translating for them, they were embarrassed when it became public. They went through the formalities of dismissing him—but could not afford to lose him. Completion of the New Testament was the signal to begin work on the Old. But Morrison now had wider ambitions. He persuaded his missionary society to set up an Anglo-Chinese College in Malacca (now Melaka in Malaysia). Many Chinese were settled there, while preserving links with the homeland. Morrison envisaged European and Chinese students living together, studying English and Chinese, and a mission press that would produce Christian literature in Chinese, much of which would be directed to China. Malacca would be a China mission in waiting, preparing the personnel and the literature against the time when direct mission work would be possible and meanwhile making use of the connections between Malacca and China. The missionary movement, as represented by Morrison, understood the significance of the overseas Chinese better than did the Qing government.

In his early years in China Morrison devoured Chinese books of any kind he could lay his hands on. But he soon realized the place that the classics held in Chinese consciousness, and especially the reverence for the words of Confucius. "In reading with me the Four Books," he wrote, "they [his informants] seem quite enraptured." He set himself to discover the source of this rapture, but found these ancient texts almost impossible to penetrate:

> The very particles, moreover, which in other books are mere expletives, are here full of meaning; and there is in the reasoning of the philosopher, they affirm, a depth which requires the utmost sagacity to fathom, and a fullness that demands a long paraphrase to unfold.

As he wrestled with the obscure old texts, Morrison recognized that the moral teaching they contained was indeed excellent. But his Calvinist training and his Evangelical reflexes conditioned him against moralistic preaching as offering no salvation. He sought to impress upon his Chinese conversation partners the barrenness of even the best moral system without Christ. His informants were not impressed by the implication that other nations had something of value that China lacked:

> The Celestial Empire has every thing in itself that is desirable either to possess or to know. As the most learned never acquire the whole of the literature of China, why concern themselves about that which is exotic? With regard to religion and morality, the depths of knowledge contained in the Four Books have never been fathomed; and, till that be done, it is folly to attend to any other.

In another illuminating passage, Morrison describes how he sought to impress on a Confucian who was denouncing the Buddhist sects that Confucians lacked religion and Buddhists lacked morality, while Christ combined morality and religion to perfection. Next day he overheard someone ask the same Confucian what the foreign religion was like. "It is like Buddhism," was the reply.

Morrison had arrived in China in 1807; he died there in 1834. His saw his work as laying foundations. Fully sharing the Protestant consensus that the Scriptures were the foundation on which Christianity would arise in China, he devoted himself to linguistic scholarship, acquired by unremitting application and severe self-discipline. The first object of those solitary years had been that pioneer translation of the New Testament. Then, with the help of his first colleague and the Malacca base, came the complete Bible that had been the task assigned in his original commission. There was a pioneer grammar, to reduce for his successors the frustration and misery that he had known of navigating the language as an apparently trackless waste. There were many tracts, service books, statements of Christian teaching. There was a *Review of China for Philological Purposes*, covering topics such as chronology, geography, government, calendar and festivals, and religion. There was a Cantonese vocabulary. And there was a multi-volume Chinese dictionary.

The dictionary is an extraordinary work. The first part has three volumes and more than 2,700 pages, and lists 40,000 Chinese characters. The explanations of some of these take up several pages. Where the words relate to social customs, a description of the custom is provided. Where they indicate the names of celebrated persons, such as Confucius or Mencius, a biography follows. The entry on government officials describes their grades and functions. This is not just a dictionary; it is an encyclopedia of China.

The second, more philological part has two volumes, lists 12,680 Chinese symbols with their different forms, with indications of the Mandarin and Cantonese pronunciations. It also gives the rendering, where available, of the manuscript Latin dictionary. There is a collection of Chinese names for stars and constellations and a separate listing of terms used in philosophy and metaphysics, science, history, and commerce. And the third part, itself five hundred pages long, gives English words and phrases and their Chinese equivalents.

In 1824 Morrison took his first and only home leave. He had a period of celebrity and acclaim: several universities bestowed honorary doctorates on this man who had never attended university, and the Royal Society from whose library the young missionary had copied the old Chinese manuscript, elected him a fellow. But Morrison's great object during his leave was to establish in the West the new studies he had pioneered. Indeed, he wanted all the languages and cultures of Asia to be studied; and he campaigned for the setting up of a Language Institute (or Institute) in London, with the objects of spreading the gospel (intending missionaries would be able to study there without charge) and of diffusing "useful knowledge."

There was an enthusiastic response to the idea. A constitution was devised, a committee (carefully representative of the denominations) appointed, eminent persons agreed to be vice presidents (including William Wilberforce, already vice president of every society under heaven). Morrison undertook to teach Chinese at the Language Institute until his return to China; a Baptist missionary taught Bengali, a friendly retired East India Company official undertook Sanskrit. And Morrison presented to the Institute his library of Chinese books, acquired at such cost and danger. But after Morrison's return to China the Institute languished, and not all its eminent vice presidents could maintain it. It was quietly wound up, and a saddened Morrison learned that there was now no one to use his library.

Morrison died before China was opened to missionary activity. Malacca was still a China mission in waiting. All his life he had known hard, grinding intellectual labor; for most of it he saw little but frustration and disappointment. But he completed the seemingly impossible task for which he was appointed; he had translated the Scriptures. His pioneering version was only the beginning, not the climax of the Bible translation into Chinese; but by initiating translation of the Christian Scriptures he had opened the possibility of Chinese appropriation of Christianity, placing the sources at Chinese disposal. He had also given a new dimension to the relations between China and the West and he had incidentally opened up a new branch of scholarship for the Western academy.

Liang Fa:
Personal and Corporate Sin

Morrison saw few Chinese become Christians during his lifetime, but one of the first, Liang Fa, shows how Morrison's standard Evangelical preaching of sin and salvation, formed against the background of Christendom, a Christian society that was not Christian enough, could find response in the very different situation of Qing, China.

Liang Fa[7] was born about 1786 in a village near Guangzhou. He received four years schooling and got a little Confucian learning, studying the basic classical texts through the morality books. At the heart of this morality lay the Five Relations: subject to monarch, child and parent, marriage partner and marriage partner, servant and master, friend and friend. He would have learned *li*, decorum, and the cardinal virtues; he would have learned to shun the vices of gambling, drunkenness, sexual license, murder, theft, and envy.

Liang had to leave school because of poverty, and went off to Guangzhou, where he fell into the vices he had learned from the morality books to renounce. He became a block cutter for a printer, and cut blocks for Morrison's New Testament. He cut them so well that Morrison offered him a post at the printing press in Malacca. Far from the vicious setting of Guangzhou, Liang wrestled with the problem of morality. He was frustrated by moral impotence, plagued by the sense of guilt at his breaches of the Five Relations. He went to a Buddhist temple and begged the merciful Guan Lin to intercede. A monk told him to overcome his guilt by building up merit, and when this did not satisfy, to meditate quietly and chant the sutras. But Liang wanted something more active. All this time he was listening to the missionaries, though not liking all he heard. He was also reading Morrison's New Testament. There he found Christian teaching reinforcing the Five Relations, but anchoring them in a filial relationship to God. The idea of divine Fatherhood, of being a child of God, actively venerating his Father, took hold of him. The root of filial relationship lay in the worship of one God. Human sins could indeed be (as the monk had told him) outweighed by merit, but the only merit sufficient was that which Christ had obtained by his sacrifice, and moral impotence could be overcome by the action of the Holy Spirit. Liang was moving into a Trinitarian theology. He turned to Christianity not to repudiate the ideals of the Chinese classical moral teaching, but to achieve them.

---

[7] On Liang Fa, see P. Richard Bohr, "Liang Fa's Quest for Moral Power," in *Christianity in China: Early Protestant Missionary Writings*, ed. Suzanne Wilson Barnett, 35–46 (Cambridge, MA: Harvard University Press, 1985).

Liang became the first Protestant pastor. He also became a volumi-
nous Christian writer. He had embraced Christianity as an answer to a
quest that had begun in the Chinese tradition, in both its Confucian and
Buddhist elements. The new component in his outlook, coming from
outside the Chinese tradition, was active monotheism, the relationship—
a relationship analogous to the Five Relations—with one God. Liang's
writings stress the Fall, which reflects human rejection of filiality to God.
This has affected all human beings since, and China most of all. Liang,
though responding to the stress on the personal sinfulness characteristic
of British Evangelical missionaries, is deeply aware of the deep corruption of Chinese society. Like some of the Buddhist sects, Christianity
appealed to some Chinese who were dissatisfied with the existing order,
and did not think that the celestial empire necessarily possessed all the
resources for a happy state.

It was as author of the omnibus tract—several tracts in one—entitled *Good Words to Admonish the Age*, that Liang had a major impact on
Chinese history. The tract provided Hong Xiuquan, "the heavenly King,"
with the concept and the vocabulary that empowered the Taiping rebellion against the Qing, which took control of much of the south and east of
China and set up an alternative government there in the crucial years that
followed the European invasion and the treaty of 1842. Liang's biblically
based expositions of the sins of China rang true with Hong, after his years
of frustration with government and the examination system. When Liang
quotes Isaiah, "Your country has been devastated, your cities lowered to
the ground, foreigners take over your land and bring everything to ruin,"
it seemed that this ancient sage was prophesying the fate of Guangzhou.
When Liang writes of the heavenly beings announcing at the birth of Jesus
"glory to the highest God of heaven (Shangdi) and on earth Great Peace
(Taiping), and goodwill toward humanity," that vision of Great Peace, and
its association with the active worship of the Highest God of heaven, filled
Hong's mind.

He had, of course, received his own vision of his divine election, perhaps
in a shamanic trance, many years before; but it was Liang's account of Christian faith, Liang's marshalling of the Christian Scriptures, Liang's biblical
analysis of the sins of China, that provided Hong with the key to his vision.
It led him to form the God Worshippers' Society, which became the nucleus
of the Taiping movement. The dynamic of Taiping lay in its vigorous monotheism. The course of the Taiping movement shows that aspects of the
Christian message fell on fertile soil in south and east China. In any consideration of the question whether Christianity can authentically take root in

China, some thought must be given to the Taiping rebellion, which many missionaries found an embarrassment.

But first we must return to the missionaries.

James Legge and Chinese Culture

The learned world gradually awoke to the academic significance of Morrison's work. It was some years before a British university established the teaching of Chinese, and it was not Oxford or Cambridge, but the learned institution, University College, London, that took up the newest academic subject in 1837. The first professor was, inevitably, a missionary, Samuel Kidd, who had learned Chinese in Malacca using Morrison's materials, and taught in Morrison's Anglo-Chinese College.

One of Kidd's first students was James Legge,[8] born in the little West Aberdeenshire town of Huntly in 1815, when Morrison was still engaged in his early translations. Unlike Morrison, Legge had the advantage of an excellent classical education at one of Aberdeen's two universities. He offered for missionary service with Morrison's London Missionary Society, studied Chinese with Kidd, and in 1839 was appointed to the Anglo-Chinese College in Malacca. But Malacca's time as China mission in waiting was nearly over. Within three years of Legge's arrival there the Opium War opened China to liberalized trade, and the missions rushed to exploit for the gospel the new situation that the Western powers had created for trade. The Anglo-Chinese College moved from Malacca to Hong Kong, the new British colony, and Legge moved with it. He was to be in Hong Kong for the next thirty-three years. He returned to Britain in 1876, when he was already past sixty, to become the first professor of Chinese at the University of Oxford, and remained there, pursuing scholarship to the last, until his death in 1897. This may sound an uneventful, if industrious, life. In fact, Legge was responsible for transforming the understanding of China in academic circles; and his object in doing so was essentially missionary.

In seeing his essential task as the translation of the Scriptures for China, Morrison was entirely in line with the core convictions of the Protestant missionary movement. His career shows that this task was by no means a

---

[8] On Legge, see Helen Edith Legge, *James Legge, Missionary and Scholar* (London: Religious Tract Society, 1904); Norman Girardot, *The Victorian Translation of China: James Legge's Oriental Pilgrimage* (Los Angeles: University of California Press, 2002); Lauren Pfister, *Striving for 'The Whole Duty of Man': James Legge and the Scottish Protestant Encounter with China* (Frankfurt am Main, Germany: Peter Lang, 2002), 2 vols.

straightforward one; it raised issues that never crossed the minds of the mission directors who appointed him in 1807. We noted that Morrison found the ancient Chinese texts particularly difficult, while he recognized that Chinese people found in them a depth and significance beyond his reach. Reading Morrison on Confucius, or on his attempts to speak about Christ to Confucians, one has the sense that he feels he is missing something dear to Chinese hearts. It is the achievement of James Legge that he identified that feature, and opened it to wider view, more fully, perhaps, than any other Western scholar. He realized that translation was a two-way process. Morrison's generation faced the problems of how the missionary could get the Christian message into Chinese. For this the Scriptures must be worthily translated and Christian missionaries must learn to speak and write good idiomatic Chinese. Legge saw a different problem for his, the next missionary generation. It was not enough for the missionary to get into China and get into the Chinese language; for the Christian gospel to be appropriated there, China must get into the missionary. Only so could Christianity penetrate the consciousness at the core of the nation. That consciousness had been formed by a most ancient literary tradition, coming into being over centuries of thought, reflection and writing, influencing millions of people who knew little or nothing of the literature itself.

In 1841, when still a raw young missionary in Malacca, Legge began to translate the Chinese classics. He continued with that task for the rest of his life, finishing his last text a few months before his death. The labor involved was immense. His translations were rigorous, and they were annotated in depth, making reference to the whole long tradition of Chinese learning. In a passage that makes a revealing contrast with Morrison's initial despair at the language of the Chinese classics, Legge describes how and why he translated a text that had already been (inadequately) translated by others:

> I undertook the labour of translating [it] afresh for myself, transcribing at the same time the original of the Chinese commentary on it, because I have learned by experience that such a process gives one most readily a mastery of the old books of China. Their reading and spirit sink gradually into mind. My long dealing with them has not enabled me to make them throw open their gates at the first reading.

Legge wanted the West to understand China, and especially that missionaries should understand Chinese culture at sufficient depth for their work to have permanence.

Today, more than a century after his death, Legge's translations and scholarly notes are still in use, in the East and the West. But their original purpose was to enable missionaries to be more effective in Chinese culture by reaching to China's heart with devoted labor at China's language and history. The process, he believed, would remove old misunderstandings; Legge, unlike Morrison, saw Confucius as essentially a religious, not simply a moral, teacher. Legge made a pilgrimage to the place where Confucius died in order to tread the very soil that had held the Master's dust. But his deepest emotions were stirred when he contemplated what he believed to be the historic heart of China's religion. Though hidden, covered over, corrupted, the old religion of China, Legge believed, had been monotheistic; the annual sacrifice now performed by the emperor on behalf of his people at the temple of heaven was a survival of that early recognition of the God of heaven. And Shangdi, the old Chinese name for God (the name used by the God Worshippers' Society at the heart of the Taiping movement) was the equivalent of the biblical Hebrew El Shaddai. Confucius and Mencius knew and safeguarded a much older tradition than the one reflected in their writings. Legge writes that Confucius was "a great and wonderful man. But I think that the religion which he found and did so much to transmit, was still greater and more remarkable than he."[9] And when he visited the place where he believed the worship of the God of heaven had been preserved in China for four thousand years, he removed his shoes (for he felt he stood on holy ground) and sang the Doxology: "Praise God from whom all blessings flow."[10]

Legge's research, undertaken as part of Christian mission, and in order to bring Christ to China, led him to the conclusion that despite the corruption and idolatry of Chinese popular religion, the God and Father of the Lord Jesus Christ had revealed himself in China, and at a period before the West knew the name of Israel's God. It was a divine pledge of China's Christian future. Chinese Christianity had roots long before Western contact brought the missionaries.

Hong Rengan and Taiping Theology

Legge describes his life in Hong Kong thus: "Several hours of every day were in spent visiting them from house to house and from shop to shop, conversing with them on all subjects, and trying to get them to converse with me on one

---

[9] James Legge, *The Religions of China: Confucianism and Taoism Described and Compared with Christianity* (London: Hodder and Stoughton, 1880), 149.

[10] Ibid., 251.

subject."[11] He made many friends, and one of the closest was Hong Rengan, a cousin of the Taiping Heavenly King. Hong and Legge preached in the London Missionary Society church, for Hong was a devout believer, well versed in Scripture. They composed poetry in Chinese together in convivial evenings, and—it is Legge who tells us this—walked the streets with arms around each other's necks. In 1858, Hong, to Legge's sorrow, left Hong Kong to join his cousin, then ruling the heavenly kingdom in Nanjing. There he entered the Taiping inner circle, becoming shield king. He was eventually arrested by Qing forces and executed in the Taiping collapse of 1864.[12]

Hong had a fuller knowledge of Christian theology than other Taiping leaders, and his presence in the inner counsels of the movement again raises the issue—which cannot be pursued here—of the indigenously Christian dimensions of Taiping. Some pieces of evidence about Hong in the six years from his journey to Nanjing suggests he was a serious theological thinker, moderating, nuancing, and clarifying Taiping language and behavior. While entirely loyal to Hong Xiuquan—he had been one of the heavenly king's earliest followers—his explanations of the relationship of the heavenly king to God the Father and to Christ carefully softened older and bolder Taiping statements that were so shocking to mainstream Christians. Some "revelations" of Taiping seers, such as those of the eastern king, he would not accept. He sought to moderate the violence in Taiping society; it was he who initiated the bans on slavery and infanticide, and he wanted to ban capital punishment, producing a more perfect obedience of the Sixth Commandment by leaving the judgment to God. Had he succeeded in this, it could have transformed Taiping society. Hong Rengan is surely a sign of Christianity authentically rooted in China within the missionary period, and a harbinger of a vigorous indigenous Christian theology.

Karl Ludvig Reichelt and Chinese Buddhism

Much of Chinese religion lay outside the scope of Legge's literary work. He was not much interested in the paper burnings, divination, and invocations of popular religion. Some missionary colleagues thought his studies irrelevant

---

[11] Quoted in Jonathan Spence, *God's Chinese Son: The Chinese Heavenly Kingdom of Hong Xiuquan* (London: Flamingo, 1996), 270.

[12] On the Taiping movement, see Jonathan Spence, *God's Chinese Son: the Chinese Heavenly Kingdom of Hong Xiuquan* (London: Flamingo, 1996); Thomas H. Reilly, *The Taiping Heavenly Kingdom: Rebellion and the Blasphemy of Empire* (Seattle: University of Washington Press, 2004).

to the contemporary religious scene; others thought it alien to China's crying need for modernization along Western lines. His late book *The Religions of China* has two main sections. That on Confucianism deals with the "higher" tradition, and has a superscription from Romans 1:21, "They knew God." That on Daoism is mainly concerned with the "lower" tradition, and its superscription is from Colossians 2:18, "Intruding into those things which he hath not seen." Legge sees no evidence of any relationship between the "noble" book Dao De Jing and the Daoism of his own day. Contemporary Daoism for him is begotten by Buddhism out of ancient Chinese superstitions; it represents the degradation of Chinese traditional religion, lamentable if understandable, as it declines into polytheism. On Buddhism, other than its influence, for good or ill, on Daoism, Legge says remarkably little. He probably did not regard it as being really Chinese. Yet, judging by conversions we know of, many of the people who became Christians in response to missionary preaching in the nineteenth century had previously been members of Buddhist sects.

Chinese Buddhism, and sectarian religion generally, did find some sympathy among missionaries; in Manchuria for instance, John Ross argued that the most fertile soil for Christian growth lay in the most extreme Buddhist sects; these were people who understood the seriousness of sin and were seeking redemption. From such people had come many of the leaders of Manchurian Christianity.[13] And the maverick Welsh Baptist Timothy Richard was able to find in China what he called *The New Testament of Higher Buddhism*.[14] But for a missionary attempting to root Christianity in the soil of Chinese Buddhism, we turn to Karl Ludvig Reichelt,[15] who entered training for the Norwegian Missionary Society in the year of Legge's death.

Reichelt's theology and piety and upbringing were solidly conservative. He belonged to the Pietist wing of Norwegian Lutheranism, and had an Evangelical conversion in his teens. He arrived in China soon after the Boxer rising, a time when the missionary movement was suffused with the thought of the modernization of China and gaining new hope from the apparent readiness of Chinese people to adopt the ways of the West. (It is common to talk of the cultural baggage brought by missionaries, but the weight of that baggage varies greatly from era to era; there have been times when it seems to be no imposition at all). In the period when Reichelt began his work, there seemed little point in studying traditional China: it seemed

[13] John Ross, *Mission Methods in Manchuria* (Edinburgh: O. Anderson and Ferrier, 1905).
[14] (Edinburgh: T & T Clark, 1910).
[15] On Reichelt, see Eric J. Sharpe, *Karl Ludvig Reichelt, Missionary, Scholar and Pilgrim* (Hong Kong: Tao Fong Shan Ecumenical Centre, 1984); R. Olsen, *Prevailing Winds: An Analysis of the Liturgical Inculturation of Karl Ludvig Reichelt* (Lund, Sweden: Centre for Theology and Religious Studies, 2007).

to be passing away. The young missionary entered into the usual routine of open-air preaching and Scripture and tract distribution.

His encounters with Buddhist monks was shattering, both because of the evident genuineness of the monks' faith and because of his inability to communicate to them his own. He describes his experience after visiting a Buddhist monastery in 1905:

> Pained and distraught, I walked about and wrestled with the question: are we permitted to believe that the Spirit of God and the Spirit of Jesus Christ may also be at work within these melancholy walls, where superstition and idolatry walk side by side with the loftiest longings for purity and liberty?
>
> It was my last night there. There was no question of sleeping— the inward struggle and pain was too great. I was thankful when I heard the bell ring at two a.m. for the monks' first worship. They slipped silently into the sanctuary. There was the soft stroke of a gong, and the long monotonous act of worship began in its usual melancholy minor key. Everything felt doubly dark to the missionary kneeling there and wrestling in prayer on the cobblestones outside.
>
> When dawn came, everything breathed the freshness of the morning and the power of resurrection. The birds began to sing. I sat down in quiet meditation. It was as though I heard the Lord's voice: God is not far from each one of us, for in him we live and move and have our being. God has not left himself without witness; long before the missionaries came to China, God was in China. What you find of glimpses of truth and points of contact, he has placed there.
>
> For the first time I began to understand what the Gospel of John states: God has been active from eternity through his Word, his Son. What has to be done is to gather all the rays of light that there are . . . [to] help the individual to go deeper and reach further, to an understanding of the Word that became flesh and dwelt among us. . . .
>
> It was a quite different missionary who walked down the Weishan Hill, a missionary whose heart was full of holy power and love.

This experience led Reichelt to the study of Chinese religious traditions. The form of study differed from the type that Legge pursued in two ways: it concentrated on Buddhism, which Legge treated almost as a bypath; and it was not only textual but interpersonal. His mission was not very friendly to innovation, but Reichelt continued to visit monasteries, spending days and weeks there, not only in worship in the temple halls but in the meditation sessions. There were, he concluded, plenty of charlatans and much perversion in monastic life; but also "so much sincere piety, wholehearted and holy devotion, and beauty of character and spirit among the monks that my soul has been filled with wonder." If these people were to come to know Christ, what spiritual heights might they attain? And what a blessing they would be to the church in China!

When he tried to talk to monks about Christ, he found that they readily accepted his identification of Jesus with the Merciful Savior from the West of Mahayana Buddhist tradition. Their response to the teachings of the Bible was to acknowledge their truth. But they found followers of Jesus, whether Western or Chinese, deficient in gentleness, the first characteristic of true religion. Christians spoke harshly about Buddha and Buddhism, and said things that were not true. The indictment, Reichelt believed, was justified. Much Christian harshness came from ignorance. He promised to do justice to Buddhists and acknowledge what they had of truth, since that truth came from the Father and his Logos. The means by which it had come was of secondary importance, but Reichelt, like Timothy Richard, believed that some of the special features of Chinese Buddhism, its idea of grace and assertion of a Savior figure, was probably the result of interaction centuries earlier with Nestorian Christianity.

In 1919, in a monastery in Nanjing, Reichelt met several young monks who showed great interest in the message about Christ. One in particular, by the name of Kuantu, responded to the idea of Christ as the Great Savior from the West (i.e., paradise). (Reichelt insisted on the historical nature of the descent of the Merciful Savior and of the actuality of the heavenly kingdom: "The West" was not just a theoretical pure land.) Kuantu got leave from his monastery to visit Reichelt, and the two spent months together in prayer, in Scripture reading, and in reading the Buddhist Scriptures. Kuantu returned to his monastery to explain what he was doing, and after much trouble was allowed to withdraw from the monastery. On Christmas Day 1919 he was baptized, making a great impression by his articulate but unusual testimony: "using words of unique richness and solemnity such as only a mind molded in higher Chinese Buddhism can use." Reichelt hailed this as a foretaste of the church universal; it was not a new form of Christianity but old, unimpaired Christianity.

Reichelt and Kuantu were the nucleus of a Christian Brotherhood among Chinese Buddhists. They were soon joined by others: an old abbot with his servants, as well as younger people. The Brotherhood acquired a temple in Nanjing and converted it into a chapel to the Thorn-Crowned Christ. Reichelt saw this as a halfway house where Buddhists could be comfortable with the ambience and the atmosphere, since these resembled those of a Buddhist temple. But the hope was that they would encounter Christ.

The plan was to have a hospitality hall where traveling monks seeking opportunities for worship and study could be received, a dormitory, a lecture hall and a library and school, a meditation hall and a prayer tower shaped like a pagoda with a bell. Reichelt envisaged a core of resident baptized monks, some of whom would be pastors, evangelists, or teachers, some nurses, printers, or with other ministries, with an open house for all who wished to study the Christian way; for in Christ the deepest aspirations of Mahayana Buddhism could be fulfilled. The theological basis for this drew on Justin's teaching about Christ as Logos Spermatikos: the seed germinating in salvation. God was providentially at work within spheres of thought outside the church; thus in China Buddhism developed a tradition of grace, of a Savior, of paradise, none of which were part of its original doctrine. The Christian task now is to lead Buddhists to recognize Christ as that Savior, within the Chinese setting—hence Reichelt's phrase "religion in Chinese garment."[16] The key Scripture passage is the prologue to the Fourth Gospel (where Logos may be translated Dao), at work in creation and giving light to humanity. The gospel is addressed to seekers; the Logos has inspired the search; and the purpose of the gospel is not to absorb Buddhism but to enlighten Buddhists from within.

The setting in which the gospel is presented should therefore fit the Chinese garment. Hence the Buddhist architecture and a Buddhist atmosphere; the ritual in chapel was reminiscent of that in a temple, with bells, incense, and meditation. There was a reading of the Christian Scriptures and also of those Buddhist Scriptures recognized as in harmony with Christian teaching. The liturgy used a version of the Triratna that pointed to the Trinity: "I go for refuge to the Father of All Goodness and Mercy, to the Mysterious Perfect Dao, to the Shining Pure Holy Spirit." The diet was vegetarian. And there was a distinctive symbol, a cruciform lotus. This caused anxiety in some mission circles, as being syncretistic; Reichelt insisted that it represented a faith centered in Christ crucified and rooted and growing in Asia.

This remained Reichelt's plan of work until his death in 1952. He had times of encouragement; a number of monks responded. One of his most interesting books is entitled *A Transformed Abbot*, the story of a conversion

---

16 The title of the English translation of perhaps his best-known book (London: Lutterworth Press, 1951).

that exactly follows the pattern of the search that Reichelt developed.[17] But Reichelt met with much opposition, both internally within the church and missions, and externally from the chaotic national situation. To some of his conservative colleagues his approach seemed syncretistic; some zealous Protestants found the bells and incense too reminiscent of Roman practice. His own mission abandoned him, and some of the more liberal supporters he attracted did not really understand him; he was not teaching that there was a single universal religion, nor proclaiming the unity of Christianity and Buddhism. He was calling Buddhists to Christ with the assurance that Christ had been in China and among Chinese Buddhists long before his time, and that thousands of years of Chinese Buddhist tradition could be turned toward Christ.

But a China in the grip of revolution, civil war, and foreign invasion was a difficult theater for activity of this sort, and Nanjing under the Japanese invaders an impossible one. Therefore some of those attracted to the Christian way were also attracted by the communist vision of a new society, and chose the latter. In earlier times Christianity offered an alternative to the Buddhist sects for those longing for change; now communism offered the same people another choice. Reichelt found his last institutional base in Hong Kong, and died just as the missionary era in China ended.

Hudson Taylor and China's Millions

The careers of Morrison, Legge, and Reichelt together cover the Protestant missionary period in China, a little under a century and a half. They also represent stages in a process in which Christianity, arriving in China in a form heavily acculturated by centuries of interaction with the languages and cultures of Europe, increasingly interacted with those of China. But there were other missionary traditions interacting in different ways, and it is necessary in closing to take brief account of them.

The transition from Morrison to Legge marks the crucial event of the war that led to the treaty of 1842, with the Western powers forcing a way into China in the interests of trade liberalization, and missions pushing through the door thus opened. But the door opened only to the treaty ports. Though the number of these expanded considerably during the nineteenth century, missions were in active engagement with only a small proportion of the population of China. Response in most areas was small; anti-foreign

---

[17] English translation (London: Lutterworth Press, 1954).

feeling was strong. The later decades of the century saw an intensification of missionary effort in the wake of a reradicalization of the missionary movement. One of the key figures in the radicalizing process was an Englishman, James Hudson Taylor.[18]

Taylor embodied new developments in theology and spirituality. The eschatology of the earlier Evangelicalism had seen missions as a long-haul undertaking, and commonly looked forward to a time of success for the gospel when "the earth would be full of the knowledge of God as the waters cover the sea." By the middle of the nineteenth century, other views of the return of Christ were becoming fashionable in the mission community. The world seemed to be getting worse; the true hope of Christians lay in the return of Christ. Their urgent task was now to preach the gospel to as many people as possible as quickly as possible before the Lord's coming. The older Evangelicalism, frequently yoked to antislavery and other humanitarian causes, had sought the reform of society; the imperatives of the new eschatology could not wait for social improvement. The same applied to many of the doctrinal and ecclesiastical issues that divided churches; these seemed of minimal importance in the light of the responsibility to spread the gospel to those who were perishing without it. Taylor was oppressed with the thought of millions of Chinese perishing without the gospel while the missions were confined to the treaty ports, doing nothing about most of those millions. He recounts in his autobiographical *Retrospect* a vision he had of four-hundred million Chinese marching four abreast around the Equator. He decided to go to China as an independent missionary, without the aid of a missionary society; later he set up an entirely new kind of mission society. His China Inland Mission (CIM) became the pattern for many other missions.[19]

The aim of the CIM was to reach millions with the gospel. That meant reaching across the whole of inland China, far beyond the treaty ports. It would involve working outside treaty provisions and risking the personal safety of missionaries. Consecration to the missionary task must include a readiness to suffer and die; and when the Boxer rising came, CIM missionaries indeed formed a high proportion of those who died, and the mission, unlike many others, refused any share in the indemnity money imposed by the Western powers on China after the collapse of the rising.

The gospel carried was generally thought of in terms of verbal communication; it was expected to issue in transformed lives. The mission sought as

---

[18] The fullest biography of Taylor is A. J. Broomhall, *Hudson Taylor and China's Open Century* (London: Hodder and Stoughton, 7 volumes, 1982–86).

[19] On this, see Klaus Fiedler, *The Story of Faith Missions* (Oxford: Oxford Centre for Mission Studies, 1994).

far as possible to avoid the establishment of colleges, schools, hospitals, and all the other institutions that had become part of the established missions in China, lest they interfere with the grand object. Missionaries should live as closely as possible to Chinese people in dress and food, and not live in a separated "Western" style.

Another stream of teaching that influenced Taylor stressed the principle of faith in God for the daily provision of all needs. The new mission abandoned the principle of fixed salaries and allowances, as well as fund-raising campaigns and public appeals, all characteristic of older missions. The mission would not ask for money, but pray and trust God to supply the needs; and its missionaries should live by the same principle. The name "faith missions" was devised for the type of mission pioneered by the CIM.

Older missions had been mostly denominational, in effect if not always in name; the CIM and other faith missions became pan-denominational, drawing from sources across the ecclesial spectrum from episcopal to baptistic. By an extension of this reasoning, the mission also became international, soon drawing its personnel from Britain, continental Europe, North America, and Australasia. Instead of having a directive committee in the West, as in other missions, there was a field missionary in China as director: decisions about the field were to be taken on the field. Women were accepted as missionaries in their own right. (The older missionary societies had sent ministers, with their wives; the minister was the missionary, the wife was not.) Women undertook evangelistic tours, usually in pairs, on the same terms as men.

By the same token, education was irrelevant to missionary vocation. If God had called a person, God would equip that person with the language skills and other necessary acquisitions. The older societies had insisted on a body of trained missionaries who were reasonably well educated and had completed a theological course; CIM threw open the gates to people of all ranks and backgrounds. The task of reaching the perishing millions with the gospel needed every available worker, provided that worker had the divine call.

In one respect, CIM differed from most of the faith missions that followed it; it had no stated doctrinal basis of belief. Taylor evidently did not think one was necessary; he would not have expected anyone to offer for missionary service in CIM who was out of sympathy with his type of theology and spirituality. CIM had not so much a creed as an ethos; and probably the theological point that Taylor held to most firmly was the belief that those who were not in Christ were perishing.

Maximalists and Minimalists
in Christian Missions

In the history of Christian missions, there have always been maximalists and minimalists; those who have seen mission in broad terms, addressed to the whole of human society and every department of human life, and those who call for concentration on one essential, one overriding imperative. James Hudson Taylor was the arch-minimalist, standing for a gospel expressed essentially in words but demonstrated in transformed lives. He was not without social consciousness; the CIM campaigned against the British export of opium to China and sponsored a campaigning magazine called *National Righteousness*; but he was suspicious of institutions and activities that appeared to divert time and resources from the preaching of the gospel.

The Baptist Timothy Richard,[20] whose name has been already mentioned several times here, may stand as the representative figure of the arch-maximalist. Starting from a theological position similar to Taylor's (he had originally wanted to join the CM), he found himself as an evangelistic missionary in the midst of a famine that called for immediate compassionate Christian action. He successfully organized famine relief, helped to make famine relief a serious concern in mission circles generally, and made a substantial impact on his locality in China, from which his mission benefited. But the experience forced him to ask why famines occurred in China so often; they were not necessary or inevitable, but were caused or exacerbated by human error and ignorance. Like most Evangelical missionaries, his message had been Christocentric and cruci-centric; without abating his beliefs about Christ and the Cross, he began to argue for a missionary theology that took account of the work of God the Father and Creator. To serve China, missions, as servants of God the Creator, should be spreading knowledge that would break the cycle of famine. The audience to reach—with meetings, teaching, lectures, and above all literature—was that of the literati, the educated gentry, hitherto the heart of opposition to missions; and the Christian legacy to China should include the provision of modern universities and medical faculties.

But in 1950, minimalists and maximalists alike were swept away. In the new China that was arising, the narrative of missionary enterprise became indelibly linked with the Western intervention in China, backed by military action, which had brought successive humiliations to the country.

---

[20] On Richard, see Andrew F. Walls, "The Multiple Conversions of Timothy Richard," in *The Cross-Cultural Process in Christian History* (Maryknoll, NY: Orbis Books, 2002), 236–56.

The association of missions with imperialism proved to be more toxic in China, which (Macau and Hong Kong apart) was never in any formal sense colonized, than in most places that had been colonies. Perhaps the sheer immensity of the missionary infrastructural investment in China, exceeding anywhere else in the world, emphasized the foreign dimension of Christianity. And when in 1950 the Chinese government made it clear that its dealings with Christianity would be conducted with Chinese Christians, without the foreign presence, it was manifest how many heads of Christian institutions, not to mention leaders of churches, were foreigners.

Conclusion

And yet, as our story has shown, even in the missionary period, that bridge between the age in which the cultural and demographic center of Christianity lay in the West and one in which it lay in the non-Western world, there are signs of Christianity authentically taking root in China. The careers of such people as Liang Fa and Hong Rengan imply not only deep conviction but an appropriation of the Christian faith in Chinese terms, and in answer to Chinese concerns. And whatever one's assessment of the Taiping movement and its relation to Christianity, its history shows that Christian affirmations could speak powerfully to nineteenth-century South China society. Nor should we forget that the Christian encounter with the Chinese living outside China, who were to include a significant presence in the late twentieth century, began in the missionary period.

What had nineteenth- and twentieth-century missions done to prepare for an authentic Christianity taking root? Our story has concentrated on three things. The first is the provision of the vernacular Scriptures, the source of Christian reflection and renewal, the task that dominated Morrison's life and work. The second is the linking of the Christian faith to the ancient past of China and its indigenous traditions of thought, to which James Legge devoted his life. The third has been active engagement with the living faiths of China, to which end Reichelt labored. To these we should add two dimensions necessary to Christian rootedness at any period: the vision of what this terrestrial world could be and should be according to God's design, which was embodied in Timothy Richard, and the uncompromising quest of the transcendent world reflected in Hudson Taylor.

It is hard to think of parallels in previous Christian history to the history of Christianity in China, nor to think of many analogies to its modern story, where such vicissitudes have been followed by such an outcome. The future of the Chinese churches, both in the homeland and in the diaspora, and their impact beyond both, is one of the critical issues for World Christianity in the present century.

From the second to the fifth century the Bible and the Christian tradition interacted with Greco-Roman thought, raising Greek questions in the Greek language, using indigenous categories of thought and styles of debate but issuing in declarations that have expressed the worshipping consciousness of the worldwide church over centuries. Perhaps we are entering a similar period, when the interaction will be with the cultures, intellectual and literary traditions, and languages of Africa and Asia. In such a process, China may yet have a formative role in the future of Christianity.

16

Building to Last

Harold Turner and the Study of Religion

What follows here was written in 1990 as an introduction to a volume of essays presented to the late Harold Turner on his return to New Zealand. Marks of date and occasion, including the names of some contributors to the volume have been retained; see the note at the end of the essay.

By the grace God has given me, I laid a foundation as an expert builder, and someone else is building on it. But each one should be careful how he builds.
—*Paul to the Corinthians* (1 Cor. 3:10 NIV)

Harold Turner is the son of a builder and the father of an architect. His own knowledge of and interest in buildings is evident in his writings, and notably in one of his finest—and most neglected—works. *From Temple to Meeting House* is about "sacred space," about the use by humans of buildings in recognition of the Holy, and as such it provides a starting point for considering the life work of its author. For as a scholar Harold Turner has been both architect and builder. He has recognized the need for certain types of scholarly construction and been a visionary designer of them. He has also been prepared to labor at the implementation of his designs, sweating with the bricks and mortar (not to mention the paint and putty) of scholarship. It has often been lonely labor, since some who might have helped were taken up with gaudy marquees that have long since collapsed. Turner's structures, like Noah's, have resisted the weather and still invite habitation, adaptation, and extension—perhaps occasionally repair—for extended life in the climate of a new generation. Those who carry on the work of this expert builder may well remember *From Temple to Meeting House.*

Turner's buildings are sacred space. They are designed not for spectacle, but for use; and they stand in recognition of the Holy. Unless this is recognized, their form cannot be understood.

At first sight his first book signals interests quite different from those with which his name is most associated now; but it was a landmark in its way, and in many respects characteristic of its author. *Halls of Residence* was published in New Zealand in 1953, and, being speedily recognized as having more than local relevance, was republished by Oxford University Press the next year. It was the first, and perhaps is still the only, monograph on its topic. It arose from the experience of the author—he was also lecturing in moral philosophy at the time—in setting up student residences in what was then the University of New Zealand. It is informed by the conviction that student residences should express life in a community with a shared purpose and with shared values. Their purpose should be formative and in the fullest sense of the word, educational. It is one of the author's sadder literary memorials, for he has lived to see the conception of halls of residence, like their architecture, evacuated of that meaning so that their buildings decline into shacks for students.

By the time *Halls of Residence* appeared, Noah was being transformed into Abraham. Africa was drawing Harold Turner; but in those days there was no obvious route whereby a New Zealand academic could reach that land of promise. Harold and Maude, with a young family, set out for Britain to find one, and after a spell of teaching at Goldsmith's College, London, reached the critical point of their great migration. Harold was appointed to a lectureship in the Faculty of Theology at Fourah Bay College in Sierra Leone, the oldest university institution in tropical Africa. At that time affiliated to the University of Durham, it was in transition between the missionary institution it had lately been and the independent university of a new nation that it was soon to become. The Faculty of Theology was crucial in that transition. It had responsibility for the training of the ministry, at every level, for the country's three principal churches. It represented theology, no longer an acknowledged queen of the sciences, in a consciously secularizing academic community. And it had to explore new frontiers that Durham theology knew nothing about. Turner, commissioned to teach biblical and theological studies—naturally, he was a warden of students as well—began by throwing himself into the first two of these tasks. They were an indispensable background for the third. In his contribution to a modest faculty publication celebrating Sierra Leone's independence he sets out a view of the theological task, and of the relationship of theology to other disciplines, which in developed form was to underlie much of his future work:

> a true knowledge of God the creator includes also a doctrine of human life and of the natural universe in which it is set. God cannot be known except through man and nature, and by this very fact both man and nature are seen in their unity and their meaning. Theology is the most concrete of all studies, since God, the creator and "constant environment" of all things, is the least abstract and isolated of beings. In former times this was recognized when theology was called "the Queen of the Sciences"; in some universities vestiges of this remain in the recognition of the faculty of theology as the senior faculty. . . . [W]e at Fourah Bay College have no such ambitions; rather would we seek to serve all branches of knowledge by providing for their consideration a comprehensive framework within which all may find their place and their unity while retaining in full measure their own responsibility and freedom.[1]

There are hints here of later themes: the "mediated immediacy" in human encounter with the divine—an idea developed from a brief discipleship with John Baillie in Edinburgh, a view of theology as an integrative discipline, and yet the recognition of the autonomy of each academic discipline within its own sphere. This view of the totality of human knowledge and the freedom to increase it, within—not supplementary to—a Christian confession about God and the world, is a keynote in his most recent thinking with its keen interest in modern scientific thought and in the historic dependence of scientific method as a Christian worldview. This declaration of the autonomy of academic disciplines has paradoxically irritated some of his critics because of its implied resistance to the subsumption of the whole study of religion under some other discipline.[2] The position he enunciates in this article is fully in the Reformed tradition in which he was reared— and Harold Turner has always valued the sense of identity, the freedom to be oneself, which comes from sharing in a tradition—and the combination of ultimate commitment and liberty of exploration has never left him. It has enabled him to enter sympathetically into cultures and religious—and

---

[1] Harry Sawyerr, ed., *Christian Theology in Independent Africa* (Freetown, Sierra Leone: Faculty of Theology, Fourah Bay College, 1961).

[2] Robert W. Wyllie, "On the Rationality of the Devout Opposition," *Journal of Religion in Africa* 11, no. 2 (1980): 81–92.

nonreligious—traditions not his own. It has opened him to insights from a variety of intellectual approaches, and his breadth of discourse has allowed him to place the results of his explorations on the general map of learning.

One day in 1957, on Lumley Beach near Freetown—a place for them of spiritual exercises—Harold Turner had met white-robed members of the Church of the Lord (Aladura) and their remarkable leader, Apostle Adeleke Adejobi. The encounter was to give Harold Turner's work a new direction and to release his richest creative activity.

It is worth remembering how little knowledge or understanding of the newer forms of African Christianity was then abroad. On the human level there were few situations where the old and new forms of African Christianity could meet on equal terms. In mission-related or "mainline" church circles the new churches were commonly regarded as "sects" or "cults," or as a syncretistic Cave of Adullam, frustrated ambition in league with polygamy, adultery, superstition, and ignorance. There were no widely recognized criteria for distinguishing one type of new church from another. The newer churches often denounced the older as powerless, mercenary, compromising with evil. Among scholarly writers Geoffrey Parrinder, as so often, was pointing the way, indicating in his study of religion in Ibadan the significance of the new churches.[3] But there were only two major studies generally available in English, and both were localized in reference. One was Bengt Sundkler's seminal *Bantu Prophets in South Africa,* then known only in its first (1948) edition. Sundkler revealed something of the size of that mass of Christianity outside the mission-related sphere and also something of its highly complex history. He uncovered indigenous religious initiatives little thought of beyond the Zulu domain, and set them in their local context. He also produced the first typology of the newer churches, distinguishing between their "Ethiopian" and "Zionist" forms. Sundkler wrote only of South Africa, where land deprivation and the sense of oppression were so intense; but others were soon finding parallels in the situation in other parts of Africa. The first academic work seriously to address the new churches in Nigeria—if we discount the section in Parrinder's *Religion in an African City* already mentioned—was by a political scientist.[4] It invests them with a nationalist political significance that sits oddly on the great bulk of them. The other major study available—less well known and often hard to find— was Efraim Andersson's *Messianic Movements in the Lower Congo,* which illuminated the thirty-year period from 1921 in which Simon Kimbangu

---

[3] Geoffrey Parrinder, *Religion in an African City* (London: Oxford University Press, 1953).

[4] J. S. Coleman, *Nigeria: Background to Nationalism* (Berkeley: University of California Press, 1958).

and the movement deriving from him was the most notable but far from the only striking phenomenon. Andersson's word "messianic" became added to words already in use, such as "nativistic," "syncretistic," "prophetic," "separatist," and occasionally "millennial" or "chiliastic," to designate what churchmen and scholars alike were beginning to realize was a vigorous part of the religious scene in many parts of Africa.

Turner's new interest thus began at a critical time. "African Independent Churches," as they are now known, have rarely been a luxuriant growth in Sierra Leone, and the Church of the Lord (Aladura) was still a singular phenomenon in Freetown. Deepening acquaintance with it revealed both direct connections maintained across West Africa and parallels elsewhere.

The mode of investigation—and how crucial that was to all that followed—grew naturally out of the first encounter. He took his new acquaintances in the Church of the Lord seriously for what they were and for what they claimed to be: as fellow believers seeking to worship God and to experience the divine presence and power. This enabled him to build trust and friendship with Church of the Lord leaders and members and to share freely with them in their activities. This form of "participant observation" was not role play but deliberate sharing, as far as the participant was able, in what he took in good faith to be Christian worship by other believers. There was a shared ground in the acknowledgment of the Christian Scriptures, however different the traditions of use. So Harold Turner accepted the risks and the personal vulnerability involved in such openness. In return his new friends took him for what he was: neither as an outsider nor as a "convert" but as a fellow believer from beyond the circle of prophet-healing churches. Doors were opened to him in branch after branch of the church right across West Africa.

This sort of ecumenism was not common in West Africa in the 1950s; certainly the resultant uninhibited participation of Apostle Adejobi and his cohorts in a Fourah Bay conference for clergy was something of an event. Throughout his career Harold Turner has acted as a bridge, a terminal that permits live contact. In an essay in his honor, Rosalind Hackett, representative of a younger generation of scholars, tells of her experience of being identified by the leader of another Nigerian independent church as "a spiritual daughter of the great Dr. Turner"—and this many years after his last visit there. She points out how many have followed his example in the simple act of taking the new Christianity seriously.

The first published fruits of the connection with the Church of the Lord were analyses and interpretations of liturgical documents, the church's litany and catechism. These studies were published in early issues of the

Sierra Leone Bulletin of Religion, a small journal begun as a vehicle for the type of local studies incumbent on the Faculty of Theology. Both have since been republished in two other places. They illuminated the way in which the new churches maintained continuity with the liturgical and the doctrinal traditions of the older churches—in this case the Anglicanism, which had been the background of most of the Aladura members a generation earlier—while reordering them and finding new elements to express notes in worship and catechism essential to them but missing from the Western liturgies. It was a first exercise in elucidating the continuity and the new departures, the assumptions and the priorities of the new churches, the "spiritual" churches, as they saw themselves.

The process was taken to a deeper level by an examination of the use of Scripture in the church. Turner worked steadily through the register of sermon texts maintained by the Church of the Lord. Contrary to what might have been expected of a body characterized by charismatic leadership, ecstatic utterance, dancing in worship, and individual revelations, the preachers of the church did preach from texts and did regularly record them in a register. Turner checked one obvious possible source, the lectionary in the widely available *West African's Churchman's Calendar*—there was no obvious correlation; the texts were their own choice. The incidence of the texts indicated the parts of the Bible most in use, and the commonest themes of preaching and items thus helped to build a profile of the concerns of the church. The outcome was *Profile through Preaching* (1965). That this little book was published for the Commission for World Mission and Evangelism of the World Council of Churches indicates the growing consciousness in the older churches of the importance of understanding the indigenous African churches and of the inappropriateness to them of the norms of inter-confessional debate developed in Western Christian history. The Church of the Lord, for example, used the Christian Scriptures and observed both dominical sacraments, two of the classic marks of the church in Protestant tradition. While the Apostle's Creed was certainly recited in services, there was a profound lack of interest in doctrinal concerns that had lain at the heart of Western agonizing, and an equally obvious concern with questions hardly raised in the West. It was the first of Turner's forays into the question of the frame of reference within which people in different cultures read the Scriptures. There are hints, too, in *Profile through Preaching* of a wider possibility. What if the same method of analysis was applied to the preaching in other African churches? Are the outlines we can trace clearly and firmly in the indigenous African churches simply the contours of an African Christianity that is discernible as a substratum in the older churches, too? Are the old and the new churches converging?

But at this time Harold Turner was concerned with plotting the contours of the Church of the Lord (Aladura). Though the articles flowed, the full published form did not appear until 1967. It is his magnum opus, or rather, magna opera, for—despite some confusion engendered by the cover and title page—it is two books rather than one. *History of an African Independent Church* is important not only as a detailed history of the Church of the Lord in four countries but for the insight it gives into the story of the whole Aladura movement. "Even now, thirty years later, the oldest churches know so little of the inner spiritual history of this great religious upheaval in their midst," writes Turner of a time in the 1930s.[5] What he describes is just that—an inner spiritual history with a very specific context, agony, and ecstasy, yearning and fulfillment, controversy and consensus, triumphs and disasters of the sort well known to the student of conventionally prescribed church history; but occurring not in the Hellenistic Mediterranean or Renaissance Europe but in the Nigeria of the influenza epidemic and the postwar depression, with taxation a burden, disease a peril, several generations of decent Anglican Christianity and a less-than-half-comprehending and periodically jumpy colonial administration. The second, larger volume of the duo explores the whole range of the life and faith and manners of working of the Church of the Lord (Aladura). The two works taken together still probably provide the most comprehensive picture we have of any African Christian body of any sort. As far as the "spiritual" churches were concerned they were soon usefully supplemented by John Peel's more sociologically orientated *Aladura,* which appeared soon after.[6]

Meanwhile, Turner had become involved in matters concerning the new churches more widely, and especially in clarifying and fixing terminology. The Commission on World Mission and Evangelism sponsored a consultation at Mindolo, Zambia, in 1962, the report of which appeared with the significant if slightly clumsy title, *African Independent Church Movements.*[7] Turner's contributions to the report are the bibliography and the first of a long series of his characteristic typological charts and flow diagrams. The report signals recognition in the wider church that Africa had churches—not just sects or cults—outside and beyond those hitherto accepted in Christendom. They were of different types but had in common that they were "African Independent" Churches, over against the "older"

---

[5] H. W. Turner, *History of an African Independent Church* (Oxford: Clarendon Press, 1967), 26.

[6] John D. Y. Peel, *Aladura: A Religious Movement among the Yoruba* (London: Oxford University Press, 1968).

[7] Victor E. W. Hayward, ed., *African Independent Church Movements* (London: Edinburgh House Press for World Council of Churches, 1963).

churches of Christendom, the sources of the missionary movements that had first brought Christianity to most of tropical Africa. At the same time, the independent churches were formally part of a series of movements indicating the interaction between African societies and the Christian faith, which itself could not be separated from the wider impact of the West; and the relationship of these movements to the Christian faith greatly. It was necessary thus to regard the flux as well as the forms. Both forms and flux are recorded in Turner's chart. It is the first version of his typology, which he was to refine over the years, and which necessarily included the terminology adopted at the consultation. The key term adopted there, "independent churches" (divided, as by Sundkler, between Ethiopian and Zionist, with Aladura added to the latter) has, despite some grumbles, been generally adopted. Flux continues; the Aladura are no longer the "new" churches of Nigeria, and some extension of categories is needed to cope with the dynamic ebullience of religion in today's West Africa and the effect of the charismatic movement both within and beyond the older, formerly mission-related churches,

Harold Turner's move to a post at the University of Nigeria Nsukka assisted the broader application of his work. Eastern Nigeria was a forest of independent churches of the Aladura type, but mostly smaller, more localized, and less hierarchical than the Yoruba-originated Church of the Lord. Eastern Nigeria had had its own separate religious history, and its own prophets; and the government archives at Enugu provided new light on the Elijah of the Niger Delta, the one-time Anglican catechist Garrick Braide. A whole long wall of the Department of Religion became devoted to a map whereon, as it was identified, was indicated the location of each congregation in Eastern Nigeria. The questions grew with the clusters of color-coded pins. Why were there 331pins (mostly white for independent) in an area marking five miles from the center of the middling town of Uyo? An extraordinary Mennonite missionary living near Uyo became the kindly Socratic midwife for a range of developments in relation to Uyo's burgeoning religious life. Mild, venerable, and not at all academic, Edwin Weaver, instead of instituting a new denominational church, had concentrated on personal relationships with and service to Ibibio independent church leaders. He also sought mutual understanding between the main representatives of the other churches of the area. With Harold Turner as consultant and facilitator Uyo became the scene of a regular and active study group with a most variegated set of participants, which stimulated research as well as reflection.

The University of Nigeria saw itself as a national institution in a religiously plural nation, and had a Department of Religion rather than of

Theology. Within this, Harold Turner was responsible for teaching a course on the forms and history of religion. It drew him back to the study of religious phenomenology, and he drank deeply from continental wells. He was to make his own contribution to the literature on phenomenology (the systematic study of the history of religion, as W. Brede Kristensen called it) but the phenomenology of religion also became an essential part of his regular tool kit in the area of study where he was now well known. He did not abandon his vocations as theologian and historian but took up a new one as well. The whole history of religion and its manifestations typologically considered became his intellectual grid. His established interest in typology, his long concern with the distinctive features of the Christian faith, the ponderings on Semitic religion and prophetic religion derived from his years as a teacher of Old Testament studies, all assisted the development. The phenomenological method had not been widely used in the study of African religion, still less in that interaction of Christian and African traditions to which his special studies had brought him.

Phenomenology has been sadly neglected in the English-speaking world, especially Britain where it has often been reduced to a survey of methods and approaches to religion. When he left Nigeria, Harold Turner seized the opportunity to initiate the study of religion at the University of Leicester, building a department around the study of the forms and history of religion. Later Harold was to teach phenomenology at the University of Aberdeen. It is significant also that teaching phenomenology of religion led him to produce (Selbstverlag) an abridgement of and commentary on Rudolf Otto's *Idea of the Holy* which has made that work accessible to hundreds of students who— by this writer's experience—rarely otherwise get beyond chapter three of the original. And we have already noted his major study of sacred buildings in the different religious traditions, *From Temple to Meeting House.*

Phenomenological method brought new zest to his studies of what he has described as the relations of the new religion of Africa with the old. Historians of religion have always tended to center on the "great" traditions of Asia and the Semitic world. But it is the primal religions, so often miscalled primitive, which underlie all the others and frequently give the clearest models of religion. Further, the clear historical relationship of the primal religions with Christianity gives them special claim to sympathetic historical study. Harold Turner's visiting appointment at Emory University, following the Leicester and preceding the Aberdeen years, gave him two years to study Native American religions, Native American Christianity, and the interactive movements (so different in their effects from those in Africa) between Christianity and the North American primal religions. His booklet, *Living Tribal Religions* (in a series mainly for schools, and therefore often overlooked) in which the primal religions are presented in terms of patterns of revelation and response, is a little classic of its kind.

But perhaps most important of all, his involvement in the broader synoptic treatment of religion took Turner from *African Independent Church* to *New Religious Movements in Primal Societies*. It is by his work on new religious movements, especially those in primal societies, that Harold Turner's name is most widely known. Many fine scholars have worked in parts of this field and produced superb studies of those parts; but more than any other one person Harold Turner has defined the field, surveyed it world-wide, identified the materials, and established the area as having a distinctive place in the study of religion.

Behind the concept lies Turner's continuing concern with the relation of form and flux. The interaction of mission-organized Christianity, other modernizing influences, and African traditional society produced a range of movements of which independent churches were not the only, but were certainly the characteristic, form. Parallel processes elsewhere— in Melanesia for instance—produced an equally luxuriant growth of new movements, but relatively few independent churches. New Zealand had a history all its own, with a large Maori movement beginning outside the Christian faith but becoming progressively more like a Christian church, while another movement that began as a Christian revival moved for a time in another direction. The Native American peoples, north and south, have a history of interactive movements; so do many widely separated parts of Asia; there are even one or two in the records of the remaining primal peoples of Europe. On this larger map, the typology Turner had used for his early work on African churches was revised and refined. There have been several versions, and it is time for them to be again revisited; but in general there are four main classes of movement in a spectrum from the old religion to the new: neoprimal, synthetist, Hebraist, and independent church. But it is of the essence of movements that they move; the dynamic components within them may draw them now further toward one end of the spectrum, now to the other. Turner's working definition of new religious movements, in the form in which it appears in a celebrated article in the *Encyclopedia Britannica*, is

> a historically new development arising in the interaction between a tribal society and its religion and are of the higher cultures and its major religion, involving some substantial departure from the classical religious traditions of both the cultures concerned, in order to

find renewal by reworking the rejected traditions into a different religious system.[8]

In principle, therefore, new religious movements can arise from the interaction of any religion from outside upon a primal society. In practice, as the article goes on to argue, Christianity has been infinitely more productive of such movements than any other faith, whereas Islam, often present within the very same societies, produces next to none.

Turner's definition—and the precise form of it quoted here may bear the marks of editorial policy—has given rise to plenty of discussion. Those concentrating on one particular religious situation may be more impressed by the adaptive capacities of indigenous traditions and thus stress continuity rather than new creations. Those concerned with a general social theory of religion may wonder why the definition is framed in terms of primal societies—the early typologies of "revitalization movements" such as those of A. F. C. Wallace had a much wider reference[9]; or they may question the meaning of "historically new"—in practice Turner's examples begin in the sixteenth century, though most are from the nineteenth or later. Church historians may similarly discuss whether "new religious movements" so defined really do introduce any fundamentally new element into Christian history. Was second-century Phrygian Montanism, for instance, different in kind, either in its manifestations or in the conditions that produced it, from many "new movements" today? Missiologists may ask whether any successful cross-cultural transmission of Christianity does not involve "some substantial departure from the classical religious traditions of both the cultures concerned, in order to find renewal by reworking."

All these may be points for discussion. They do not in the least affect the usefulness of the definition, for it marks the boundaries of a field that everyone must recognize consists of cognate items.

It is at this point that one of Harold Turner's most remarkable achievements begins. So far we have seen the architect of the study of new religious movements. But he has also been its master builder. Over the years, by hard travel—often involving a heavy program of lecturing, conferences, and other duties into which the literary quest had to be packed—intense application, and insatiable curiosity, he has assembled a massive corpus of material relating to new religious movements in every

---

[8] H. W. Turner, "Tribal Religious Movements, New," *Encyclopedia Britannica* 18 (1974): 698.

[9] Anthony F. C. Wallace, "Revitalization Movements," *American Anthropologist* 58 (1956): 264–81.

continent, in a multitude of languages, and in every conceivable genre. He has recognized that in this field the scrap of information or comment in a newspaper or missionary magazine may be just as revealing as a learned article. So he must capture the newspaper, the magazine, and the learned article. From this ocean of literature he has distilled a series of scholarly, annotated, user-friendly bibliographies. When it appeared in 1967, the *Bibliography of Modern African Religious Movements*, which he prepared with Robert Mitchell, seemed vast; when ten years later the first volume of his series *Bibliography of New Religious Movements in Primal Societies* appeared, we learned how much more grain there was in the girnal. And that represented only a selection from a still larger collection, and the quantity of material collected since 1977 is colossal. Turner's bibliographies are the starting point for any serious student of the new movements, and a reference point for anyone enquiring into many an aspect of African or Native American Christianity.

A conventional scholar would have considered his work for posterity done with the bibliography, and might legitimately reserve the actual materials gathered with such labor for his own ongoing researches. Harold Turner determined to make his whole collection, the literature itself, available and accessible. In the first instance it was to be available in a center specifically dedicated to the study of the movements. But he also wished it to be available throughout the world, available above all to those in Africa and Asia and Latin America and Oceania whose religious history the materials reflect. And he wished it available without long journeys, or costly technology, or high-priced multivolume sets which only major libraries could afford. Hence the painstaking investigation of various intermediate technologies and the laborious establishment of a sort of cottage industry that makes the corpus available in modest microfiche form and distributes it worldwide. Harold has insisted that the material properly belongs to the people of the areas whose religious activities produced it. The most invidious colonialism of our day is the colonialism of information, the establishment by large Western agencies of proprietary rights over it, the fencing of it with logistical or financial barriers. In this matter Harold Turner has always been a pugnacious anticolonialist.

All this required sustained vision and sustained toil. The large foundations and the learned establishment did not soon warm to the idea of a Centre for the Study of New Religious Movements in Primal Societies, and several noteworthy locations lost the opportunity to become the base for exciting developments. As the Project for New Religious Movements in Primal Societies, it found a traveler's tent in the Department of Religious

Studies at Aberdeen and then a home in the Selly Oak Colleges (from meeting house to temple?).

In the early days of his worldwide paper chase, Harold was usually alone in the work—no, never alone, for Maude sailed cheerfully into the quest as she had into all the earlier ones, whether they involved transporting a family across continents or entertaining prophets (and other angels) unawares. For the establishment and maintenance of the Centre, Maude has always been ready to acquire what few skills she did not already possess. Aberdeen brought the energy and sharp eye of Jocelyn Murray to the project. Gradually a miscellaneous corps of volunteers emerged, from very diverse sources, to bind, to file, to pack, to translate—one aspect of Harold's plan for general accessibility of the materials was that key items in languages other than English should be translated.

Toward the end of the sojourn in Aberdeen Harold Turner had another encounter that recalls the meeting on the beach in Sierra Leone three decades earlier. It led him into engagement with post-Christian religious movements in the West. There is no space to talk of what has followed: the defense of vulnerable groups and the activity on behalf of religious liberty. The Centre he founded broadened to the Centre for New Religious Movements.

Now Abraham has lifted his tent pegs again. His intellectual concerns, so long concentrated on cross-cultural situations, reverted to the place of the Christian faith in the great non-Christian culture of the modern West. In Harold Turner's concerns as he now returns to his homeland we hear some of the notes that sounded out in earlier years, including that Fourah Bay manifesto of 1961, but with a sonority that comes from all that has happened in the intervening years. The expert builder is still at work, and we may expect to see new walls rising.

His buildings have always been such as other people may live in and adapt for their own needs; indeed, he has always welcomed others to join him on the site, where Maude would never be far away with refreshment. Nor, rigorous scholar as he is, has he restricted that welcome to professional academics; he has known how much of the knowledge and skill required are in other hands. The contributors to this volume are merely representatives of a host of his associates from different periods and places who are in debt to his inspiration, his assistance, and his achievement. They are well aware that the best tribute they can pay the expert builder is to take care how they themselves build.

When the words above were first written the Turners were about to set off on another Abrahamic journey, this time to their native New Zealand. It proved to be the beginning of yet another chapter of intellectual and literary life for

Harold, after so many years of engaging with primal societies over issues of concerning the relationship of Christianity to contemporary Western culture. He returned to his original academic discipline of philosophy, finding much stimulus in the work of Michael Polanyi. He picked up once more the theme he had sounded decades before in his Sierra Leone manifesto, the place of theology among the academic disciplines, and especially its relations with the natural sciences. He wrote a book on the history of the relations between Christianity and science. He engaged in a long and fruitful correspondence with Lesslie Newbigin, in whom he found a kindred spirit, and whose concern for the gospel as public truth he shared. He founded the DeepSight Trust to pursue the issues of Christianity and Culture, and found time for a memoir, titled The Laughter of Providence, describing how he and Maude had been led into encounters that had far-reaching consequences. He died in 2002, Maude some years later.

Conclusion

The Future of Missiology—
Missiology as Vocation

Missiologists are the magpies of the academic world; they invade the scholarly territory of their neighbors and steal their topics. Geographers, as anyone who has worked in a social science faculty knows, do the same; but geographers can at least claim maps as their peculiar territory. We have no equivalent possession; we invade the biblical field, the theological field, the historical field, and the practical field in the name of the study of mission. When the theologians, the biblical scholars, the church historians, the practical theologians are alert to the missiological aspects of their task, we are not really needed; but as with washing up, what everyone is meant to do, no one does. So, in practice, missiologists voluntarily undertake everyone else's washing up.

This also makes us academic subversives, upsetting harmony by raising new issues; introducing new perspectives and new data; identifying new questions and problems within established fields; exploring the missiological dimensions of topics already discussed by our theological colleagues; and for those of us who work in universities, placing issues raised by Christian activity before our colleagues in the humanities and social sciences.

Missiologists are also intellectual brokers, enabling exchange across cultural or national or regional boundaries. In their day, missionaries were themselves cultural brokers; they were representative Westerners in non-Western society, representatives, however inadequate, of the host societies when in the West (often the only organs by which the church in the West ever took the rest of the world into account), and representative Christians in non-Christian society. Those responsible for the study of mission accordingly have, in the original sense of the word, an ecumenical function—that is, a function in relation to the whole inhabited world. One of the prime tasks of academic missiologists is to create and maintain cross-cultural Christian contact and understanding.

The need for this process derives from the essential nature of the church. The model of the church presented in the New Testament is bicultural. Certainly, the earliest church of all, the church of the apostles and elders in Jerusalem, with its converted Judaism, its Jewish life lived in the light of the Messiahship of the Jesus, reflects a coherent cultural whole.[1] But from the time that those unnamed Jerusalem refugees who came to Antioch decided that their Greek pagan neighbors needed to know about Jesus,[2] and the apostles and elders agreed that such Gentile believers in Israel's Messiah entered Israel without Torah or circumcision, there were two Christian lifestyles in a single church.

On the one hand, there were old-style Jewish believers, like the apostles, who kept the Sabbath and the food laws and ritual purity; on the other, there were new-style believers practicing the sort of Christianity we see under construction in Paul's letters—a converted form of Hellenistic family and social life. It was this working biculturalism that defined early Christianity. It was in Antioch that it first appeared, and it was in Antioch that the name Christian was invented.[3] In Jerusalem, the Jesus community, Israel in the Messianic age needed no name; it was the emergence of a bicultural community that was unique in its own world that made one necessary.

The Epistle to the Ephesians insists that the two segments of converted social reality belong together, that Jewish believers and Gentile believers—not just two races, but two cultures, two different ways of being Christian—are necessary to each other, necessary for building the new temple, necessary organs in a functioning body of which Christ was the head.

In later Christian consciousness, this awareness faded. The great ecumenical tragedy of the sixth century effectively split the church permanently along cultural and linguistic lines, and opened the way for this process to take place again and again in Christian history. Part of the present missiological function is to facilitate the return of the plural cultural Christian consciousness of the New Testament, since certain features of the present time suggest directions in which missiology may proceed.

First of these features is the cumulative effect of several interlinked developments of the twentieth century. The World Missionary Conference

---

[1] Though even here, differences of upbringing, reflected in different attitudes to the Greek language and aspects of Greek culture, were present, and could cause tensions which needed deliberate action to resolve. Cf. Acts 6:1–7.

[2] Acts 11:19ff.

[3] Acts 11:26.

which took place just ten years into that century, represents the high-water mark of the missionary movement from the West. The delegates, as they left the Assembly Hall with renewed dedication and huge enthusiasm, had no idea of the cataclysms before them. Filled with new vision they could not hear the beating of the wings of the approaching Angel of Death. War and economic depression overturned the world order on which the assumptions of the Edinburgh 1910 Conference were based. Nevertheless the vision that dawned at Edinburgh of a great expansion of the faith of Christ in the non-Christian world was a true one; the vision was fulfilled, and the church on earth was transformed in the process. But the transformation did not come about in the way, or by the means, or in the places that even the best observers in 1910 expected.

It is a truism that the missionary movement operated in the ambience of colonialism; but colonialism was itself the child of a larger movement, a huge movement of population, that we may call the Great European Migration. This migration began, on a small scale, early in the sixteenth century; it ended in the middle of the twentieth. Over those four and a half centuries, millions of people left Europe for the lands beyond Europe. They formed whole new nations, including all the nations of the Americas. Empire, conquest, and domination were less important motors for most migrants than the desire for a better life or a more just society for themselves or their children.

The new nations that they formed adopted the languages and cultural norms of Europe, eventually giving English a special status as an international language for which it is perhaps not in all respects suited. The migration provided a platform that enabled Europeans and their descendants to assert economic and political hegemony over the rest of the world. The process produced other migrations as Chinese were taken to the Caribbean, or Indians to Fiji, and a huge piece of Africa transported to the Americas. Religion was profoundly affected by the Great European Migration. One can argue that Hinduism as we know it today is a product of the British Raj in India; and colonial rule did more to further the spread of Islam than all the jihads. The primal, or ethnic, religions were transformed as they became the substructure of the religion of large numbers of Muslims and especially of Christians; African Christianity can be viewed either as the African chapter of the history of Christianity, or as the Christian chapter of the history of African religion. The cultural and demographic composition of Christianity was changed beyond recognition; once a Western religion and the religion of the West, it entered a steady decline in Europe, becoming a principally non-Western faith with new centers of energy in Africa, in Latin America, and in some parts of Asia.

The Great European Migration was the ultimate source of the political and economic order under which we grew up; but that order began to unravel in the very era of the World Missionary Conference as the competition between the European nations exploded in the First World War. By the middle of the twentieth century, the Great European Migration had effectively come to an end;[4] the creation of the state of Israel was its last great manifestation. The unraveling of the world order that began with the First World War seems set to continue; if we may use the language of the Book of Daniel, the Great Beast constituted by the Great European Migration is still able to roar and lash his tail, but is being gradually moved from the center; other Beasts, perhaps with Asian stripes, may replace him at the center before the Son of Man comes with the clouds of heaven.

But the twentieth century saw the beginning of another development. Around mid-century, the Great European Migration went into reverse. Another people movement began, as thousands upon thousands from Africa and Asia and Latin America came to Europe and North America. All the evidence suggests that this process will continue for the foreseeable future. As in the Great European Migration, those engaged in it seek a better future or a safer society for themselves and their children. Already the process has brought Africa and Asia to Europe, whereas once they lay at the end of a long sea voyage. It has brought Latin America to North America with immense force. It has made Hinduism and Sikhism and Islam Western religions, and it has brought vast numbers of Christians of non-Western origin to Europe and North America, often bringing with them expressions of Christian faith and practice new to the host societies in the West.

The significance for Christian mission of this Great Reverse Migration is incalculable. To take one or two examples: there is much current discussion of a hospitality model of mission; there is abundant need for its exercise, and in a variety of forms. And there will clearly be implications as and when what are at present migrant congregations addressing other migrants discover a mission to their host communities. And for the church in Europe and North America, the Great Reverse Migration offers an opportunity to rediscover the multicultural model of the early church. Indeed, the whole shift in the Christian center of gravity to the world outside the West opens a possibility of escape from some of the effects of the ecumenical failure of the sixth century that cut off the Christians of Europe from those of Asia and Africa,

---

[4] Migration from European countries has continued and is currently manifest; but it is directed within Europe, or to nations such as Australia, Canada or the United states that were themselves constituted by the Great European Migration.

and from the resultant train of division of the church along linguistic and cultural lines. It is likely that the great Christian issues of the current century will be ecumenical; and ecumenism is no longer a story about denominations, but a matter of *oikumene,* of the whole inhabited world. It is a matter of how African and Korean, Chinese and Indian, East and West European, North and South American Christians cohere, live, and learn together, all functioning as necessary organs in the body of Christ; hearing each other's stories, getting an inner realization of the stories of others who live under the cross.

Our faith is incarnational; Christ is to be formed among those who receive him in faith; the Word is to take flesh again. And the Word does not take flesh in a generalized humanity, for there is no such thing. Humanity is always culture specific, reflecting the conditions of a particular time and place, and with an identity formed by a particular past. Our various segments of social reality are to be converted to Christ, turned toward him; and, when converted, all the segments are necessary to one another. They are stones to build the new temple in which the Spirit of God dwells. The representations of Christ that arise in our various segments of reality can only be partial; only together can we realize the full stature of Christ.[5]

There are many theaters of mission in the world—many theological workshops where the ancient cultures of Africa and Asia will produce issues as far reaching, and perhaps as painful to settle, as the issues that arose from the encounter with the Greek intellectual tradition in Christianity's early centuries. But Europe and North America, in a period when the West is post-Christian and Christianity post-Western, present the obvious laboratory for the experiments that can help realize the New Testament model of the church, or that neglected or ill performed could shatter it. Europe and North America now host Christian communities, each with its own discourse, from all over the world. In the United States, there is even a fellowship of Somali churches; it might be difficult to find one in Somalia. But the Christian interaction with the older churches of the host countries has, for the most part, been minimal. Here are the stones to build the new temple of the Spirit of God of which Ephesians speaks; but at present, they are lying side by side, separated on the ground.

The new missiology, as it becomes the remembrancer to the churches about the mission into which they are called, has this domestic task, to facilitate a return to the cultural comprehensiveness of the New Testament Church,

---

[5] Compare Ephesians 4:13. An attempt to explore this idea is made in the essay "The Ephesian Moment" in Andrew F. Walls, *The Cross-Cultural Process in Christian History* (Maryknoll, NY: Orbis Books, 2002), 72–81.

which embraced both Torah-keeping Jews and ex-pagans of the nations, accepted in the Messiah without the Law.

Some other issues for the new missiology can only be mentioned much more briefly than their importance warrants.

One arises from the polycentric nature of the church. When the Edinburgh Conference of 1910 issued its call to bring the gospel to the whole of the non-Christian World, it could foresee Christian initiatives from only one quarter, and addressed its call for the mobilization of the resources of the Christian world and for international cooperation to achieve it, essentially to the churches of Europe and North America. Today initiatives for mission may begin almost anywhere in the world and be directed to almost anywhere in the world. The effects of such initiatives are as unpredictable as their source. It may be well to remember that, by the New Testament account, the mission to the Gentiles did not begin with the apostles, or with some strategic decision of the Jerusalem church, or even with the calling of Paul. It began with a group of refugees in Antioch, and we do not even know their names, who interpreted Jesus to their Greek neighbors, and in doing so changed the course of Christian history.

Another major area of missiological concern is a likely explosion of theological activity, for which the theological academy as a whole is not at present well prepared. The activity is likely to arise through the progressive interaction of the biblical material and Christian tradition with the cultures of Africa and Asia. Already the limitations of Western models of theology in Africa and Asia are evident, since those models result from the long interaction of Western Christianity with the themes of the European Enlightenment, and theology has been made to fit into the framework of the Enlightenment universe. But the Enlightenment universe is small in scale; in particular, it has no real space for the demonic. Africa and Asia know much larger and more populated mental maps of the universe, where the frontier between the empirical world and the spirit world is constantly being crossed and recrossed. Accordingly, Western theology is left with nothing to say to a whole range of human situations, including some of the most distressing that people face; it is just not big enough. African pastoral practice has for many years been engaged with the issue; but reflective theology has not yet caught up with pastoral practice, giving rise to dangers, excesses, and sheer confusion. Disciplined African theological activity may help all of us to a larger "ecumenical" theology of evil,[6] a theology dealing

---

[6] The idea is explored in Andrew F. Walls, "Christian Scholarship and the Demographic Transformation of the Church," in *Theological Literacy in the Twenty-First Century*, ed. Rodney L. Petersen with Nancy Rourke, 166–83 (Grand Rapids: Eerdmans, 2002).

seriously with what Paul calls the "principalities and powers" that underlie what we more obliquely call structural evil: those world rulers defeated in Christ's death and resurrection.[7] A fuller theology of the principalities and powers might also assist in those sterile Western disputes as to whether the gospel is addressed to structural evil or to personal sin and guilt—and if both, which has priority.

In addressing another area of potential creativity for a polycentric church, I am led to reminiscence. I recall visiting a branch of one of the oldest Zulu churches in South Africa, arriving on the Saturday before Easter. The members were in the Lenten fast—on Good Friday it had been absolute—and Saturday night was kept in prayer and vigil. But as dawn broke on Sunday, drums and shouting tore the air, and the community moved into a joyful dance. The Lord had risen, and rejoicing, we broke the fast with goat meat and bananas. I remember it as one of the most "eucharistic" experiences of my life—an occasion of high thanksgiving. Yet we did not take bread or wine. The church in question observes a communion service with bread and wine, but no one seemed to think of it as belonging to this, hugely significant, event.

The reason for this may lie in the peculiar history of the sacrament of communion in Africa. The great majority of Christian traditions have reserved the administration of the sacrament to a priest or minister; in Africa, even missions that were not tied to such ideas, and loudly asserted the priesthood of all believers, tended to be cautious with communion. But, speaking generally, the number of ordained clergy has usually been small in proportion to the number of believers and of congregations. A high proportion of services therefore were—and in many areas still are—conducted by catechists or other unordained people; so, even churches with a strong sacramental emphasis have not been able to give the Eucharist in practice the place it has in their theology. African Christianity has developed as a Christianity of the Word. Another factor affecting the place of the sacrament from mission days has been its use in discipline, the widespread use of exclusion from the sacrament as punishment. There has been little calling of sinners to the gospel feast, nor has the table been seen as a converting ordinance, a visual, tangible presentation of the gospel. Yet what feature of African life is more significant than that of eating together? The communal meal is a statement of community and harmony. Commonly, it pulses with life. And if, as on that Easter morning in Kwa-Zulu, the communal meal honors the risen Lord, does it not become a proper vehicle for the sacrament, an occasion for bread and wine in remembrance of him?

---

[7] Colossians 2:15.

In much of the world the communion has lost the characteristics of the common meal. Cultural factors induced changes in sacramental use very early in Christian history. The joyous common meals that were such a feature of the early church in Jerusalem, once transferred to the Hellenistic world, too easily became occasions for ostentation, gluttony and excess, and in 1 Corinthians we see them being stripped down to essentials.[8] Western Christianity, too, has had its own struggles over the sacraments and quarreled about how many there are, and now often stresses the individual rather than the communal participation. Perhaps Africa can make the Christian common meal possible again, and help us to understand better what it means to take bread and cup together in remembrance of Christ.

A final word must be on the possibilities of the theological process being carried on in African and Asian languages. There is no small danger of English becoming the new Latin, the ecumenical language for ecclesiastical thinking. Increasing use of mother tongue theology in African and Asian vernaculars might have an effect like that initiated by the second (French) edition of Calvin's *Institutes* in sixteenth-century Europe.

Is there any more exciting vocation at the present time than missiology? I, who am nearing the end of my course, must envy those of you with many years to serve. May God speed you.

---

[8] 1 Corinthians 11:17–33.

Sources .

1. ***World Christianity and the Early Church.*** Originally appeared as the Foreword to *A New Day: Essays in World Christianity in Honor of Lamin Sanneh*, ed. Akinade E. Akintunde (New York: Peter Lang, International Academic Publishers, 2010), 17–30. Reprinted with permission.

2. ***Origen, the Father of Mission Studies.*** Originally published as "In Quest of the Father of Mission Studies," *International Bulletin of Missionary Research* 23, no. 3 (1999): 98–102,104–105. Reprinted with permission.

3. ***Worldviews and Christian Conversion.*** A revised version of a chapter under the same title in *Mission in Context: Explorations Inspired by J. Andrew Kirk*, ed. John Corrie and Cathy Ross, chap. 11 (Aldershot, UK: Ashgate, 2012).

4. ***Toward a Theology of Migration.*** The original form of this article appeared in Frieder Ludwig and Kwabena Asamoah-Gyadu, eds., *The African Christian Presence on the West: New Immigrant Congregations and Transnational Networks in North America and Europe* (Trenton, NJ: Africa World Press, 2010), 314–32. This book is a collection of studies of African churches in migration, many of which illustrate the issues discussed in the essay.

5. ***Globalization and the Study of Christian History.*** The original form of this essay appeared in Craig Ott and Harold A. Netland, eds., *Globalizing Theology: Belief and Practice in an Era of World Christianity* (Grand Rapids: Baker Academic, a division of Baker Publishing Group, 2006). The book was a tribute to Paul Hiebert. Reprinted with permission.

6. ***The Cost of Discipleship: The Witness of the African Church.*** Appeared in *Word & World* 25, no. 4 (2005): 433–43. Reprinted with permission. With regard to the section on Sudan, it should be noted that it was written before the emergence of the new state of South Sudan in 2011.

7. ***A Christian Experiment: The Early Sierra Leone Colony.*** Appeared in G. J. Cuming, ed., *Mission of the Church and the Propagation of the Faith: Papers Read at the Seventh Summer Meeting and Eighth Winter Meeting of the Ecclesiastical History Society,* Studies in Church History

(Cambridge: Cambridge University Press, 1970), 107–27. Reprinted with permission.

8. ***Christianity and the Language Issue: The Early Years of Protestant Missions in West Africa.*** The original form of this article appeared as "West African Christian Proclamation: The Early Years," *The Bible Translator* 55, no. 3 (2004): 389–400. The issue was a tribute to the work of Paul Ellingworth. Reprinted with permission.

9. ***The Discovery of "African Traditional Religion" and Its Impact on Religious Studies.*** First appeared in Gillian Mary Bediako, Bernhard Y. Quartier, and J. Kwabena Asamoah-Gyadu, eds., *Seeing New Facets of the Diamond: Christianity as a Universal Faith. Essays in Honour of Kwame Bediako* (Eugene, OR: Wipf and Stock, 2015), 1–20. Reprinted with permission.

10. ***Kwame Bediako and Christian Scholarship in Africa.*** First published in *The International Bulletin of Missionary Research* 32, no. 4 (2008). Reprinted with permission.

11. ***Missions and the English Novel.*** This is a previously unpublished lecture delivered Liverpool Hope University.

12. ***World Parish to World Church: John and Charles Wesley on Home and Overseas Mission.*** First appeared in Darrell Whiteman and Gerald H. Anderson, eds., *World Mission in the Wesleyan Spirit* (Nashville, TN: Providence House, 2009; Franklin, TN: Seedbed Publishing, 2nd ed., 2014). Reprinted with permission.

13. ***Missions and Historical Memory: Jonathan Edwards and David Brainerd.*** The original form of this essay appeared in David W. Kling and Douglas A. Sweeney, eds., *Jonathan Edwards at Home and Abroad* (Columbia: University of South Carolina Press, 2003), 248–65. Reprinted with permission.

14. ***Distinguished Visitors: Tiyo Soga and Behari Lal Singh: In Europe and at Home.*** First appeared in Judith Becker and Brian Stanley, eds., *Europe as the Other: External Perspectives on European Christianity* (Göttingen, Germany: Vandenhoeck und Ruprecht, 2014), 243–54. Reprinted with permission.

15. ***Western Christians in China: A Chapter in a Long History.*** An earlier portion of this essay originally appeared as "Scholarship and the Missionary Movement: The China Experience," *Journal of African Christian Thought* 9, no. 2 (2006): 34–37.

16. ***Building to Last: Harold Turner and the Study of Religion.*** In 1990 a group of friends, colleagues and former students of Harold Turner (to whose memory and that of his wife's Maude, this book is

dedicated) presented him with a book of essays honoring him and commemorating his many-sided work. This essay forms the greater part of the opening essay Andrew F. Walls and Wilbert R. Shenk, eds., *Exploring New Religious Movements: Essays in Honour of Harold W. Turner* (Elkhart IN: Mission Focus Publications, 1990).

Conclusion: *The Future of Missiology—Missiology as Vocation.* The original form of this essay appeared in Viggo Mortensen and Andreas Østerlund Nielsen, eds., *Walk Humbly with the Lord: Church and Mission Engaging Plurality* (Grand Rapids: Eerdmans, 2010), 230–37. Reprinted with permission.

Index